THE SOCIAL SKILLS BASIS OF PSYCHOPATHOLOGY

CURRENT ISSUES IN BEHAVIORAL PSYCHOLOGY

Series Editor

Robert S. Ruskin, Ph.D.

Chairman, Department of Psychology and
Director, Center for Personalized Instruction
Georgetown University
Washington, D.C.

THE SOCIAL SKILLS BASIS OF PSYCHOPATHOLOGY
Alternatives to Abnormal Psychology and Psychiatry

E. Lakin Phillips, Ph.D.

Professor of Psychology and
Director, Counseling Center
The George Washington University
Washington, D.C.

Founder and Executive Director
School for Contemporary Education
Springfield, Virginia

GRUNE & STRATTON
A Subsidiary of Harcourt Brace Jovanovich, Publishers
New York   San Francisco   London

Library of Congress Cataloging in Publication Data

Phillips, Ewing Lakin, 1915–
    The social skills basis of psychopathology.

    (Current issues in behavioral psychology)
    Bibliography: p. 250
    Includes index.
    1. Psychology, Pathological. 2. Psychotherapy.
3. Social interaction. I. Title. II. Series.
[DNLM: 1. Adaptation, Psychological. 2. Problem
solving. 3. Psychopathology. 4. Psychotherapy.
WM100.3 P558s]
RC454.P48   616.8'9'07   78-23505
ISBN 0-8089-1126-0

Grune & Stratton, Inc.
111 Fifth Avenue
New York, New York 10003

Distributed in the United Kingdom by
Academic Press, Inc. (London) Ltd.
24/28 Oval Road, London NW 1

Library of Congress Catalog Number 78-23505
International Standard Book Number 0-8089-1126-0

Printed in the United States of America

Contents

Acknowledgments

Many persons have contributed to the development and writing of this book. Special thanks are due Linda Scott, Steven Sowards and Geraldine Lyons, all of whom helped formulate early versions of this writing. Appreciation for his statistical help is due Dr. Charles E. Rice. Geraldine Lyons collaborated with me on the research and writing of Chapter 3. George Cherry assisted in the writing of the section on Biofeedback in Chapter 7. Piper J. Phillips was an unflagging supporter of my efforts and did important editorial work on the manuscript.

Foreword

The phenomenal interest in behavioral psychology over the past decade has stimulated a vast amount of debate, research, and theory. One effect of the ever-growing effort to organize and understand the complexity of human activity in behavioral terms has been a greater acceptance and utilization of the behavioral approaches to psychological therapy. For many years, behavioral techniques have been successfully implemented in a wide variety of environments—from the hospital setting to the out-patient clinic. Indeed, behavioral techniques have become so important an addition to the clinician's arsenal, that their usage has essentially redefined the clinical area. Almost every important clinical activity has been touched by the rising acceptance of a methodology based on carefully controlled research and empirical data.

In addition to many other beneficial changes in the field, researchers and therapists have seriously questioned the usefulness and accuracy of traditional diagnostic classification systems, investigated the efficacy of therapeutic strategies, and challenged the basic theoretical underpinnings of traditional therapy. Such a rigorous review of both traditional and behavioral strategies can only continue to improve the empirical structure of the field of psychology.

Respected professionals in this dynamic field of study have formulated varying methods of organizing the existing research, leading to differing theories of human behavior and appropriate strategies for therapeutic treatment. This series, *Current Issues in Behavioral Psychology*, while not intended to be limited to behavioral applications in clinical settings, will certainly emphasize such usage. The issues necessarily raised and examined cannot be ignored. They will have ever-growing impact, not only for specific treatments, but also in understanding and defining society as a whole.

It seems most appropriate to begin this series with Dr. Phillip's contribution. Past attempts by psychologists to behaviorally define the complex nature of the individual in the context of his or her social milieu has often proven to be a thorny task. Dr. Phillips presents an organized analysis of individual behavior in terms of interaction with a changing environment. Emphasis is given to the situationality and transience of both behavior and environment. This perspective on the individual's social skills in relation to a day-to-day environment is a much needed addition to the psychological literature.

Dr. Phillips has approached the issues of behavioral treatment in a social context with the solid credentials of a highly successful practicing clinician and teacher. His book combines a well-documented theoretical foundation with basic common sense that can be developed only after many years of clinical experience. Those of us who are concerned about the field of psychology will gain from Dr. Phillip's presentation a new and useful perspective on the state of behavioral theory and treatment.

Robert S. Ruskin, Ph.D.

Preface

Writing a book with a new slant on the subject matter covered is no easy matter. Nor is it without risks. For several years, I have been noticing that as a therapist and a "behavior changer," I was primarily teaching, promoting, or encouraging in various ways the development of social skills among my patients and among those I consulted with in schools or other institutions. This growing emphasis on social skills constituted a complete abandonment of anything close to the traditional medical model; for it essentially foreclosed the need for diagnosis, classification, nosological groupings, and put the emphasis entirely on an analysis of the behavioral situation (the person interacting with his or her environment). While the person/environment notion is far from new, very few clinicians or therapist/theorists have actually carried out its implications. Since social skills are learned and practiced in the environment, pivoting a consideration of human functioning in terms of their adequacy seems an entirely useful and heuristic notion.

Social skills form a nexus between the individual and the environment; their subtle, far-reaching nature can account, I believe, for much if not most of the current recourse to cognitive explanations in clinical and social contexts. Social skills also form a nexus between the individual and the environment, in that recourse to studying these skills takes the place of trying to find diagnostic categories to explain, control, and change psychopathological behavior. In short, with valid and functional social skills analysis, the individual's behavior need not be explained by cognitive models nor be understood in terms of nosological categories; social skills become the connecting links in both instances.

Behaviorally oriented psychologists have not placed the study of social skills squarely in their empirical, clinical, or therapeutic frameworks. It is proper now to call attention to these lacks and to suggest ways of going about the study of social skills to meet many of the demands for better understanding, control, and prediction of human clinical and social interactions. Doubtlessly other behavioral therapists will take different vantage points from the present one; stimulating a need for variety in approaching these problems is one task of this book.

Science marches ahead on both empirical and theoretical fronts. The study of social skills requires considerable empirical study and will, in time, be given this study. Meanwhile, some theoretical clarification of how the study of social skills is important and how their investigation offers promising alternatives to many present practices is in order. If this book contributes even slightly to this broad effort, I will consider my task well begun.

E. Lakin Phillips, Ph.D.

Introduction

Science is always looking for new knowledge and for more parsimonious ways to view knowledge already in hand. The study of psychopathology offers an unusually good opportunity for a new look at old problems and for ways to attack traditional problems that have not yielded to standard practices.

Clinical tradition built up over the past several decades in psychology and related areas has placed a high premium on diagnosis—it has been the presumed link between the person's biosocial and psychological history on the one hand and prognosis or treatment on the other. The diagnosis of psychopathology has been the pivotal consideration in all studies of abnormal psychology and psychiatry, a large part of counseling and psychotherapy, and a strong contributor to personality theory. This has been a burden. It is argued herein that the study of psychopathology has not been met successfully.

This hoary tradition is now changing. This book is an attempt to recognize a change in our view of psychopathology, an effort to accelerate the change, and a proposed reconceptualization of psychopathology in terms of social skills that will hopefully prove revealing and challenging.

There are several reasons for changing views of psychopathology. One is that the diagnostic enterprise has never been very successful or encouraging. It has had a preoccupation with the wrong problems based on asking the wrong questions. Diagnosis of psychopathology has been more a static classification, a searching for disease entities, rather than a dynamic view of how the individual and society play out their dance of life. Psychopathological diagnoses have not shown how unwanted behaviors were formed (learned), how they were maintained (reinforced), or how they might be economically altered (through psychotherapy, behavior change, or whatever).

A second objection to abnormal or psychopathological classifications is that, being static, these classifications have never been stated in behavioral language—or in any other language—that could lead to an understanding of the process of change, that is, change into or out of psychopathology. There has been no continuity between descriptive terms and process terms. Labeling a person "a hysteric" or "a paranoiac" has not led to any suggested or useful change plan or process.

Most diagnostic enterprise has located the variables describing psychopathology inside the person, with perhaps some speculation as to how the person may have developed the observed behaviors. If the presumptive causal condition were located in the person, then an encapsulation in the psyche would often result, with no suggested way of overcoming this impasse. How could one understand the observable behavior (in some social context), yet attribute causality to inner (i.e., non-social) conditions? And how could one then "do therapy" in an avowed interpersonal context on the basis of unobservable inner causes?

Yet another general reason for taking a new look at psychopathology and abnormal psychological classification is to emphasize the interrelationship between so-called abnormal and normal behavior. Aren't the laws and principles governing behavior—as well as we know them—applicable to both abnormal and normal behavior? To assert that there is a difference in lawfulness or in principle places the burden of proof on one who makes this assertion. Even extremely abnormal persons are occasionally normal—in some ways and for some periods of time. Likewise the most normal of us may behave abnormally at times—for example, in temper or anger outbursts. As we begin to view abnormal or psychopathological behavior along with normal behavior, we immediately look for evidence of the person's capacity to cope, for knowledge of the social context, for problem-solving skills and the like. Basically, this is a social skills problem.

How does one cope? We all meet problems—passing ones, recurrent ones, persistent and formidable ones. Those of us who "get along fairly well"—how do we solve problems? How does one meld personal resources with environmental opportunities, or limitations, and arrive at some degree of adequacy?

Enter here social skills. If one can cope, that means one must have at least a modicum of skills—skills in managing oneself, in dealing with others, in aligning situations so as to reduce friction and optimize problem solving. The person who copes possesses the requisite skills; the "un-coper" lacks these skills. This fact can be easily observed in our own behavior and in the behavior of others. If we want to teach better coping behavior, we must teach skills—skills in recognizing a problem, skills in seeing the contexts in which the problem occurs, skills in seeing our own contribution to the problem, skills in viewing the demands of situations (interpersonal and otherwise), and skills in relating effectively with others. These all add up to a complex of social skills or social competencies.

Let us, then, ask new questions: What social skills does the complaining person lack? What social skills deficits does the hospitalized psychotic show? What social skills improvements might each of us cultivate in order not only to solve problems but to live more fully and fulfillingly? Are these skills now available in the person's repertoire—that is, do existing social skills simply have to be upgraded, applied more saliently to given situations? Or, are the social skills deficits more seriously lacking—that is, does the person have to learn now what he or she might have learned earlier in life? Are the opportunities for learning the requisite skills present in the natural environment, or do special environments have to be created for remedial purposes? Will the learning of the apparently needed social skills then overcome the deficit, the psychopathology?

Can we say that social skills deficits *cause* psychopathology? Perhaps not with great assurance, although setting up social skills training that leads to a correction of the presumed or described inadequacy can often lead to better coping, better self-understanding and generally better functioning. We can compare persons with and without social skills of a given type and see if they fall into different (psychopathological or diagnostic) categories (depressed versus non-depressed, and so forth). Or, we can compare extant depressed persons with non-depressed ones and ascertain if there are substantial social skills differences between these groups. We can assert in some cases that relieving or overcoming "condition A" by means of "method M" goes a long way toward establishing a connection between the two. Irrespective of one's view of psychopathology, we must remember that we do not literally treat "depression" (or other diagnostic categories) by any therapy—we, rather, use various methods to overcome the observable or reportable behavioral deficits (sluggishness, expressed unhappiness, disinterest in socializing, disorderly living, etc.). Any diagnostic category or psychopathological condition, in the present meaning, is a collection of items relating to social conditions, to social skills deficits. If corrected, these deficits would lead to greater adequacy. Whatever methods we use to overcome an unwanted or abnormal condition are, presumably, related to the particular diagnostic condition under study, otherwise we would be proceeding randomly.

In some studies we can go further in connecting social skills training with particular deficits. We can manipulate the presumed causes of a condition—the presumed independent variables—by presenting the suspected causal condition under controlled circumstances; then removing the independent or causal condition to see if the dependent condition (psychopathology in this case) changes in discernible ways; then re-presenting the independent condition again, and observing anew the dependent or resultant abnormal conditions. As we manipulate the presumed independent or causal condition, this should have an off–on effect on the dependent condition: as we turn up the heat, the water boils; as we turn down the heat, the water stops boiling. When we teach social skills, we can reduce psychopathology; when we do not teach or reinforce social skills in an observable setting, we note that the psychopathology can again increase in likelihood; this is part of the rationale.

Not only are the above methodological considerations important in the understanding of social skills and their relationship to psychopathology, the study of social skills is also important for other reasons. Such a study will lead us into observing finer and finer details about human behavior and human social interaction. We are learning more each year about how very subtle and far-reaching gestures, expressive behaviors, arm /face /bodily movements (often rhythmic), eye contacts, stance, carriage, sitting / standing /walking postures, etc., go a long way toward telling what we think of ourselves and others, and how much mutual influence between people is carried in these subtle ways. We speak not only with our tongues but with our whole bodies—and all of the time. The nuances here are many and varied. Listen to a tape of a socially withdrawn male patient as he verbalizes his problems in contacting and relating to women—how he is hesitant and awkward in making conversation, in sustaining a social interaction, in terminating and /or carrying over to another time the social exchange. Similarly with women who have opposite-sex-interpersonal-skills deficits. One can often observe these behaviors firsthand at a dance, during social introductions, during conversations, and in a myriad of other human interactions. In such human social interaction settings, we might be inclined to diagnose the man as "depressed" or as "hysterical" and similarly for the women; "paranoid" might even come into the diagnostic picture if a person believed that others hated him or her, especially if the degree of distress were great and persistent. In all cases, however, we might teach the person social skills to overcome the specifically identifiable deficits, noting changes for the better in these types of interactions. We would thereby avoid a psychopathological diagnosis which, in any case, would not instruct us on how to overcome the deficits in question—it would only put a label on the deficits.

Why don't people learn social skills in the first place—while growing? As part of maturing? Some do; some don't; some falter more or less seriously. The failure to learn social skills may derive, of course, from a variety of circumstances: The interpersonal and social environments may not be instructive; conflicting expectations between social requirements and "payoffs" may often exist; skills that may serve one well in a very limited circumstance (say, in the ghetto) may ill-equip one to function broadly in the larger society; and so on. The reasons are legion. Parents as models for the child, may be deficient, or very idiosyncratic. Or, the culture may promote exorbitant expectations that lead to disappointment, self-rejection, and failure patterns. At all levels of social interaction—society at large, social class or group settings, the school, the family, friends—there are "good" and "bad" social skills instructional consequences. All of them are bound to have affected the individual who arrives at some place and time as a "social deficit."

Conflict lies at the root of psychopathology—conflict between what the individual produces in the way of social skills behaviors on the one hand versus what both the individual and society "expect" as normative, desirable, or highly commendable. One cannot have a disturbance, it is hypothesized, without conflict. All theories of psychopathology give at least a nod to that premise, but few theories of psychopathology or psychotherapy make conflict central as we do in this book. Social skills training helps to overcome the conflict by reducing the contrast between approach and avoidance conditions which make up the conflict.

Various theories of psychotherapy are based on somewhat different notions of psychopathology. Rogerian theory emphasizes the warm and unconditional acceptance of the client by the therapist; a condition, it is stated, that allows the client to grow toward self-understanding and self-fulfillment. Although psychopathology, in the sense of conflict, exists tacitly in Rogerian therapy, the therapeutic emphasis is placed on client-therapist relationships needed to bring about change in the client. This change, it is asserted, will come about without special effort, training, or deliberate intent as far as social skills education is concerned.

In Freudian theory, despite several modifications and revisions, it is believed that psychopathology lies in the unconscious and in developmental abstractions which, if properly uncovered in therapy through transference and other efforts to overcome "defensiveness," will free the patient to engage in mature behavior. The use of social skills in the psychoanalytic context would be both unwelcome and a hindrance, it would be argued. Social skills efforts would disturb free association, destroy the transference, and confuse unconscious and conscious processes.

Most behavior therapy practices appear to take up where other more "depth" theories of psychopathology and psychotherapy leave off, viz., at the juncture of taking the patient or client here and now as primarily being in conflict. They then proceed by skills training—but do not neglect how the patient views his or her problems (which itself is part of the social skills deficit)—and attempt to shift the reinforcing contingencies in the direction of better problem solving. The whole thrust of this book is a set of propositions and procedures for describing, promoting, and explaining how social skills efforts answer simultaneously the traditional problems associated with psychopathology, and how they supplement, augment, and foster therapeutic change in more practical, functional, and heuristic ways.

Social skills objectives appear to deal with many of the theoretical and practical problems associated with cognitive views of behavior and personality disturbances. In conflict, the person searches for solutions, vacillates between pros and cons, fails to check out fully and reliably the possible fruitfulness of the available options and thereby gets lost in the subjective elements of the situation. Worry, rumination, self-abnegation occur in lieu of social solutions to problems; anxiety states, in the form of constant vigilance, seem to inundate the person. The less adequate the behavior, the more pronounced the in-the-head preoccupations. Attempted solutions, however, of a subjective nature, narrow and redundant as they are, seldom lead to gratifying and viable results. "I took these mental-mucking-around situations and brought order into the chaos by learning social competencies" were the words of a psychotherapy patient after he was able to develop suitable social skills and then look back on his former anxiety and ruminative state as no longer controlling him. In short, the greater the conflict, the more pervasive the anxiety; the more persistent the anxiety, the more "mental" (cognitive) the preoccupation, and the greater the searching for relief. Contrariwise, the better the conflict is handled, based on ever finer analysis and control of the social skills and interpersonal processes, the less the anxiety and the more the person is encouraged to develop and be reinforced in terms of social skills adequacies.

Social skills approaches to abnormal conditions are, then, an alternative to traditional views. The viewpoint proffered here posits the lack of social skills as the essential behavioral deficit, owing to conflictful person–environmental conditions, and sets out to promote change through better understanding of, and alterations in, the environmental contingencies regulating behavior. To bolster this set of propositions in this book, we will have to look into the nature of social skills, into psychopathology, into some psychometric and other methodological considerations, into anxiety and conflict and their interrelationship, and into parallel lines of evidence for a social skills viewpoint by drawing on related research. We will look briefly and suggestively at society's efforts to regulate behavior (the law in relation to psychotherapy). And, we will try to understand the need for a social curriculum that might guide the socialization process so as to optimize social skills adequacy. Gaining a foothold in this conceptualization of psychopathology and behavior change (and/or psychotherapy) will require new lines of research and practice, will pose new problems, and will lead, one hopes, to a better understanding of human behavior.

THE SOCIAL
SKILLS BASIS OF
PSYCHOPATHOLOGY

1

It might be better to begin the first chapter in this book with a discussion of social skills *deficits*, since such deficits are more pronounced, more easily observed, and far more frequently reported in the literature. However, the emphasis in this book is on positive social skills acquisition, or utilization, hence, the negative side of the matter will be deemphasized.

Enough has already been written about the psychological ills of mankind, with diagnostic encyclopedias comprehensively covering these ills. In the area of children's distresses, Hobbs (1975) has addressed the unfortunate consequences of labeling children, assigning them to a kind of educational perdition, and the seeming intractableness of those who are responsible for labeling children, thereby denying them better educational opportunities. In reviewing Hobbs' book, Becker (1977) comments on the predominant American system of labeling:

effects of
wrong or' ineffective
labeling .

> This book is a brilliantly argued indictment of the American classification and its wide abuse. It is now very clear that the damage done to no doubt millions of American children by virtue of reckless, indifferent, insensitive, or casual assignment of descriptive syndromes of maladjustment, intellectual incompetence, or cognitive disorder may now be beyond help. (Becker, 1977, p. 180)

It is one intention of this book to show that the prevailing preoccupation with diagnostic classifications is not a doomsday for us all, and that drawing attention to social skills and how they may be improved will be the way out of the diagnostic morass, not only for children—recognized clearly by Hobbs (1975)—but for adults as well. Emphasizing social skills is an alternative to abnormal psychology and psychiatry, insofar as they are preoccupied with theories, causes, and descriptions of deviant behaviors.

What Are Social Skills?

SOCIAL SKILLS DEFINED

Social skills are legion, encompassing nearly all aspects of our daily lives, from teaching the toddler to pick up his toys before bedtime to the diplomatic handling of intense conflict among couples, groups, or nations. If fair and effective interpersonal relations depend on how we handle ourselves and how we respond to others, then social skills are at the heart of the matter.

Social skills are more often taken for granted than they are explicitly defined. There is no "diagnostic manual" for social skills as there is for human distress and psychological problems (*Diagnostic and Statistics Manual—II*). Unfortunately, much emphasis in psychotherapy has been on diagnosis, even while purporting to change behavior toward more constructive ends.

Defining social skills is not easy, except in an immediate, common sense way. Developing definitions that will be pervasive and workable are not only tasks we confront now, but they are obligations for the future. The literature on social skills does mention objectives, target behaviors, and offer some succinctness in regard to operationalizing research or clinical use of social skills. Some of these definitions follow.

DEFINITIONS OF SOCIAL SKILLS

1. Behavioral measures of social adequacy in heterosexual situations (Arkowitz et al., 1975; Bander et al., 1975; Boles 1976; Clark & Arkowitz, 1975; Curran, 1975; Libet & Lewinsohn, 1973; McGovern, 1973; Pendelton, Shelton, and Wilson, 1976; Shaw, 1975; Shinedling, Terry, & Ravsten, 1975).

These include studies where (usually) males are taught *social approach* skills toward women, sometimes using women as confederates, sometimes giving out "assignments" or "homework" for the males to carry out between therapy training sessions, as well as they are able to do so in their natural environments. These programs may be packaged, in that a finite set of topics and a limited time span are involved, or they may be more open-ended wherein the nondating or nonsocially skilled males are allowed to talk about their social anxieties in group sessions and then to come up with specific target behaviors to be carried out in relation to women.

2. Social competence (in males vis-à-vis females) as shown by shorter latencies in responding to social stimuli and in carrying on more conversation (more words per response in heterosexual interaction) (Arkowitz et al., 1975; Arbes & Hubbell, 1973; Brendel, 1974; Curran & Gilbert, 1975).

The term "social competence" appears repeatedly in the literature, may be used in place of social skills referents, and usually applies to situations in which "dating," heterosexual exchanges, and conversational skills are required. Since many of these studies are carried on in college and university settings, usually with clients from out-patient counseling centers or other mental health facilities, it is to be expected that social skills will refer to heterosexual social competencies and that the problems will have grown out of clients applying for help with their social anxieties.

3. Social skills (or social competence) as defined by "attending skills" (Boles, 1976; Clark, 1975; Curran & Gilbert, 1975; McGovern, 1973).

These skills, part of a broad spectrum of social interactions, focus on teaching the person to attend more sensitively, to intersperse comments in conversations, to maintain eye contact, and to generally "look at" or "pay attention" to the correspondent in a social interaction (Orford, 1976, p. 63). One way we all have of "turning off" another person is not to appear to listen to that person, to turn eye contact and other signs of attention away from the participant, or show boredom—all of which are the antithesis of listening skills. Often, when we are tired, bored, or disinterested in others, we inadvertently turn them off by lack of attention. We may utilize these types of social interactions so often as to blunt our social skills and not realize it until others say to us, "I didn't know you like me," or "I thought you discounted me and my conversation," or "If you are interested in what I have to say, you don't show it very clearly," and similar remarks by others indicating they have sensed a lack of social interest and/or skill from another person.

4. Social awareness contributes in some studies to the general concept of social skills (Dye, 1974), also sometimes referred to as "group awareness."

In this case, students were taught broad social skills in order to overcome reported or measured anxieties in social situations as assessed by such instruments as the Tennessee Self-Concept Scale or various anxiety scales. Generally speaking, social skills or group/social awareness efforts tend to be very broadly based and implicitly considered to be generalizable to work and social situations, a generalization that does not always occur.

5. Self-actualization skills are also subsumed under general social skills (Connolly, 1975), along with assertive training (Boykin, 1975), as a way of helping one learn to develop and actualize one's self. The overlap here is quite in evidence as between one kind of self-development objective and another, regardless of the particular methods used to bring about social skills changes in the individual.

It can be noted that some efforts to change social skills derive from a focus on the individual's "internal" state (self-actualization, for example) and sometimes from a focus on the individual in explicit relation to others (e.g., learning to assert oneself in stores, public places, when others attempt to take advantage, and so on). All of these attempts result in overt behavioral changes that we call social skills, since the one who is "actualized" is, perforce, able to accomplish what he intends to accomplish, and the one who is "assertive" is able to hold to an equitable and effective set of relationships with others in at least some critical areas of daily life.

6. At the risk of playing a semantic game—calling the "same thing" by a lot of different names—it is to be noted that "encouraging transactions" with others is also recorded as a social skill (Brendel, 1974).

In this case—encouraging transactions—hospitalized psychiatric patients were instructed along Adlerian lines to develop interest in others and thereby to increase self-esteem, although it was reported that no statistically reliable results were achieved toward this goal.

One difficulty with many studies of groups given instruction in social skills is that the ultimately *individual* nature of the social skills involved are not properly nurtured in the skills training sessions where the focus is on the group instruction. Even if social skills, defined in some of the various ways cited above, were well-tailored to meet individual cases, the group setting and group support of these skills passes out of existence when the study is over, hence, the individual may be left without his own relatively independent repertoire of social skills; therefore, whatever skills may have been developed in group settings do not readily generalize to other situations. Moreover, the criteria for many social skills training objectives are often spelled out in psychometric terms—reduced anxiety, as shown on an inventory, or increased self-esteem /self-concept, as seen through questionnaire results—which bear a tangential, or possibly even an unknown, relationship to social skills as exemplified in actual social interactions in specific settings (dating, in-hospital living routines, among social skills practices in group interactions, etc.). As far as can be told from the literature, there is no clear advantage in teaching individual social skills via a group setting (giving instructions in a group) in preference to individualized instruction and practice: it is only a matter of economy of time and effort. In fact, the initial group setting as the modality in which social skills are learned and practiced may even be a deterrent to generalizing the *individual's* skills to later situations, since the supporting efforts of the group are forfeited when the individual is on his own. The mootness of this point tends to vitiate many attempts to teach social skills and to have them generalize to other situations. Generalization is too often taken for granted; it, too, must be programmed, perhaps through fading techniques of some type, where attempts are made to actually put the person through the skill requirements he or she needs in daily life. These may be fostered initially in group settings but should be carefully monitored to cover each individual's particular social needs and opportunities. Both settings—group and individual—are needed to teach social skills, but the demands of training and the entering repertoires of persons, as well as the circumstances of generalization to criterion life situations, need to be studied from a variety of standpoints utilizing various procedures.

In circumscribed environments, such as a mental hospital, social skills training can often be prepared in capsule form. The most familiar format here is the "token economy" (Ayllon & Azrin, 1968; Kazdin, 1977), which is a massive social skills program intended to cover a very wide variety of behaviors (Ulmer & Lieberman, 1970). They point out that society at large is a token economy where rewards and punishments are transacted around and through the use of money, and that teaching social competencies among hospitalized patients (or anyone, for that matter) can be accomplished by setting up miniatures of what goes on in society at large.

7. Very simple social skills among institutionalized patients include such behaviors as shaving, showering, joining work units, asking to have needs met (asking for keys to a shower area, asking and answering questions of staff, etc.) (Farina, Arenberg, & Guskin, 1957, Ulmer & Lieberman, 1970).

From the development of these minimal social skills, come larger social skills of a conversational nature, the understanding and carrying out of more complex directions, and perhaps the ability to go on "pass" from the hospital to the outside world, or even live outside the hospital. The motto of much training in minimal social skills might be: "Start small but think larger." Social skills training is the hard-rock competency that serves as a bulwark for further social development.

8. Although overlapping with some of the above citations, the use of "systematic homework" to increase social interaction was advanced by Pendelton, Shelton and Wilson (1976). They used 8 weekly 2-hour sessions to promote relaxation, skill training, cognitive control and systematic homework assignments, the latter being the bridge to behavior change outside the clinical setting. The authors report widebased changes of a reliable nature and generalization to other situations.

In the Pendelton et al. study (1976), the generalization problem was well used, in that the homework feature provided for social skills applications to settings beyond the therapy or training sessions. Some "bridge" of this type is necessary if the intensive efforts promoted in clinical settings are to bear fruit in terms of overt behavioral changes elsewhere and provide evidence of anxiety reduction, self-evaluation improvement, and the like.

9. Providing a broad, sweeping definition of social skills, Libet and Lewinsohn (1973) defined these skills as the ability to emit both positively reinforcing behaviors toward others and to avoid emitting be-

haviors that invited punishment by others. They studied these contrasting behaviors among depressed and nondepressed persons and found that depressed persons were less socially skilled. Interpersonal behaviors of a verbal nature were coded and cross-validated, showing that in more operational measures of social skill (activity level, rate of positive reactions emitted, action latency, and interpersonal range) the nondepressed exceeded the depressed persons.

Of the multiplicity of social skills that might be operationally defined, those mentioned in the Libet and Lewinsohn (1973) study are of special interest inasmuch as they point to the specific behaviors that have to be measured (counted, at least) in operationally defining social skills; and this research also purports to relate social skills to clinical or pathological behavior—depression in this instance.

Inherent in the Libet and Lewinsohn work is the earlier work on social behavior by Gouldner (1960) and Homans (1958, 1961), in which reciprocity was considered to be an important element in social functioning. Social behavior or social skills, however stated, imply reciprocity, interaction, and mutual reinforcement. Those who lack these functional skills are, perforce, less able to socialize and reap rewarding experiences in relationship to others. These shortcomings lead, in turn, to various pathological states, or incline one in such directions. Thus, psychopathology derives from the lack of social skills, from failures in the environment to provide social learning opportunities, and further failure in the environment to provide opportunities for relearning commensurate with broad societal demands.

10. Social achievement might be cited as an example of social skills (Craighead, Kazdin, & Mahoney, 1976, pp. 363–368). Different kinds of failures to achieve social skills or competence resulted in different clinical disorders (Phillips & Zigler, 1961), where hospitalized patients with ruminative and obsessive complaints tended to be more socially competent than patients with suicidal tendencies, temper tantrums, and unreliable behavior. Sometimes the degree of social skills attained by the person before hospitalization was more significant in promoting recovery than the particular diagnosis proffered.

References to social achievement tend to be mentioned more often in studies of hospitalized patients where it is immediately noted whether a person can perform in ways relating to self-care (shaving, bathing, eating, etc.) so as to fit better into the hospital routine. Persons with verbal social skills are more amenable to oral and written instructions, whereas patients with lesser skills either do not follow and attend well to such instructions or they tend to develop negative and oppositional behaviors in response to verbal instructions. The presence of verbal skills allows not only for social skills management (regulation concerning hospital routine), but may also admit persons to group therapy sessions and to vocational and educational instruction more readily. The more skills the better; and with more social skills, the patient is more likely to have out-of-hospital privileges and/or to be discharged with greater confidence and perhaps get a job if other life considerations are in order.

People are more often liked by others when the attending person's listening skills are well developed. The person who is paying attention to another's comments only to find a point to interject his/her own comments, whether they relate or not to what the other person has said, cannot be an example of showing good "listening skills," (this is similar to "attending skills" cited above). In professional settings, a therapist, a physician, lawyer, or teacher is often judged informally on how well the professional listens to what a client or patient has to say and demonstrates this awareness by returning appropriate conversational remarks.

11. Boles (1976) experimented with the listening skills and with exploratory conversational skills among 53 medical students and tried to ascertain, among other questions, whether personality type influenced such skills acquisition. Results indicated that personality type descriptions used in this study did not influence the acquisition of exploratory and listening skills but that the learning environment of the training course did positively influence such skills. These skills, then, were trainable.

One might point also to assertiveness as a set of skills that teach one to approach, interact, support, deny, and otherwise cope with the person or situation with which one is interacting. Failures at assertiveness not only disallow a person's interacting with others in a given situation, but also suggest a repertorial lack, a skill deficit that is more general than the circumstances at hand.

12. The absence of assertiveness skills, clinicians and researchers say, represents a lack in a variety of social skills and may account for much pathology (Wolpe & Lazarus, 1966). The concept of assertiveness (or its lack) may be as broad as the notion of social skills; they are often used interchangeably. Assertiveness training may cover such varied skills as learning to say "Yes" and "No" appropriately, ability to

express anger, noting and expressing disappointment, speaking up for one's rights, realizing that depressive aftermaths may represent a failure in interpersonal relations to act on what one covertly feels or intends, and so on. One of the most succinct ways to increase social skills generally is to proceed through assertiveness training (Craighead, Kazdin, & Mahoney, 1976, pp. 363–365).

The emphasis on assertiveness will be considered again in this book, but it is important to say that the passivity, acquiescence, discouragement, and muted anger that often accompanies lacks in social relationships are directly approached and attacked in assertiveness training. The individual tends to remain underassertive because of the anxiety associated with assertiveness ("others will disapprove of me," "I will hurt their feelings," "I won't be correctly understood," and so on). Underassertiveness preserves an emotional status quo but fails to move the person toward others; as the social skills deficits become habituated, the person comes to think of him- or herself as a failure (which in fact may be the case up to a given point, but it need not remain so) and despairs over "getting a fair hearing from others."

The use of other persons, sometimes peer counselors or confederates of some kind, can often help patients or clients acquire social skills. This kind of effort is sometimes referred to as "systematic human relations training" (Balzer, 1975) and may be directed to various target groups and target problems.

13.   Balzer (1975) used psychiatric in-patient peer helpers to develop interpersonal skills (empathy, respect, warmth); and subjects were trained by nurses on the staff. Pre- and post-test results using checklists, the Minnesota Multiphasic Personality Inventory, a behavioral adjustment scale, and ratings indicated that the training in human relations skills was useful in producing peer helpers able to function in some ways at levels commensurate with trained therapists. Male psychiatric patients to whom the training was directed also improved in their skill levels.

Perhaps one of the main issues in producing constructive social skills training results is that of targeting the desired behavior change specifically and appropriately enough to increase the likelihood of success. Not any social skills training will do; only those skills identified as germane to the social context and to the repertoire of the subjects or patients, with an appropriate match between these two complex sets of conditions, will produce desired changes.

14.   Willingness to self-disclose may be considered an important social skill, especially among peers with otherwise fairly competent social behaviors. Persons disclosing their feelings, problems, etc., to
friends, spouses, employers, and others tend to be warmer, more
likeable persons (Jourard & Lasakow, 1958). Spouses tend to disclose
to one another more than to others. Ability to disclose feelings is a
social skill bearing a relationship to self-confidence, trust in others, and
assertiveness and is indicative to one's self and others that one can
share all manner of positive and negative characteristics with fellow
human beings without being misunderstood or taken advantage of.

Self-disclosure might be interpreted by some as indicating
that one feels free to assert not only overt interactional matters
("I'm sorry, I was in line here first," "Ma'am, I've been waiting a
long time and you are still not taking my order"), but also covert
or closely guarded ones as well. Students will often disclose to
one another how they feel about a teacher or other students, a
course, or even the way a school handles commonly felt problems.
Self-disclosure is a way of expressing not only trust toward
another person, but is also a way of noting that two or more people
share a common problem and may need to share the burden derived therefrom.

15.   Acting firmly, fairly, and consistently toward others (Orford, 1976;
Phillips & Wiener, 1972) places one in an assertive and equal position
with others, prevents one from being condescending or aggrandizing,
and provides for means of handling aggression, social pressure, and
rejection from others. Coopersmith (1967) found that relatively high
self-esteem among high school students and their mothers in middle-
class settings was related to firm, clear, and structured or demanding
parental behavior toward the adolescent, plus a belief in democratic
practices, which is to say the discipline was firm (and even demanding) yet the exchange was fair and consistent between them.

For many years there have been discussions in the child-
rearing literature about permissiveness and structure in parent–
child relationships (Phillips & Wiener, 1972; Phillips, Wiener, &
Haring, 1962). Generally, a parental attitude of firmness, fairness,
and consistency toward the child bodes better for the development of social skills, personal self-esteem, and happiness in the
child than does a parental attitude that is always permissive,
giving-in, and non-contesting of the child's motives and demands. How else is the child, who is often petulant and demanding, to learn the limits and bounds of his emotional stance unless

he or she is dealt with firmly, fairly, and consistently by responsible adults?

16. One could argue that self-esteem depends upon exercising relevant social skills. Self-esteem is probably a composite of social skills, a derivative of many skills acting on issues important for the individual. Many clinicians—Freudian analysts, the self theorists, as well as behavior modification practitioners—all agree that self-esteem is important in social functioning and that self-esteem may, in turn, be based on a variety of factors: A feeling of *personal worth; social competence* based on past and current success in social functioning; the experience of a modest sense of *personal power* or *strength* in carrying out social roles that have relevance to the individual; and a sense of *virtue* in holding to one's own standards and values (Orford, 1976, p. 53).

In discussing social skills in complex settings among psychotherapy patients, one will often hear recitals of social deficits that relate to the conditions cited above: "I don't feel I am *worth* much, therefore, I don't speak up in social or public settings," one patient reported (lacking a feeling of personal worth); "I know I have something to say but *I am afraid I'll muff it*, get confused, stutter, or act like a fool," another person remarked in therapy (social competence in self-assertiveness, although an underlying belief that one has something to say is stated by the patient); "Every time I try to talk to her I feel my opinion is worthless, that what she has to say is somehow right and I am wrong . . . so I just never get out what I want to say," remarked a patient in discussing her mother (lacking personal strength, power, and conviction); and "I felt it was important for me to stand up for what I believed in the group discussion, even though my ideas were not popular with them," a patient reported about a contentious group discussion centering around ethical issues in her profession (displaying a feeling of virtue in holding to one's standards and values despite opposition).

17. Gradually increasing social skills complexity through successive steps. King and others (1960) progressively taught schizophrenics to first depress a lever for sweets and cigarettes (accompanied by statements of "good," "very good," etc., by the experimenter); second, to have the patients move on to more complex motor responses; third, to move further on to giving and responding to verbal cues and instructions; and fourth, to use team work, where all steps were reinforced appropriately by social and material consequences.

The study by King et al. (1960) is similar to many studies with retardates and autistic persons in which fairly complex social skills are taught on a gradual, step-by-step basis, with each step clearly reinforced and well solidified in the client's repertoire before moving on to the next stage. The successive approximations route is essential when repertoires of social skills are particularly meager at the beginning, and an end result is sought that cannot possibly rely on verbal instructions alone as reinforcement.

18.   Simulation, role playing, and modeling have proliferated in so many studies that an adequate review of them would take a separate volume or two (Bandura, 1969; Bandura, 1973). Studies of social skills training using these techniques, and others akin to them, are usually based on verbal and action-oriented instruction, and acting-out roles by models, with trainees (patients) then simulating what they have seen and understood to be their objectives. Often, video and movie versions of social behavior are utilized to present to the patients the end results of the behavioral skill under study (McFall & Lillesand, 1971).

The use of modeling techniques generally applies to more complex social skills and to people with more complex social repertoires already in use, where verbal instructions alone are not as economical as visual models. Social skills modeling in relation to opposite sex skills might be far more useful than simply talking about such relationships in a therapeutic context and might be expected to come more to the point as to what behaviors are functionally useful.

SOCIAL SKILLS AND COMMUNICATION WITH OTHERS

What, then, are social skills, social competencies, assertiveness, and other equivalencies? A person is socially skilled, competent according to:

the extent to which he or she can communicate with others in a manner that fulfills one's rights, requirements, satisfactions, or obligations to a reasonable degree without damaging the other person's similar rights, requirements, satisfactions, or obligations, and hopefully shares these rights, etc., with others in free and open exchange.

This definition, while not intended to be all-encompassing, may fit a variety of situations: asking the opposite sex member to share an experience such as a dance; carrying out one's daily role in an institution with minimal friction; not letting another person usurp one's rights; speaking openly about anger, disappointment, unfair treatment; not being taken advantage of; saying positive things to another person without feeling insincere or condescending; being free to initiate an interaction with another person without embarrassment; being capable of continuing on with an interaction (or discontinuing it) without feeling pressure, estrangement, or rejection. Social skills also include knowing what to say, to wear, how to behave in a variety of situations extant in our culture, where deviations from the norms are ably handled but are not engaged in for wholly selfish purposes. All of these details do not mean that one has to be niggling, compulsive, or overly formal; flexibility and adaptability are also important social skills, as one's individual style and grace are more than minimally acceptable in social interaction.

RELATIONSHIPS TO SOCIAL PSYCHOLOGY

The previous section covered briefly some representative research approaches and findings concerning social skills. Many of these studies have taken place in hospital or out-patient clinic settings, usually where some kind of intervention purporting to overcome psychopathology has occurred. In addition, there is a vast range of studies from social psychology that bear on social interactions, social skills, and competencies that seldom reach the eye and ear of the clinician. A separate volume or two would be needed to integrate these social psychology studies into the clinical field, and trying to apply them to clinical practice would take a good deal of research—one cannot simply borrow from social psychology and apply techniques whole-cloth to clinical settings. However, a reminder that many areas of research and application can be derived from social psychology and made useful to clinical practice is clearly in order. In the following discussion, a few topics of possible interest to clinical psychologists studying abnormal behavior and looking to social skills remediation will be mentioned and considered.

Many of the behaviors subject to change in the clinical setting could be partly described as face-to-face interactions (or the absence of such interactions among grossly isolated people). Duncan and Fiske (1977) have delineated many areas of research with discussions of theory and methodology, in reference to face-to-face interactions. Methodologically, the much earlier study of group interactional processes by Bales (1950) might serve as a model for some types of analysis of group processes and applications to the change process in clinical practice. Barker's work on the stream of behavior (1963), which cited detailed interactions between persons and their environments in terms of "acts" as discrete units of behavioral analysis in relation to the physical environment, may also be reviewed and considered by clinical psychologists.

Duncan's work on nonverbal communication, on signaling when it is another person's turn to take up the conversation, and related topics might be of considerable importance in assessing social skills among patients and in remediating the attendant skill deficits (Duncan, 1969, 1972; Duncan & Niederehe, 1974). These small interpersonal acts may be the building blocks for many aspects of social skills as reviewed previously.

Rather than using verbal retrospective reports to assess the degree of social skills and competencies among patients, hospitals at least, and perhaps out-patient clinics as well, could be the setting for conducting video tape studies of social interaction in real or simulated settings (Duncan & Fiske, 1977, pp. 148–149; Ekman & Friesen, 1969). Many social interactions are so fleeting and subtle, yet often of such far-reaching importance, that they cannot be readily and reliably captured by the human eye. Their more detailed measurement and extension into social skills areas await more sophisticated recording, as is afforded by video or movie cameras; these records are then preserved for further research and reliability checks.

Interpersonal attraction has been considered in a comprehensive review by Duck and his associates (1977). A large number of behaviors are subsumed under interpersonal attraction, many of which at least touch base with the social skills topics cited above and many more of which could form the basis for further social skills studies that are of importance to clinical situations and to social functioning of both disturbed and nondisturbed persons.

One could consult some of the comprehensive volumes on social psychology to gain access to other topics bearing on social competencies and skills (Argyle, 1969, 1975; Berkowitz, 1972; Clore, 1975; Homans, 1974; Kelvin, 1970; Murstein, 1974, 1976). Broadening one's clinical perspective through the study of social processes of many kinds could go far toward encouraging new research and clinical practice in the area of social skills as they bear on psychopathology.

SOME CONTRASTING FAILURES IN SOCIAL SKILLS

It may be useful to delineate some contrasting instances of failure in social skills, as we sometimes understand concepts, as well by their absence as by their presence.

It is often recognized that people who lack appropriate social skills are often regarded as "peculiar," as "odd balls," with diagnostic labels being applied to the socially incompetent by peers as well as professionals: "He acts skitzy," one man said of a fellow worker; "She's really flaky and I expect her to break down any time," another averred about his female secretary; "I think she's crazy—at least terribly immature—the way she acts most of the time," one student said of her roommate. We judge another person largely by and through social behaviors; we add to or take away from that judgment from what a person might disclose to us about his or her life in confidence. Sometimes we discount personal disclosure of people who report that their private lives are strongly in contrast to the facade they may present in limited interactions: "Oh, you don't look to me like you have any problems" or "I think it is your imagination—you seem to get along so well," both remarks made to persons who disclosed feeling states and personal problems apparently contrasting with their public behavior.

We are often struck by news reports of serious crimes perpetrated by persons who otherwise, superficially, seem adequate, until we get into the details of their social and personal lives. We often note after-the-fact that a murderer of several people ". . . seemed to be a loner . . ." or "he sometimes came up with some pretty weird things but I never thought he'd do *that*." We cannot readily understand bizarre behaviors, summary destructive acts unless we know more fully the person's social and personal functioning; when we know that, we can better understand the preemptive acts that are so startling and shocking. Most serious social offenders and perpetrators of serious crimes lack social skills: "I could never get a date with a girl," one murderer was reported to have said to the press; and another said, "I hate people because they never pay any attention to me." Examination shows such persons—lonely, resentful, vindicative—to have contemplated criminal-like recriminations on many occasions, perhaps even performed some of them and escaped apprehension, only to continue on in their isolated vein, eventually committing a crime that brings their very serious disturbance to full recognition.

EXAMPLES OF POOR SOCIAL SKILLS

Some milder versions of poor social skills may be addressed in the following examples. These are not as dramatic or destructive as murder and other heinous crimes, but they do help to fill out the picture of social skills adequacy by contrasting examples of inadequacy.

> *Excessive self-references.* A person talks about him- or herself most of the time, telling long stories about him or herself and boring others with the rendition. Sentences usually begin with "I," and reactions to another person's conversation take up not where the correspondent left off but where the "I-user" left off (Orford, 1976, pp. 64–65).

We all know people with these monotonous social presentations of themselves. We usually try to avert continuing interaction, often avoiding some interactions at all costs. We may remark that we feel sorry for such people, recognizing that they tend to dominate others with their single-track social interactions without seeming to recognize the impact such unilateral behaviors have on others.

> Playing an *interrogative* role. Asking questions excessively, giving the other person the "third degree," not waiting for replies, and seldom continuing the conversation by including how the other person in fact replied. It is as if such a person had a long list of questions and requirements in social interaction and the other person's reactions were unilaterally ignored and seldom shared (Argyle, 1969).

Such interrogation quickly leaves the impression that the question-askers do not really care about interacting with other people, but have ulterior motives to satisfy that are hindered by reciprocity and free exchange. The question-askers in such instances may appear to be very selfish, domineering, and controlling—which they usually are.

> Showing great difficulty in *opening* and *closing* conversations. The inhibited person here is so self-

occupied—similar to the instances cited above—that others' remarks and nonverbal stance are not noted or reacted to with relevance. The co-respondent may be trying to look at and encourage the inhibited person to converse; or one person in a social duet may be trying to leave, while the other continues to hold the first to the conversation to the extent that the interaction becomes aversive (Duncan & Fiske, 1977).

One individual, commenting on a person who had great difficulty in starting and sustaining conversation, said: "I just never know if I am speaking *with* him; he seems to attend but then I never can be sure—it's painful, it seems, for him to say anything but grunts or yes/no reactions." Another person observed that she had trouble getting a friend to terminate phone calls—"She'll keep me on the phone all day if I let her—she never knows when to stop and she says the same things over and over and over . . ."

Egocentricity. All so-called mental disorders involve egocentricity, although the latter may exist without the former among people whom we describe as "unusual" or "different," not quite specifying egocentricity. Small degrees of egocentricity make people interesting, but the dividing line is hard to discern (Foulds, 1965). Egocentric means "self-centered." A person's self-centeredness may be interesting for a while or to some people, e.g., the artist who is always coming up with something new; the inventor who talks a lot about what he's doing or going to do, and so on. The abiding question in such cases is whether the self-centeredness is only momentary and the person will come up with something useful, interesting, or remarkable, or whether the egocentricity merges into boring recitals and bespeaks a person with many social inadequacies.

People who are momentarily or intermittently egocentric may display on occasion remarkable ingenuity and social awareness. People who have to perform their main occupations in relative social isolation—poets, writers, composers, artists—may often come off in some social settings as egocentric, yet display remarkable social dexterity in other settings. One has to see such people broadly and deeply in order to decide when egocentricity is simply a selfish, redundant, narrow set of interactions and when it is simply an interlude in a limited social context with a person possessing a remarkable repertoire that does not easily show itself to any observer [see Clark's (1975) biography of Bertrand Russell in this connection].

> The *schizophrenic non-society* represents an extreme case of social skills deficit. These patients do not engage in, or make up, social interactions as we know them; they use few or no signs (verbal or nonverbal) toward one another; they have no explicit leadership that is acknowledged or followed; they do not cooperate, trade off, or barter; they do not pick up from or renew an interaction with another (Orford, 1976; Sommer & Osmond, 1962). Social skills training in such institutional groups must begin at the most elemental level. The novel *Lord of the Flies*, may represent in part a kind of social deterioration back toward a non-society where inputs from the outside world are minimal (as they often are in institutional settings).

There are also examples of very narrowly constructed societies in penal and correctional institutions (Stanton & Schwartz, 1954; Szasz, 1961). While these societies are not non-societies in the sense of institutional schizophrenic social behaviors, the penal and correctional institutional societies are often extremely narrowly focused and, depending on the institution, may seldom encourage behaviors other than those based on immediate supremacy over others, domineering and threatening tactics, sexual assaults, and other nonconstructive interactions.

RELEVANCY OF SOCIAL SKILLS TO CLINICAL PROBLEMS

What can we now say about social skills and their relevancy to the study of psychopathology and to clinical problems in general? Several generalizations flow tentatively from the foregoing: Social skills are a new area of study having much promise for understanding abnormal or pathological behavior and for replacing a largely time-consuming preoccupation with diagnosis and classification (see later chapters for more detail on this topic); social skills are referred to only tangentially and infrequently in much of the literature in abnormal psychology, behavior modification, and training, but are occasionally mentioned with such cogency as to demand serious attention; social skills are extremely numerous and cover almost every facet of one's life but, as yet, there are no agreed-upon guides for defining social skills, since they exemplify more of a common sense, observational basis for assessing behaviors that relate to the individual and to his or her social context; social skills are composed of examples of very flexible and functional notions about how people interact in ways that are interdependent and potentially mutually satisfying to the participants; they help to spell out the differences between normal and abnormal functioning; social skills efforts offer a more parsimonious way of changing behavior than that of institutionalization or prolonged therapy; social skills offer a specific way of entering into and enlarging upon the person's repertoire in constructive ways so that simultaneously individual subjective experiences and social functioning are enhanced; and they are a viable way of connecting the so-called inner world with the outer world, a way of connecting subjective experience and evaluation with objective criteria of change. Social skills study also relates notions about how people are now trained (educated) to fit into a social context under a potential set of criteria, with how people might be educated so that social skills development and a social curriculum might become a more salient feature of human development and functioning. A social skills viewpoint is a more positive, constructive, testable way of looking at human social problems and foibles than those that tend to locate causality inside the person with few or no ways of examining these presumed causes with testable procedures.

Not all existing techniques and procedures in clinical study are immediately adaptable to a social skills viewpoint. Some nod must be given to traditional assessment procedures, which is done in the next chapter, relating as best we can at this time the more orthodox viewpoints to a social skills one; a rapprochement is sought in chapter 2.

2

The study of personality and psychopathology have never been without a plethora of theories, hypotheses, and clinical hunches. Over the last several decades there have been more books written about personality and its various facets, including abnormal psychology and psychopathology, than almost any other topic in psychology. With the growing importance of clinical psychology during the past 2 decades, there has been a renewal of diagnostic studies, mostly psychometric, in the effort to find categories that might improve reliability of nosological groupings, relate better to the patient's history, and be of some predictive value as to the outcomes from various kinds of treatment, including psychotherapy. Many of the efforts to improve psychodiagnosis stemmed from the growth of psychometric instruments that promised greater objectivity and possibly to replace clinical judgment (Meehl, 1954). Attempts to place the diagnostic enterprise squarely between the patient's past and present (and future) have never suffered from neglect.

The diagnostic enterprise, however, has not proved entirely satisfactory; nor have psychometric efforts to bolster diagnosis been without serious limitations. Diagnosis and psychometric devices have certain strengths and limitations: a social skills approach may offer some improvement on diagnosis and psychometric evaluations—although these will probably never be wholly abandoned—by both feeding on the former types of efforts and striking out in new directions at the same time.

Diagnosis, Psychometric Evaluations, and Social Skills: A Rapprochement

DIAGNOSIS

Diagnosis, in one form or another, has been with us for decades, perhaps centuries if we allow for the inclusion of the Greek notion of humors—blood, phlegm, black bile, and yellow bile—which were thought to depict not only fundamental body states but also to display a relationship with what today we call psychological factors or predispositions.

Kraepelin was an early diagnostic theorist who developed a complicated nosological or diagnostic set of categories that has influenced diagnostic efforts ever since, even though today few would subscribe wholly to the Kraepelinian system. His system was intended to relate body type and psychological characteristics of the "mentally ill" and to provide a reliable classification for treatment and disposition as well as for diagnosis.

Sheldon (1954), in the tradition of Kraepelin, developed a "somatotype" theory[1] in which three major body types—endomorph, mesomorph, and ectomorph—were correlated with certain behavioral and personality inclinations or predispositions. This was an attempt in one gigantic effort to relate "mind and body" in a way that purported to help not only the clinician in

---

[1] Sheldon's three somatotypes (body types) were: ectomorph—lean, small-boned, esthete, intellectual, shy; mesomorph—brawny build, large bone, muscular, and athletic; and endomorph—fat, rotund, "jolly," or "happy-go-lucky." 23

treatment and diagnostic postures but also was intended to increase knowledge about personality functioning in general, including, of course, in normals.

It is not necessary to elucidate all the trends in diagnosis that have characterized psychological and psychiatric thought over the years; it is sufficient to say that the attempts at classification have been numerous, without any of them standing out in terms of validity, reliability, or simple clinical usefulness. In fact, the whole diagnostic enterprise has been an essentially disappointing one with few redeeming features. We must eventually leave it to history, rather than pursuing constant refinement of an approach that may have already had its time.

Some of the reasons that diagnostic classifications of nosological groupings have proved unsatisfactory are the following:

1. Trained observers in the same hospital or clinical setting often come up with different diagnoses based on essentially identical data (Beck, 1967b, Beck et al., 1962).

2. Often, when a patient is rediagnosed by the same clinician after the lapse of a period of time, the two diagnostic results may differ noticeably (Kleinmuntz, 1974, p. 31). This may be a function of some or many changes in the data-base (e.g., the patient may get better or worse) as well as diagnostic unreliability.

3. Diagnostic labels, as such, may replace better and more complete understanding of the patient: the clinician may assert, "Well, what do you expect—he's a schizophrenic!"

4. The diagnostic label does not tell us how the patient became disturbed, how treatment should be planned, what the expected outcomes from a variety of treatments are, or what the treatment of choice would be. (In physical medicine, the diagnosis either fulfills these criteria or closely approximates them.)

5. Present and recent, as well as historical, attempts at psychodiagnosis stem from a disease model of illness, where both the terms "disease" and "illness" have a physical ill-

ness implication. Nondiagnostic views, nonmedical and nonillness, of human maladaptation follow a social learning model that states that the person has learned his or her maladaptive behavior in a manner similar to how other (adaptive) behavior is learned (Calhoun, 1977; Coleman, 1976; Davison & Neale, 1974; Martin, 1977; Nathan & Harris, 1975).

6. Diagnosis is based on the assumption that symptoms often "go together" (form syndromes), whereas individual differences, especially in the "milder" disorders, are extensive and many commonly observed symptoms associated with given classification (e.g., neurosis) are known to vary widely with age, sex, social status, education, ethnic background, and so forth (Maher, 1966, pp. 24–28).

7. Apropros to no. 6, state hospitals versus private hospitals and out-patient psychiatric services versus state hospitals tend to display different "diagnostic styles," in that the state hospitals accumulate more organic, psychotic, and severe disorders than private hospitals or private out-patient facilities (Page, 1975, pp. 37–38, 172). These differences may reflect selection or social stratification differences based on cultural circumstances (Zax & Cowen, 1972), as well as diagnostic unreliability.

8. Diagnosis may not only be unreliable, as per many points cited above, but it may be unnecessary; diagnosis is not necessary to begin or carry out treatment or psychotherapy. As a corollary, a misdiagnosis may hinder treatment by placing a spurious emphasis on some and not other aspects of the patient's behavior.

9. A significant number of therapists and theorists hold that all functional (i.e., nonorganic) or learned maladjustments have a common basis, and their descriptive differences reside primarily in exigencies and

shaping conditions in the lives of patients rather than fundamental differences in the various disorders (Maher, 1966; Zax & Cowen, 1972).

10. Clinicians having high level confidence in their own diagnostic skills often move to support their predilections and resist evidence to the contrary, setting "diagnostic styles" that may subsequently have an impact on whether and how the patient is treated. Thus, diagnosis can become a kind of "self-fulfilling prophesy" rather than a descriptive or objective assessment of the patient.

11. A clinician's diagnosis may not only give rise to a self-fulfilling prophesy, but may also act so selectively in how he or she responds to the patient that the patient "learns" to develop and show the symptomatology alleged in the diagnosis (Zax & Cowen, 1972, p. 14).

12. The psychological and social realities governing the lives of persons (patients included) tend to ebb and flow. How a person appears at any given time (e.g., during a depressive reaction to the loss of a loved one) may be more a function of the particular circumstances under which he or she was diagnosed than any abiding characteristic.

13. If we attend properly to the issue of analyzing the patient's behavior, life situation, current exigencies, age, sex, intelligence, education, social status, and so on, we are likely to focus on many specifics in the person's life (e.g., depressive aftermath, hysterical reactions to stress, a "breakdown" following trauma). We can try to be very practical in helping the patient respond constructively to these conditions, keeping in mind the descriptive relevance of age, sex, etc., and putting far less emphasis on a label or diagnostic category. In this case, the clinician or therapist would be emphasizing the pa-

tient's capacity for problem solving and recovery, not placing the patient in a diagnostic category.

14. With the increasing importance of behavioral methods the diagnostic /treatment enterprise attunes itself to the patient's environment (family, job, living conditions, close relationships, etc.) and what can be done in the environment to aid the patient's recovery; emphasis is put on the patient-environmental interactions, not on some hypothetical "inner" state of the person.

15. When more primitive, or as yet developing, countries show changes toward industrialization and urban congestion, they take on the neuroses of the Western world (Carothers, 1953; Page, 1975; Tooth, 1950; Wallace, 1966) and develop problems and symptoms comparable to those developed in urban settings in Western societies. Their "neuroses" were presumably nonexistent until stress and conflict supervened in their social lives and gave rise to symptoms and syndromes which, in our society, we would "diagnose" as neurotic or the like. These diagnosable symptoms, then, were not indigenous to the persons, as persons, or even to the society, until changes in the form of the conflicts and pressures of industrialization overtook the inhabitants.

16. Social skills programs apply across the board to all types of clients or patients. Psychotherapy has often been criticized because of its primary application to the young, attractive, verbally intelligent, and successful (YAVIS) types of patients (Sloane, et al., 1975, pp. 43–46). Truly effective behavior change methods have to minimize the preferences of therapists for the YAVIS types and tailor efforts to cover patients in hospitals and other institutions, out-patient mental hygiene cases, inner-city cases, university /college counseling center cases,

and early /middle /late adolescent populations from working families and the less
well educated.

17. In the social skills approach to changing
psychopathological behavior, somewhat different problems with validity and reliability
occur, including problems with specificity
of target behaviors and with generalization
(Craighead, Kazdin, & Mahoney, 1976; Phillips, 1977a). Since the teaching or training
situation that purports to communicate social skills and competencies can be readily
observed, data can be collected on procedures and communicated to other researchers with high accuracy. The kinds of
schedules used, what reinforcers are apt for
given individuals or groups, problems related to discriminative stimuli, and so forth,
are challenging technical issues, existing in
connection with any behavior modification
project. However, these are experimental
problems and not problems related to diagnosis.

18. If diagnosis is supposed to lead to further
change in the patient's status and to contribute to psychotherapeutic or other treatment, then it largely misses the objective. It
has been shown (Meehl, 1959) that over 80%
of typical clinical diagnostic information is
of little value to psychotherapy. Diagnosis
tends to stand alone, to reside in the patient's folder, to contribute more to bulk than
to enlightened planning for the patient.
Peterson captures this point when he says,

> ... it is growing more and more apparent that
> there are serious flaws in the traditional approach
> to psychodiagnosis and that the means by which
> clinicians have studied personality need to be
> complemented and possibly replaced by im-
> proved procedures. (Peterson, 1968, p. 2)

Some backup data and support for these reasons for casting
doubt on the diagnostic enterprise follow. In connection with

agreement between two diagnosing clinicians (psychiatrists in this case), Table 2–1 shows greater inconsistency between the psychiatrists in regard to "characterological" problems than in regard to organic diagnoses (Schmidt & Fonda, 1956). This table supports point no. 1, above, and has implications for points nos. 3, 4, 5, and 6.

Another table (see Table 2–2) shows further support for point no. 1, as well as for the additional points already cited (3, 4, 5, 6), in that the agreement between two psychiatrists offering diagnostic opinions among six categories—Neurotic-Depressive Reaction, Anxiety Reaction, Sociopathic Disturbance, Schizophrenic Reaction, Involutional Reaction, and Personality Trait Disturbance—vary widely with the type of diagnosis (Beck et al., 1962).

Point no. 7 relating to diagnostic predispositions and biases between out-patient psychiatric services and state/county mental hospitals, is shown in Table 2–3. Although selective factors operate as to who goes to what hospital, under whatever conditions, there are rather large differences between the two types of institutions as to diagnostic category frequencies, with some categories—among hundreds of thousands of cases—being extremely small or nonexistent (NIMH Survey and Report Section, 1971).

There are other reasons why diagnosis may be unreliable. A diagnostic category, like any category, test, measurement, or descriptive label, must meet two criteria of usefulness: *reliability*

Table 2–1
Showing Agreements Between Pairs of Psychiatrists Diagnosing Same Patients, State Hospital Populations[a]

GENERAL DIAGNOSIS	PERCENT	SPECIFIC DIAGNOSIS	PERCENT
Organic	92	Acute brain syndrome	68
		Chronic brain syndrome	80
		Mental deficiency	42
Psychotic	80	Involutional	57
		Affective	35
		Schizophrenic	51
Characterological	71	Neurosis	16
		Personality pattern	8
		Personality trait	6
		Sociopathic	58

[a] From Schmidt and Fonda. *Journal of Abnormal and Social Psychology,* **52,** 262–267. Copyright 1956 by the American Psychological Association. Reprinted by permission.

Table 2–2
Percent of Agreement between
Psychiatrists for Six Diagnostic
Categories[a]

CATEGORY	NUMBER OF DIAGNOSES	PERCENT AGREEMENT
Neurotic Depressive Reaction	92	63
Anxiety Reaction	58	55
Sociopathic Disturbance	11	54
Schizophrenic Reaction	60	53
Involutional Reaction	10	40
Personality Trait Disturbance	26	38

[a] From Beck et al., 1962. Quoted by permission from the American Psychiatric Association, copyright, 1962. *American Journal of Psychiatry,* **119,** 354.

Table 2–3
The Incidence of Disorders by Diagnosis
and by Treatment Facility (Admissions to
Out-patient Psychiatric Services and to
State and County Mental Hospitals, 1969)[a]

	PERCENT OF TOTAL ADMISSIONS	
	Out-patient psychiatric services ($n = 881,000$)	State and county mental hospitals ($n = 368,000$)
Diagnosis		
Neuroses	19	09
Schizophrenia	17	27
Transient situational reactions	15	—
Personality disorders	11	07
Alcoholic disorders	05	26
Childhood behavior disorders	05	—
Conditions without manifest psychiatric disorders	05	—
Affective psychoses	03	04
Other organic brain syndromes	03	11
Drug disorders	02	03
Mental retardation	03	03
All other disorders	12	10

[a] From the National Institute of Mental Health, Survey and Reports Section, Statistical Notes 26–50, Sept. 1971.

and *validity*. A reliable category, test score, label, etc., is one that yields the same results (or score) on successive occasions. Think of measuring a floor for a rug or linoleum. If each time you measured you got a different square footage figure, you would not know which to use; the measure would be unreliable and your actual rug or linoleum might be too small or too large as a result. If every time you gave a test, you obtained a considerably different score, one would not know which score to use—the reliability or consistency among the scores would be so varied as to be wholly confusing. If diagnostic categories are arrived at through inconsistent or unspecified evaluations because two or more clinicians cannot generally agree on the diagnosis, or if the same clinician disagrees with him- or herself on different occasions, we have a lack of reliability. Hence, the knowledge and usefulness of a diagnosis obtained is more confusing than enlightening.

Validity is equally important. Validity refers to the extent to which an assessment, measure, score, label, etc., means what it says it means. It is a matter of calling something by the "right" name: A mechanical ability test should validly measure mechanical ability, performance, etc.; a test bearing the name of "intelligence" should demonstrably measure intellectual acumen, not some other factor or factors. Since diagnoses do not actually refer to organic conditions or processes, they are perforce based on social, behavioral, and interactional data about the person or patient. Thus, what we call "neurotic" may mean different things to different clinicians, compared to a "high temperature" or a "swollen gland" in the organic sense of these categories.

Validity may be further broken down into types: predictive validity, concurrent validity, content validity, and construct validity. Each of these types may have some bearing on understanding the problem of diagnostic classification. *Predictive* validity allows for accurate statements about future conditions—Can the diagnosis predict treatment outcome or what kind of treatment will work best with a given diagnostic classification? If we have low validity in general, as is the case with diagnostic classifications, then predictive validity—the most functionally useful validity—will suffer, and predictions will have low probability of correctness. *Concurrent* validity means that other, or concurrent, measures in addition to (say) an interview procedure, will give diagnostic results comparable to the interview; perhaps psychometric findings would serve as concurrent validity to diagnostic interviews. However, as we increase the types of measures we use in diagnostic work, the discrepancies become wider, not really concurrent. *Content* validity refers to the extent of attention given to typical aspects of a diagnostic category in making the diagnosis. For example, sluggishness and poor sleep may be important aspects of depression; making sure these items of behavior are assessed in interviewing or testing would apply to the notion of content validity. However, clinicians and diagnosticians may vary considerably in what they consider to be the essential elements of any category. Hence, content validity suffers from lack of prior agreement or orientation as to what is important, thus making for diagnostic unreliability. Finally, construct validity refers to whether the definitional or theoretical aspects of a diagnostic category can be verified objectively or operationally. If "low self-esteem" is a construct of compelling importance in diagnosing "neurosis," the measurement of this concept or construct is then required. Usually the less objective the construct (the more it is located inside the person's thinking and feeling), the less well it serves as a valid construct because it becomes too hard to assess.

What is scientifically and clinically necessary is predictive validity. If we have predictive validity, we have the other validity notions in hand, and we can say with assurance that given assessment procedures from interview or psychometric data will give the information needed to predict treatment outcome, the preferred choice of treatment, or the like. Lacking predictive validity, we tend to fall back on the less rigorous notions of validity and muddle through as best we can. Actually, none of the four types of validity fare particularly well in affording confidence in diagnostic categorization. Concurrent validity is very difficult to obtain because test or psychometric findings are often initially validated on the basis of "clinical evidence," interview material, or the like. Content validity raises a problem in reliability in that different clinicians cannot agree reliably on what they consider to be the quintessence of neurosis, depression, schizophrenia, or any other diagnostic or nosological classification. Construct validity is often more a theoretical exercise than it is a constructive lead to better empirical evidence. So what are we left with in the diagnostic effort? Several authors have summed up the sentiments of this discussion. Carson (1969) said, "Disorders of behavior . . . are unrelated to physical pathology . . . I regard these classifications of behavior (such as schizophrenia and obsessional neurosis) as being very nearly meaningless when used in anything but a purely descriptive way . . ." (pp. 220–224). It is doubtful if the diagnostic enterprise has improved much since Cameron (1944) expressed his somewhat discouraged view of it over 30 years ago:

> All current attempts at classification of functional personality disorders are unsatisfactory; this is true for the neuroses as well as the psychoses. No causal organisms have been implicated, hence we

cannot fall back upon them as we can in the specific infectious diseases, and the central nervous system exhibits no consistent changes that can be correlated with the syndromes as in neurological disorders. (p. 870; also, see Cameron, 1947)

Nathan and Harris (1975) commented:

Although a mental status examination and a review of the patient's personal history are still the touchstones on which diagnosis, treatment, and research are based, these methods have long aroused controversy. The dispute revolves around their subjectivity and resultant potential for unreliability. In fact, research has shown that the age, sex, race, and socioeconomic status of the patient, the examiner, or both can effect the conclusions drawn. . . . (p. 123)[1]

Peterson (1968) shows how complex diagnoses may occasionally be, resulting in confusion and unreliability: "It [diagnosis] may consist only of a Kraepelinian APA-style disease name such as 'Schizophrenic reaction, paranoid type, with obsessive features, in a passive-aggressive personality' . . ." (p. 2). How a clinician can keep track of such a diagnostic opinion in treatment, how he or she can convey its meaning clearly to another clinician, or how the same clinician can ferret out the same diagnostic features on another occasion (without access to his or her previous diagnosis) remains a mystery (Meehl, 1954, 1959, 1960).

Examples of how diagnostic efforts can give rise to reified concepts, to the positing of internal forces or entities acting in assumed (and infectious) ways, where the diagnosis acts as its own explanation, can be seen in the following statement by Baruch (1949):

When pus accumulates and forms an abscess, the abscess must be opened and drained. If it isn't done the infection spreads. In the end, it may destroy the individual. Just so with feelings. The "badness" must come out. The hurts and fears and anger must be released and drained . . . when unwanted NEGATIVE FEELINGS have been emptied out sufficiently then—warm and good POSITIVE FEELINGS flow in. When muddy water, which has dammed up, drains out from a pool, then fresh, clear water can flow in. So it is with these feelings. (pp. 38–45)[2]

Are there any redeeming values for the diagnostic enterprise? Some would say yes, some would say no, and others would be extremely doubtful. To give credit that may accrue to the diagnostic enterprise, we must mention that diagnosis may be useful

---

[1] From Nathan P.E. & Harris S.L. *Psychopathology Society.* Copyright 1975. Used with permission of McGraw-Hill Book Company.

[2] From Baruch D. *New ways in discipline.* Copyright 1949. Used with permission of McGraw-Hill Book Company.

in differentiating between psychotic and neurotic persons, that diagnosis may have an administrative value in hospitals and out-patient clinics, and that however unreliable diagnoses are, they may still point to some significant data about the patient and thereby help (in however limited a way) with possible assignment to therapy and other dispositions. The more the diagnostic enterprise moves away from internal states and focuses on the environment of the patient, the more we may be able to point to these factors as important in the causality and in the remediation of disturbances.

CONSIDERING PSYCHOMETRICS

Many efforts to improve psychodiagnostics during the past 3 decades have sprung from developments in the psychometric field. Psychometrics, of course, refers to measuring "mental traits" or characteristics, taking clinical hunches about important variables and converting them into measurement scales of one sort or another, and analyzing statistically the results from varied approaches to the problem of diagnosis. We will see now how psychometric activities may be applied to the problem of diagnosis and how, in turn, psychometrics can be shown to give way to the study of social skills as an alternative to both diagnosis and psychometrics.

In their own right, psychometric approaches to diagnosis may be somewhat superior to interview and life history assessment (although the latter also retain some advantages in terms of flexibility), in that the reliability and validity problems are more in hand and can be more encouragingly and objectively mastered. Any item or life survey procedure that obtains in psychiatric or diagnostic interviewing can be included in a psychometric procedure, with the latter affording a better grasp on the validity and reliability problems inherent in any assessment.

The problem of reliability is more easily approached among psychometric devices than is that of validity. Validity measures fall back on the extent to which the test or inventory agrees with "clinical opinion," or some other presumably independent assessment already extant, and thus pivot on somewhat insecure bases. However, in psychometric instruments, we have the option of seeing what items or constellations of items agree with independent assessment; we can always "clean up" the psychometric device, refine it here and there, and constantly obtain feedback on its usefulness in a variety of clinical settings. We do not have that same kind of control on subjective interview findings.

As to reliability, the psychometric device can be assessed readily for its status—test–retest measures can be taken over varying periods of time (1 day, 1 month, 1 year, as examples). This is where the same test is administered under the same set of conditions to the sample population on two different occasions which are narrowly or widely separated in time. The psychometric instrument can yield a split-half reliability figure in that on two occasions, each half of the test is administered; or the whole test can be administered and the odd–even items correlated for reliability status. In the latter case, we would expect the score from the odd-numbered items (1, 3, 5, etc.) to give about the same result as the even-numbered items (2, 4, 6, etc.), thus showing internal consistency or reliability.

The procedures for developing a psychometric instrument are well known. It is decided on the basis of observation, that some variable might, in fact, exist and that this variable is presumably related to other important aspects of human behavior. For example, "quickness in responding" might be construed in natural settings as related to intelligence; note that we said "related to intelligence," not equated with intelligence. Such an observation does not mean that "trigger-happy" responding is required for intelligent behavior but, other things equal, the sooner one responds to a problem, the more likely a solution will be reached. Thus, with most intelligence tests, time limits are inherent in the testing, and extra credit is often given for dispatchful correct answers to questions in arithmetic, solving missing elements in pictorial problems, or telling how figures are alike or different.

Following the decision that a given variable might be a useful and predictive one, the test-maker will then assemble as many instances of this proposed variable as possible, this being an example of construct validity at the outset: It is necessary to select, or formulate, as many items as possible that constitute "intelligent" behavior, or "introversive" tendencies as constructs to follow, seeking as many empirical examples as can be mustered. Even if there is no explicitly stated construct validity notion, the test-maker assumes one or works as if such a construct were a guide.

Having assembled a large number of instances of the variable to be measured, the items are then culled through to weed out any duplications and to ensure that the items are clearly written so that the persons taking the test or responding to the psychometric instrument can gain the same impressions that the test-maker does. Semantic confusion should be avoided. If the resulting test consists of 100 items, another variable must be considered: test-taking time. A test or measuring instrument should not be exhausting or boring.

The next major step is to present the 100 selected items to a suitable criterion population. If the test-maker's objective is to differentiate between "introversive" and "extraversive" tendencies, the preliminary test should be given to people whose extant status is that of being introverted or extraverted. Finding criterion populations is often not easy, especially with personality-type variables such as introversion/extraversion, but assuming that such populations are known and available, the preliminary form of the test is administered to these criterion populations and those items differentiating between the two extant populations are identified. Not all of the 100 initial items will be valid in the sense of truly representing introversive and extraversive behaviors as reported by those responding to the test; the test may identify 40–50 "good" (i.e., differentiating) items. So far so good. These are the beginnings of some evidence that the variable is extant in populations of people, and the test-maker can proceed with statistical refinements that may be extensive, and need not be explicated here.

The main point here is that a possible variable related to behavior in general—or perhaps related to some very specific behavior considered important—has been observed in nature (in clinical work, say), and there is some evidence that a large number of samples of this important variable can be assembled in a way that can be converted into a test or psychometric instrument. In short, the variable is measurable and does not have to be dealt with at arms length only through clinical (i.e., interview) assessment, conjecture, or speculation. When people interview persons for hospital assignment, class assignment, job placement, psychotherapy, or any similar placement, they tacitly assume that they have a collection of items in their minds that correspond or contribute to the task of making judgments about these assignments; the making of a psychometric instrument simply culls out all the tacit assumptions and explicitly tests them among suitable populations of people. Later tests of the validity of the resulting test or psychometric instrument have to be made on other (cross-validating) populations; the better the test stands up against these cross-validating instances, the more confidence is placed in it. Interviewers often do not cross-validate their clinical hunches and so may go on indefinitely believing that the way people, or patients in particular, answer questions is valid enough information on which the interviewer or diagnostician can base his or her judgment. This is, of course, one of the main reasons why diagnostic or psychiatric interviewing, or the like, is relatively unreliable (and therefore invalid).

The use of tests and psychometric devices somewhat refines the cruder, but sometimes more flexible, clinical or interview approach and puts on the table, so to speak, the assumptions and conditions related to the variables under study and their relationships to other variables or to specific problems in understanding and predicting behavior. Tests allow for a "leg-up" on assessment, evaluation, and prediction problems compared to interview techniques, because the problems of reliability and validity are more understood and under better control.

UNDERSTANDING PSYCHOMETRIC METHODOLOGY

The number of tests and variables measured by tests and psychometric instruments are legion. To list them all would take several volumes; the interested reader can consult the work of Buros (1972) to see how many tests exist within several domains (intelligence, personality, ability) and to gain some understanding of how tests are reviewed, criticized, and used. Within each of these domains, a number of tests measuring a large number of variables exist. Our example will take one or two variables in order to more fully understand test methodology.

It is important to realize that from time to time certain promising variables surface and create some interest in research, measurement, and understanding of personality. Consider Jung's (Jung, 1923; Wilson, 1977) early clinical and theoretical work on introversion/extraversion. This work spawned many tests and psychometric measures. Research has related introversion/extraversion to learning readiness, to conditionability, to sexual attitudes and behavior, to intelligence, and a host of other topics (Wilson, 1977). Such studies on introversion/extraversion have promoted interesting and useful stimuli to clinical practice and to personality theory and research.

The study of authoritarianism (Cherry & Byrne, 1977) has also held a revered place in personality study and has shown considerable clinical usefulness. If change in personality and behavior are important, and if we can identify refractoriness to change (rigid, authoritarian personalities), then we have a jump on the problem of change in psychotherapy, in social belief systems and attitudes, and in understanding personality more completely.

It is questionable, however, to what extent inventories of the introverted/extraverted and authoritarian types (as well as any other types) really elucidate behavior change; whether they indicate how change can be fostered and under what conditions.

Psychometric applications, in spite of their value compared to interview and subjective assessment practices, tend to be very abstract and result in data primarily based on the responding person's memory and on other reports as to how and whether one's own behavior occurs in given ways. While the relatively systematic questioning and examining that occurs in tests and psychometric devices is to be preferred in most instances over more subjective approaches, psychometric devices need to be brought closer to the actual behavior change (and predictive) situations on which they purport to give data. There are ways in which psychometric evaluations can be brought closer to the person's actual behavior so that these instruments can serve as bridges between self-reports and abstract personality variables on the one hand and as a basis for behavior change on the other. Some ways in which psychometric instruments in general may be conceptualized (or reconceptualized) to aid in pinpointing behavior change, especially efforts in the direction of social skills improvement, will now be considered.

It has been noted that psychometric devices and tests, covering variables from self-report or direct examination, are abstractions and often have a relatively static quality that makes it difficult to apply to one's daily life, especially where actual behavior change is sought. Their abstract quality is seen in terms of yielding a score—for example, the seventy-fifth percentile on some variable such as extraversion—and the meaning of such a score obtained by an individual. We can say the person receiving such a score falls at a point described as more extraverted than 75 % of a reference population (adults, people in psychotherapy, executives in moderate-sized businesses, etc.). This seventy-fifth percentile score is based on a norm or a set of statistical values that cite average scores and deviations from these average scores. It is not a score that tells us how the extraversive tendencies actually come to life for the person, whether the extraversive tendencies are socially functional and of satisfaction to the person. The percentile score is also not a score that describes the individual's behavior in situations relevant to some desired change, e.g., meeting anxieties in connection with some interpersonal interactions, dealing with social rejection, and so on. The score may mean no more than that the person acts in an "out-going" manner most of the time according to his or her answers (based mostly on memory or abstract generalizations about one's behavior), with little regard for the social intricacies involved. The seventy-fifth percentile score does not tell anyone what the person would have to do to raise or lower the achieved score, what aspects or items in the inventory or psychometric instrument were the most amenable to change, or other issues relating to change. There is no way to directly move from the percentile score to the individual's actual behavior in important social situations that are reflective of skills and /or personal satisfactions.

The reasons these limitations exist for the study of introversion /extraversion (or any other similar variable) via psychometric instruments lie in the nature of the normalization of scores that is statistically necessary if we are to have an instrument of the type described. We are seeking the typical introversive /extraversive behavior of some limited and defined group of persons (we may limit the measurement's applicability to college students, to employed adults, etc.), and we want to know generally (on the average) how a person answers questions, and how these answers vary around a central tendency or average score. A psychometric device, thus developed and standardized (normalized, given statistical descriptions), cannot evaluate a particular situation, a specific set of social and interpersonal behaviors relating to a given person under a set of observable circumstances (neither can an interview or subjective clinical assessment do these things with known reliability and validity).

The statistical constraints here, although useful in many ways, are not individually centered. For example, if an introversion /extraversion measurement is supposed to describe differentially the behaviors of people who have "satisfying interpersonal relationships" versus those who do not, we are forced to use the questionnaire itself as the norm, rather than the way a given person actually interacts with others in observable circumstances. Figure 2–1 describes this relationship and contrasts direct observational methods with psychometric methods in the study of behavior.

Following from Figure 2–1, we note that the items on an introversion /extraversion measure are answered "+" (agree) or "−" (disagree) and that each individual thereby gets a score. If, on the average, high-scoring extraverts otherwise are shown to have more "satisfying interpersonal relationships," we have some information of value. We do not know how a given individual fares, however. We compare a group of high-scorers with low-scorers and, among these high- and low-scorers in (for example) a hospital setting (with varying amounts of time in the hospital), we may determine statistically that high-scoring extraverts have more satisfying interpersonal relationships; or we may examine the same relationship in a college or high school population, and so on. As Figure 2–1 indicates, statistical tests will tell us if the

Various Individual Responses to Introversion/Extraversion

Questionnaire Items

Item No.	Individual A	Individual B	Individual C
1	+	–	–
2	–	–	+
3	+	+	–
4	+	–	+
5	+	–	–
6	+	+	+
7	–	+	–
8	+	–	–
etc.			

(A)

Observations of individuals (or groups) in specific settings (hospital, home) as per criteria social behaviors:
"Approaching Others"
"Handling Conflicts"
"Taking Turns"

vs

... In Relation to Behavior in a Hospital Setting ....

	Introversive Cases		Extraversive Cases	
	Mean	SD	Mean	SD
Hospital 1 year	25	07	21	06
Hospital 5 years	39	10	17	07
Hospital 10+ years	44	12	12	07

(B)

Training sessions, various types, duration to remediate specific social skills lacks

(C)

Later observations of same social skills in same (or closely similar) situations, based on frequency data relating to observable change

Figure 2-1. Hypothetical schema showing methodological differences between a psychometric approach in terms of some items from a personality questionnaire versus a more direct social skills training approach in specific populations open to observation by attendants, parents, teachers or others.

differences in satisfying relationships among high- and low-scoring extraverts (group averages) is a reliable or significant one.

In contrast, we take three comparable steps in the same figure and see how direct observational measures of social behavior in any one or more of several settings can tell us about the social skills behavior of the individual, how we can think about teaching or training the person in social skills, and, in due course, how we can examine the presence of these social skills in closely similar situations to see if changes have taken place. (We might want to statistically check out the significance of these changes, or we may want to compare each individual with his own earlier and later record of behavior in definable social skills situations.)

What, then, have we done in a methodological way as exemplified in Figure 2–1? We have made several changes in the methodology, to wit:

1. We have asked a different question. We ask in the bottom part of Figure 2–1 what the exact social skills are in reference to given behaviors ("approaching others," "handling conflicts") and have further asked about the later status of these skills, after a training period.

2. We have put the emphasis on the individual's behavior, not on memory or conjecture.

3. The use of a term, such as social skills, is distilled down to point to specific behaviors that are observable, i.e., reliance on the behaving person's memory is eliminated.

4. We are interested in changes comparing the individual with himself (using the individual as his or her own control) and not on statistical averages (although the latter operations can be performed if required).

5. We particularize the question of changing behavior by centering it on the individual as he or she behaves in given, objectively observable situations.

6. We gain considerable confidence in knowing that if psychotherapy and other behavior change efforts are important, we can measure these changes directly without resorting to abstract general measures that have validity and reliability only in a statistical or group comparison sense.

Another reason why a more particularized approach to changing behavior should be used is that in the development of psychometric instruments, a great deal of preliminary work has to be accomplished before the test or inventory can be used. Several complex steps are needed to develop a test: developing a large pool of items, much statistical work at each stage, and a final selection of items that make up the test or psychometric instrument that are later cross-validated on different populations. How much simpler it is—unless there is already a very useful and well-prepared test available (such as the Minnesota Multiphasic Personality Inventory, to name perhaps the best known and most thoroughly tested measure of personality and clinical behavior)—to delineate and observe the *actual behaviors* considered important in a given setting or for a given purpose, to set up pre- and post-measures ("pre" measures are baselines extended over time, not just a one-time cross-section of behavior taken on a given occasion), and, of course, to identify ways in which the behavior is changed by some training or instructional course. The matter of behavior change generalizing to other situations is certainly important but is an issue we need not go into extensively at this point.

One could then proceed with introversion /extraversion measures, or any other personality variables, without reference to questionnaires or psychometric devices, and could follow the bottom half of Figure 2–1. As it is possible to work on behavior change in a variety of clinical settings in this methodologically different way, it might become apparent that some kinds of behavior are more important in some settings than in others, e.g., in hospital settings it is important that patients be able to follow at least a minimal routine (getting up on time, washing, dressing, preparing for and going to meals). Among behaviors in more complex situations, as in schools and families, we identify those that relate to initiating contacts with others, taking turns, sharing, and sustaining these contacts, so that problems and interactions are consummated. Also important is being able to redirect or terminate these interactions in ways that are not destructive to the persons involved but that may, moreover, be mutually agreeable to all (see definition of social skills, chapter 1). As we pursue these larger and more complex objectives via behavior change methods, we come into direct contact with important relationships in people's lives and thereby discover the strengths and weaknesses of the individuals we are studying or helping therapeutically. We thereby enter a different kind of "diagnostic study" of the individual—observing the person who is weak and underassertive in typical situations and thinking of ways to overcome these unwanted behaviors.

One more contrast must be mentioned in order to compare psychometric instruments and their interpretation with a more individualized, social skills approach to changing behavior. It is often assumed that because an objectively usable test or psychometric device is available, the amount of a score indicates a greater amount of a given tendency: the higher the depressive or extraversive score, the greater the amount of depression or extraversion, or whatever. Unless a scale or test variable is constructed along equal incremental lines where each answer is summative, this assumption is not defensible. Rather as tests are constructed, a higher score indicates a greater probability that a person can be included in a given category. Figure 2–2 illustrates this point. Person A has answered eight out of a larger number of items in a scorable or significant direction. Person B has answered more items in the significant direction, and Person C still more. The differences in their scores resides not in Persons B and C being "more" depressed, extraverted, or whatever, than Person A, but in Persons B and C probably being more likely to belong to the class (depression, extraversion, etc.) or category that is under study and that is exemplified by the total collection of items in the category.

The incorrect and less useful notion of psychometric devices and the interpretation of their results is shown in the bottom half of Figure 2–2. In this latter instance, it is assumed that each item is equal to every other item and that the items are additive and linear, thus the more items answered positively, the greater the "amount" of the variable or tendency in question. Unfortunately, many clinicians use psychometric devices as if they were of the latter type and thus are led to making statements about one patient being "more depressed than" or "more disturbed than" another. When we utilize a social skills approach to understanding and changing pathological behavior, we escape the tendency to use probability results additively, and we center not so much on the "amount of" some variable but on its frequency and the conditions under which the variable or tendency in question occurs, and on how it can be modified by and through various techniques.

Following our effort to move toward rapprochement of these clinical methods we are now in a position to bring some summary statements forward in the interest of using clinical and subjective measures, as well as psychometric measures, to lead into direct social skills types of behavior modification of unwanted (or pathological) behavior.

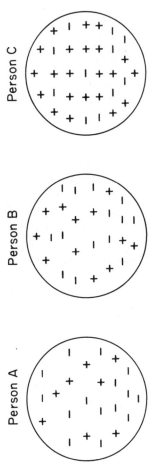

Person A   Person B   Person C

Figure 2-2A.   Demonstration of how three persons answer varying amounts of positively scored items on a personality inventory, thus showing varying probabilities of belonging to the category. The probability that Person C belongs to the category (e.g., Depression) is greater than either Persons A or B, as shown by the density of responses.

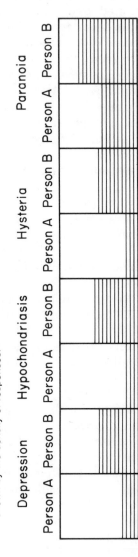

Depression   Hypochondriasis   Hysteria   Paranoia

Person A Person B Person A Person B Person A Person B Person A Person B

Figure 2-2B.   Based on four clinical measures, the graph shows how Persons A and B might be (erroneously) considered to be "more" or "less" depressed, etc., where the number of items answered positively (as shown by the horizontal lines) are thought to be equal in value, linear, and additive; in contrast to Figure 2-2A.

PSYCHOMETRIC MEASURES AND
THE SOCIAL SKILLS APPROACH

COMPREHENSIVENESS

Let us begin with coverage or *comprehensiveness*. The interview, even though it is essentially subjective in its methods and outcomes, lends itself to an accumulation of a comprehensive set of questions and observations. The interviewer need not keep all his questions "in his mind," but may well have checklists or sequential lists written out that can be followed. The patient will doubtlessly answer yes or no, or qualifyingly, under these circumstances; but a fair degree of comprehensiveness is possible. Also, the items covered in an interview or subjective evaluation can lead to *hypotheses* about the individual's behavior that might be central to change, e.g., helping the person get over depressive reactions by checking the notion that the depression is a reactive state that is elicited following situations where the person has to perform before others, or in testing situations where the individual is depressed because he fails to perform perfectly or receive great praise. This hypothesis, then, could lead to specific social skills change methods whereby the individual worked on his "expectancies" in overt, behavioral ways before he or she entered the testing or proving situations.

Psychometric instruments may also provide for comprehensiveness. After all, we have started our psychometric instruments with possibly several hundred items and have distilled them down to perhaps a hundred or fewer items, knowing that we have been both comprehensive and also economical. These items, too, can be pulled out, so to speak, and made the subject matter of direct behavior change methods in the sense of increasing social skills in order to overcome the assessed psychopathology. Figure 2–3 illustrates how these procedures might work in actual situations. In both cases—the interview and the psychometric device—we are dealing with comprehensive screening surveys in order to identify behaviors that are being considered for change, and we use the ready data from interviews or tests to get started on the behavior change project. When we have identified items of particular importance for a given person, we can then enter into the direct observations needed for pretesting or baseline determination prior to the actual behavior change effort.

The transition to social skills from interview and subjective techniques on the one hand and psychometric instruments on the other requires some further discussion. Why the social skills

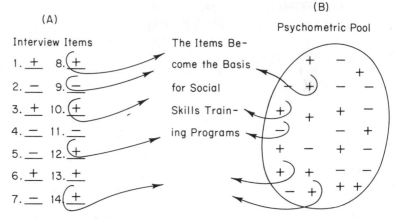

Figure 2-3. Demonstration of how items from the interview (A) and the psychometric/diagnostic pool or category (B) can be identified, pulled out, and used as target behaviors for specific training in social skills. One or more items from an interview checklist or from an inventory may thus be selected for specific social skills training; perhaps in some cases making up interrelated symptoms (or a syndrome) such as "... avoiding people I know because I do not want to speak first ...," "responding in conversation only when another initiates the conversation ...," and "... not knowing how to end a conversation without feeling embarrassment, anger, or guilt. ..."

route? Why not simply improve upon the other two methodologies? Several replies to this query are possible.

1. Many authors have noted that disturbed, hospitalized, clinical, or other descriptive accounts of patients or clients do, indeed, point to social skills deficits (Craighead, Kazdin, & Mahoney, 1976; Levine & Zigler, 1973; Zigler & Phillips, 1961) Whether the social skills deficits come first is unknown, but is of secondary importance if such skills can be identified and described and brought under some control through a behavior change plan. The less the patient is "pathology ridden," after such social skills training, the more this allows us to place some confidence in this approach and to say that social skills may be pivotal (whether they are prior in time or not) in overcoming some psychopathological conditions.

2. Social skills are behavioral, that is, they are readily accessible for observation and description, although the extremely large number of potentially identifiable social skills can lead to some confusion and overlap.

3. It is not necessary to be a trained psychologist or psychiatrist to observe and make constructive use of social skills data; even psychotic patients can often understand the importance of their own progress in acquiring social skills. The importance of social skills to the out-patient populations found in mental hygiene clinics, counseling centers, and the like is at once apparent. People often describe their problems in terms of social skills deficits ("I lose my temper too easily," "I get depressed too easily," "I am too often hurt by the comments of others," and so forth) and readily make efforts to reach specific behavior change goals for themselves.

4. Social skills are, for the reasons cited above, functionally related to life situations of importance to the client or patient: learning how to dance, to initiate and carry on conversations, to fulfill or deny requests from others, to function on jobs, and the like. We do not need an intervening (psychometric or interview) variable such as introversion / extraversion, ascendance /submission, or activity /passivity in the general ways in which such variables are commonly used; we need only to specify the functional relationship between the person's repertoire of skills and the demands of the specific situation(s).

5. The ability to identify specific social skills that are lacking, or that are otherwise important (e.g., they may not be wholly lacking but may need to be considerably upgraded), suggests their amenability to change. As the particular social skills are noted and de-

scribed, their amenability to change is increased, since we know the circumstances under which they occur (or might occur) and how to alter these circumstances to produce the desired results. It is less clear how we might change broad psychometric categories such as introversion /extraversion or ascendance /submission, and what results we might expect if we were able to change these variables (see discussion below for further ideas along this line).

6. Social skills are dynamic in the sense of changing or being subject to change (not "psycho-dynamic" in the traditional sense of unconscious causality). Social skills are different from one situation to another, and some situations where skills are adequate can serve as models or examples for other situations where skills are less polished (e.g., a person knows how to play cards and thus socializes well in such a context, yet lacks important conversational skills, knowing how to dance, how to introduce people, etc.). Thus, the individual's repertoire, in its stronger and more adequate sense, can bolster "weaker" behavior—the Premack principle (Phillips, 1977a; Premack, 1959, 1965, 1971).

7. As a corollary to no. 6, social skills as behavior can be subsumed under general behavioral laws based on reinforcement theory (Craighead, Kazdin, & Mahoney, 1976; Phillips, 1977a, 1977b). Thus, reinforcement contingencies, schedules, the handling of extinction problems, dealing with anxiety as an interfering or inhibiting condition, etc., may be considered in relation to behavioral principles.

8. Conceptualizing social skills in terms of behavioral principles suggests, but is not exclusively based on, viewing unwanted behaviors (social obtuseness in the absence of adequate skills, anxiety as an inhibiting and

distracting influence, and the like) in terms
of developing *alternatives*, rather than in
terms of extinguishing the unwanted behaviors as a first step prior to the encouragement and reinforcement of more
adequate behaviors. That is, the unwanted,
obtuse, and inappropriate social behaviors
(which, by definition, are social skills deficits) are often simply side-stepped, not
reinforced, not paid attention to, so that alternative behaviors, through reinforcement,
gain precedence and serve more appropriate
ends. For example, it is not necessary to ex-
tinguish faulty diction or inarticulation
when learning to improve one's speech before learning more acceptable diction and ar-
ticulation; one simply learns to discriminate
more refined, more relevant behaviors, and
the old, unwanted behaviors are lost in time
due to non-reinforcement.

9. Contrary to what many say, a social skills /
behavioral approach does not eschew subjective ("private events") factors in behavior
but, rather, takes them into consideration as
their relevance is progressively demonstrated, when the person's behavior changes
toward more realizable social goals
(Wachtel, 1977, pp. 115–120). One does not
first have to take into consideration the private (subjective, cognitive) events before
moving ahead along the lines of behavioral
objectives, but can incorporate the former
along with, or as, the behavioral efforts become active. For example, a person who says
he is too anxious at a party to try to speak
with an attractive female is taught how to
take *preliminary* steps under some very
minute and practical guidance, such as that
offered by surrogates or confederates, rather
than being cajoled into one or another social
effort or left to flounder at a party when the
person's anxiety level is already at its peak.
There are many models in the literature for
breaking down the steps needed to acquire

social skills in various settings and then building on these more minute steps gradually in a successive approximations way. As these overt steps become functionally related to the social skills objectives, the anxiety, which in the past has acted in an inhibitory and distracting way, is lessened, and the individual moves directly toward desired goals.

10. Anxiety and social skills are closely intertwined, as much of the discussion above suggests. It appears that anxiety and social skills (Phillips, 1977b) are reciprocally related: As anxiety decreases, social skills adequacy becomes more apparent; as anxiety increases, social skills are diminished, may become functionally lost for a time, or may, under chronic conditions, fall into virtual disuse (Craighead, Kazdin & Mahoney, 1976, pp. 363–368; Mahoney, 1974, 1977).

11. Social skills are also closely related to another common and often perplexing clinical area: depression. Perhaps more has been written about depression than any other diagnostic area (Beck, 1967; Ferster, 1965, 1973; Levitt & Lubin, 1975; Phillips, 1977a; Seligman, 1975), but its relevance to social skills deficits has only recently come into focus. Depressed people tend to exhibit the most glaring lacks in social skills: withdrawal from others, failing to initiate and sustain conversation, failing to gain satisfaction from social intercourse, and the like. As social skills improve, persons formerly depressed begin to make more approach behaviors toward others, learn to gain the satisfactions from relating to others they previously may have lacked, and learn to be more assertive where their rights, privileges, and obligations are concerned (see chapter 3).

12. It is likely, also, that other commonly used clinical or diagnostic categories—

psychasthenia, hypochondriasis, paranoia, hysteria, etc.—are closely related to social skills deficits. The complaining that is so common among hypochondriacal persons, the tendency to "somatize" psychological distress and unhappiness, are often closely related to social skills lacks. The ways in which patients relate to others around suspicious, ruminative, negative and stressful (rather than positive and shared) items in their lives also represent social deficits. More will be said on this topic in later chapters.

13. The relative specificity of social skills is both an asset and a liability. The specific nature of social skills (or their lacks) aids clinical effort and research, points the way to remediating many of the person's deficits in social functioning. On the other hand, such a profusion of social skills makes them hard to identify as being the "same" skills used by others in clinical practice and in research. Many different social operations that are basically different may nonetheless go under the same name (e.g., assertiveness training may include such a variety of specific social operations and skills that the broad term quickly loses some of its specificity and usefulness). The great variety of social skills training and research examples keeps the clinician and the researcher busy keeping track of the semantic problems involved; this may be an intriguing occupation or it may lead to considerable frustration at times. There are no straightline social skills training programs that lead directly from personal inadequacy to personal adequacy; although social skills are often a bridge between social adequacy and inadequacy, it may at times be a swinging, sagging, and unsteady bridge. Still, a social skills approach to overcoming social, clinical, and personality difficulties is the most heuristic approach we have, and it avoids the even

greater pitfalls found in the traditional approach where diagnostic entities, disease categories, and alleged basic inadequacies preoccupy the clinician and dull the sensitivities and inventiveness that lead to better therapeutic intervention.

THE CONCEPTUAL ISSUE

One final point—the conceptual issue. Items from interviews or from psychometric procedures, as well as from actual individually centered social skills efforts, do not come to the clinician or researcher /theorist all packaged and meaningful, ready for application (Sullivan, 1954). The items or the conditions of change have to fit into some theory or conceptualization. Actually the role of conceptualization is well recognized among those who offer theories of personality, psychotherapy, and behavior change; here we need only reemphasize the importance of conceptualizations (Henle, Jaynes, & Sullivan, 1973; Patterson, 1973; Phillips, 1977a).

In Freudian theory, the conceptualizations arise almost exclusively from experiences with patients—from what they say in interviews and how and what they report on their lives—and not from independent empirical evidence. Today, the conceptualizations of Freud seem cumbersome and overly theoretical, i.e., without empirical support, but they are conceptualizations that have appealed to many clinicians and theorists. Similarly, with psychometric instruments, the theory is inherent in the measurement, empirically well grounded in research on individual differences, trait theory, and the analysis of the interrelationships among trait variables. However, both the interview-derived (mostly from Freudian theory) and the psychometric-derived conceptualizations are heavy on abstractions and *less well prepared to guide actual behavior change.* We now need to interlace theory and practice based on efforts to change behavior, not simply to describe behavior or speculate about its origins and meanings.

The conceptualizations from interview material tend to be wispy and hard to verify empirically. The conceptualizations from psychometric theory seem to apply almost entirely to group trends, mean differences, with little guidance as to how to achieve individual behavior change. The social skills approach to changing psychopathology is conceptually more clear on several points: that social skills may underlie psychopathology; that social skills can be changed by way of individually programmed behavioral efforts; that measurement and the meaning derived from change in the case of social skills modification are closer to the empirical data and remain so throughout a change effort; and that social skills approaches fit closely with the larger domain of behavior modification, contributing to and gaining sustenance from this movement.

The whole diagnostic enterprise is a conceptualization based on a number of assumptions: that diagnostic entities or at least classification exist in nature; that the diagnostic groupings are meaningful bridges between the individual's past development and future predictions as to the course of behavior under various conditions (e.g., psychotherapy or other treatment); and that these classifications are reliable enough to allow for a variety of practical and administrative decisions. We have seen in this chapter—and it is the thrust of this book—that diagnoses have severe limitations; we are, then, mindful of the importance of looking for new conceptualizations that overcome the limitations of diagnostic or nosological groupings and center more on empirically available data on human behavior, not only in settings of importance to the person's problem solving and general welfare, but also for our more comprehensive understanding of human behavior.

In an effort to further overcome the limitations of traditional diagnostic study, in the next chapter we approach the study of depression through the Minnesota Multiphasic Personality Inventory, looking for the social skills implications therein.

3

Over the years, observations of depressed patients in psychotherapy settings led to the notion that many persons with ostensibly the "same" elevated scores on the Depression scale of the Minnesota Multiphasic Personality Inventory (MMPI) were, in fact, quite different clinically. Most of this notion of the clinically noted differences in depressive posture revolved around social presence, social skills, and social competence in general. The depressed patient who maintained eye contact, worked on his depressive state, recognized that depressive reactions resulted from (in theory) ascertainable and discernible conditions, simply appeared different from the depressive patient (with the same MMPI depression scale score) who was non-social or asocial, querulous, and complaining to the point of overlooking the likely conditions that led to the unhappiness.

While these clinically observed differences in depressive patients might have related to the familiar dichotomy—endogenous

This chapter was researched and written in collaboration with Garaldine Dalesandro Lyons.

Types of Depressive Reactions on the Minnesota Multiphasic Personality Inventory and Their Relationship to Social Skills

versus exogenous causality or history—it appeared that the observed depressive states were more reactive ones and that the differences between the apparent subtypes of depression hinged more on social skills, on a history of having dealt somewhat successfully with past depressive reactions, and on a posture that suggested a problem-solving attitude toward the experienced depression. In a more behavioral language, the depressive cases differed in their repertoires and behavioral economy for dealing with many kinds of problems, especially ones that seemed to have more obvious social consequences.

RESEARCH ON THE DEPRESSION SCALE OF THE MMPI

The present research then derived more from the clinical setting, per se, than from a known (or suspected) etiology in the exogenous versus endogenous sense. It did not stem from suspected functional versus organic causality except in cases where the   55 basis of hypothesizing differences in depressive states stemmed from a social skills framework.

METHOD AND SUBJECTS

Minnesota Multiphasic Personality Inventory profiles, which had elevated depression (D) scores of at least 70 and which had been administered within a 5-year period, were selected from about 1000 MMPI profiles. Two populations of patients, delineated as "older" and "younger," comprised the total sample of 138 cases, the basis of the present research.

The older population consisted of 57 patients (11 males and 46 females) who had been admitted to two area hospitals. The mean age for this group was 40.14 years (SD = 8.43 years). The younger population consisted of 81 outpatients from the George Washington University Counseling Center (55 males and 26 females) who applied to this center for psychotherapy over a 3-year period. These younger subjects were all students with a mean age of 21.53 years (SD = 5.83 years).

In all cases, the patients who took the MMPI did so as part of a general workup during the intake process, whether for in-patient or out-patient service. The University Counseling Center population of 81 patients was gleaned from a larger intake population of about 200 student applicants for mental health services, but the non-selected cases—as with the in-patient hospital population—were eliminated solely on the basis of lacking an elevation on the D scale of the MMPI; no other criteria were employed.

TREATMENT OF DATA

In order to categorize the depressed patients, a typological analysis (Ward, 1968) was performed on the two populations separately. From this typological analysis, six groups were derived from the older population of 57 patients and seven groups were derived from the younger population of 81 cases. In order to replicate the types in the older and younger populations, a distance measure, comparing each of the older groups with each of the younger groups, was computed. This step resulted in the formation of a 13 × 13 matrix with zeroes in the principal diagonal. A distance coefficient of less than 3.0 in any pairwise comparison signified that the groups were similar. Similar groups were then classified together, forming discrete types. These types were used to examine the hypothesis that there are clinically different depressive responses to the MMPI, despite similarities in overall standard score values (Drake & Oetting, 1959).

To cross-validate the types using additional data, viz., the remaining MMPI clinical scales, a one-way MANOVA was also performed.

RESULTS

Based on their index of similarity, nine groups from the 13 × 13 matrix were classified together, resulting in four types of depressive patients on the MMPI. Type I depressive cases consisted of three groups, while each of the remaining three types were defined by two groups each. In order to categorize these four types, the means and standard deviations on each MMPI scale for the individuals in each type were computed and appear in Table 3-1.

Table 3-1 displays means and standard deviations for all MMPI scales other than the D scale. In examining the hypothesis that social skills deficits figure in depressive reactions, it can be noted that only Type II depressive cases show a high elevation on the Si (Social Introversion) scale, the mean here being 79.11, with a standard deviation of 17.33, the latter showing the most dispersion on the Si scale among the four depressive types. Although this evidence is suggestive for Si elevation in relation to depressive types, it is not highly convincing.

Table 3–1
Means and Standard Deviations for the 12
MMPI Scales for Each of 4 Depressive
Types (n = 138)

SCALES	TYPE I		TYPE II		TYPE III		TYPE IV	
	Mean	SD	Mean	SD	Mean	SD	Mean	SD
L	47.40	6.52	46.11	11.59	52.75	7.79	53.00	9.07
F	63.72	8.10	67.22	17.10	61.05	11.35	55.94	7.17
K	50.30	6.28	44.48	10.54	54.45	7.35	61.42	6.82
Hs	58.97	11.92	60.96	19.58	70.75	16.08	62.45	10.58
Hy	66.06	10.75	64.74	16.03	73.90	10.71	67.97	8.92
Pd	69.57	12.21	66.89	18.91	66.35	11.86	67.74	13.03
Mf	61.30	17.91	62.44	19.36	52.25	13.27	62.35	11.32
Pa	61.58	8.43	64.54	18.20	61.30	10.19	60.81	9.51
Pt	74.57	9.85	73.93	19.08	69.85	11.10	66.97	9.84
Sc	71.95	11.31	75.37	23.88	71.95	15.51	63.19	10.87
Ma	52.20	10.84	60.30	15.41	60.05	12.05	56.29	8.74
Si	57.47	10.19	79.11	17.33	54.20	11.40	52.97	9.73

Figure 3-1 presents a plot of these mean profile scores on the MMPI for the four types of depression. It can be seen from Figure 3-1 that the overall pattern of the profiles for the four types of depression are somewhat similar, yet there are peaks and valleys that help distinguish the types.

Figures 3-2 to 3-5, inclusively, graphically display the mean vectors on all MMPI scales for each depressive type, taken separately. Included in these plots are the means of the four types on the D scale: 80.22 (Type I), 81.71 (Type II), 77.05 (Type III), and 76.58 (Type IV). It can be seen from this plot that the Depression scale scores were elevated for each of the four types of depression, as well as showing other profile similarities and differences. By examining both Table 3-1 and Figures 3-1 through 3-5, it is possible to interpret the four types with respect to the other scales of the MMPI.

As indicated in the plots of mean profiles, all the types demonstrate considerable scatter with respect to the 13 MMPI clinical scales. Comparing the shapes of the profiles further illustrates the variability among the four types. Graphically speaking, Types I and II are most similar in shape. The profiles seem to follow the same basic trend, differing in elevation with respect to the Pt (Psychasthenia) and Sc (Schizophrenic) scales. Type I's mean on Pt (74.57) exceeds the mean value noted for the Sc scale (71.95). In contrast, for Type II, the mean value on Sc (75.37) was higher than the mean value on Pt (73.93), although this difference is not outstanding.[1]

Types III and IV resemble each other with respect to their means on the D scale (77.05 and 76.57, respectively) and on the Si scale (54.20 and 52.97, respectively). However, in terms of the other MMPI scales, the shapes of the profiles characterizing Types III and IV are very distinctive from each other, and each is distinct from Type I and Type II.

Based on the multiple discriminant analysis, an overall F (36,364 = 3.99, p <.01 was obtained, indicating that the four types were significantly different with respect to the MMPI scales, taken jointly, but excluding the D scale. Furthermore, the data yielded

---

[1]The Pt /Sc relationship merits some discussion. When Pt (Psychasthenia) is higher than Sc (Schizophrenia), the general interpretation is that the pathology is more benign than when Sc is the higher score. Pt elevations describe compulsive, irrational, self-devaluative, ruminative, and self-doubting behavior; many of these tendencies assume a holding action when Sc is lower than Pt. When Sc is the higher score, this may portend a more likely psychotic condition, especially if the "neurotic triad" (Hypochondriasis, Depression, Hysteria) are not elevated.

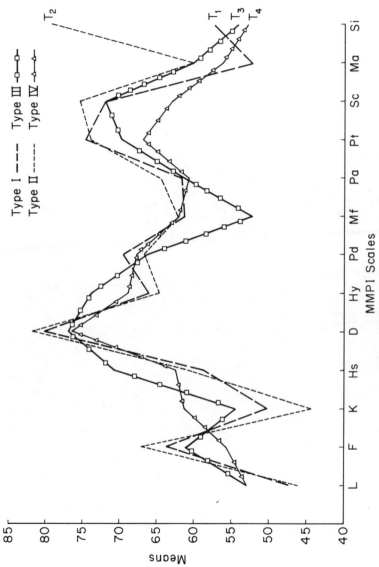

Figure 3-1. Plot of the mean vectors for four types on 13 MMPI scales.

59

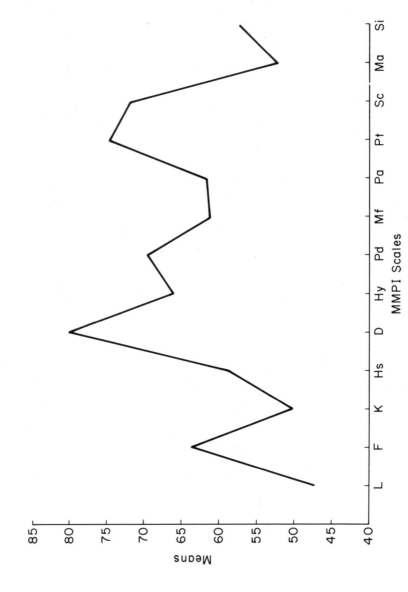

Figure 3-2. Plot of the mean vectors for Type I on 13 MMPI scales.

60

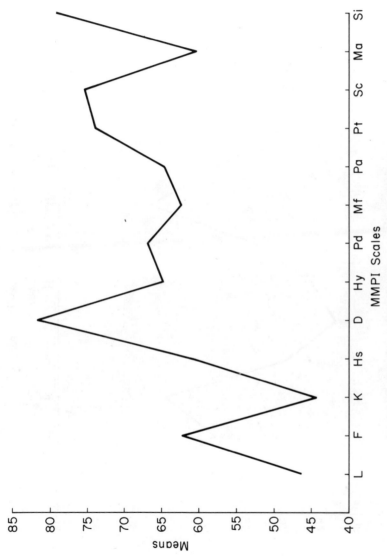

Figure 3-3. Plot of the mean vectors for Type II on 13 MMPI scales.

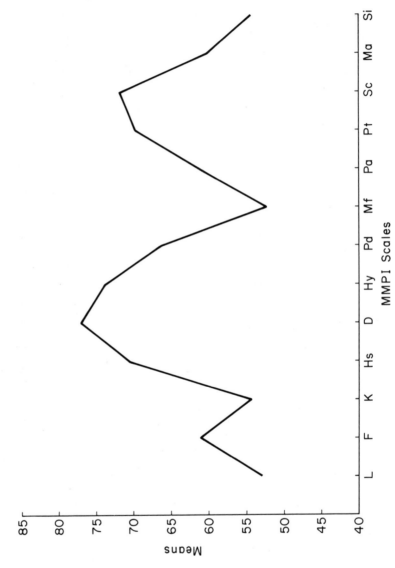

Figure 3-4.   Plot of the mean vectors for Type III on 13 MMPI scales.

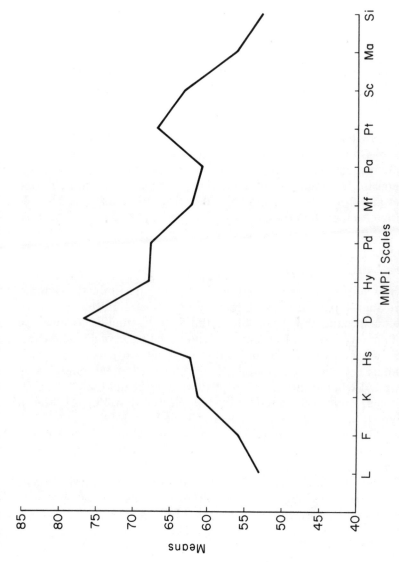

Figure 3-5. Plot of the mean vectors for Type IV on 13 MMPI scales.

two statistically significant dimensions of difference on which the four types can be discriminated ($\chi^2 = 90.09$, $p < .01$; $\chi^2 = 27.83$, $p < .01$). Dimension 1 accounts for 75% of the variance and Dimension 2, 18% of the variance. Together they account for 93% of the total variance.

Table 3-2 presents the vector of canonical weights. Function 1, a bipolar dimension is dominated by the K scale with eigenvector $= -0.89$, and by Pt (eigenvector $= 0.32$). Function 2 is also bipolar. On the negative side, it is dominated by the Hy and Sc scales with eigenvectors of -0.52 and -0.38, respectively. On the positive side, Pd (eigenvector $= 0.40$) and Pt (eigenvector $= 0.44$) are featured.

Switching now to more qualitative findings, all of the 60 Depression scale items are presented in Table 3-3; Tables 3-4 and 3-5, respectively, delineate further the endorsed and rejected items for the four types of depressed patients. The items in Tables 3-4 and 3-5 further support the descriptions selected to characterize each of the types.

DISCUSSION

The K and Pt scales resulted in the highest discrimination among the four types and therefore play the most significant role in characterizing the types. Since the K scale intends to measure "defensiveness" in test-taking attitude, the issue of social desirability becoms a key factor in this typology. In particular, the F versus K index, i.e., "looking bad" versus "looking good," was applied when F minus K was positive and greater than 11. The F versus K index calculated for the types is as follows: Type I (13.42); Type II (22.74); Type III (7.60); and Type IV (-5.48).

Because the second dimension accounted for only 18% of the total variance, the scales that dominate this function, viz., Hy (Hysteria), Sc (Schizophrenia), Pd (Psychopathic Deviate) and Pt (Psychasthenia),[2] play only a minor role in the characterization of the types. Both Table 3-1 and Figures 3-1–5, inclusively, also contribute to the descriptive profiles that follow.

TYPE I. This group can best be characterized as obsessive-compulsive with highest mean elevations appearing on the Pt scale ($M = 74.57$). People in this group appear tense and obsessionally worried, and express difficulties in making deci-

---

[2] Pt is the exception here, since it is featured on the first dimension.

Table 3–2
Vector of Canonical Weights for 12 MMPI
Scales

SCALES	DIMENSION 1 EIGENVECTORS	DIMENSION 2 EIGENVECTORS
L	−0.05	−0.18
F	0.25	0.13
K	−0.89	0.29
Hs	0.08	−0.17
Hy	0.02	−0.52
Pd	−0.02	0.40
Mf	−0.02	0.22
Pa	−0.18	−0.08
Pt	0.32	0.44
Sc	0.02	−0.38
Ma	0.10	−0.08
Si	0.01	−0.02

sions and in concentrating. Sometimes they may be characterized clinically as "agitated depressives." When an elevated score on the Depression scale (the mean in this type was 80.22 on the *D* scale) accompanies a peak on the *Pt* scale, self-deprecation, intropunitiveness, constriction, and nervousness are also common. The ruminative self-doubt and self-devaluation characteristic of those characterized as Type I is further reflected in their endorsement of *D* scale item 20, "I'm certainly lacking in self-confidence" (see Table 3-4). According to the other *D* scale items highly endorsed, Type I patients report no appetite (rejecting *D* item 1, "I have a good appetite") and perhaps, by inference, some trouble expressing anger (rejecting item 6, "At times I feel like swearing"). Because high elevations on *D* and *Pt* may imply a difficulty in responding to psychotherapy (at least among conventional modes of therapy), other forms of therapeutic intervention may be indicated or well worth exploring (e.g., specifically targeted behavioral methods aimed at social skills deficits).

Type I patients' scores on these scales suggest that these people are so agitated, worried, and tense that concentrating on and adjusting to highly verbal forms of therapy may be difficult for them. Also, therapy of a verbal and uncovering nature may act to reinforce the subjectivity of the patient and increase the self-abnegating and ruminative aspects while purporting to do just the opposite. Since Type I patients achieve the second highest *F–K* index, it is suggested that these individuals may be either deliberately attempting to "look bad" or somehow exaggerating their

Table 3–3
The Entire *D* Scale Set of 60 Items, the Mean Item Score Differentiating Items for Depressive Type, the Scoring of Each Item, and the Items Verbatim

MEAN ITEM SCORE[a]	MMPI ITEM NO.	D SCALE CONSECUTIVE NUMBERING	DEPRESSIVE TYPE	MMPI SCORING	ITEMS VERBATIM
1.12	2	1	I+	F	I have a good appetite.
	5	2		T	I am easily awakened by noise.
	8	3		F	My daily life is full of things that keep me interested.
	9	4		F	I am about as able to work as I ever was.
	18	5		F	I am very seldom troubled by constipation.
1.13	30	6	I+	F	At times I feel like swearing.
	32	7		T	I find it hard to keep my mind on a task or job.
	36	8		F	I seldom worry about my health.
	39	9		F	At times I feel like smashing things.
	41	10		T	I have periods of days, weeks, or months when I couldn't take care of things because I couldn't "get along."
1.87	43	11	IV–	T	My sleep is fitful and disturbed.
1.90	46	12	III–	F	My judgment is better than it ever was.
	51	13		F	I am in just as good physical health as most of my friends.
1.85	52	14	III–	T	I prefer to pass by school friends, or people I know but have not seen for a long time, unless they speak to me first.

1.10	15	57	III+	F	I am a good mixer.
1.85	16	58	I−	F	Everything is turning out just like the prophets of the Bible said it would.
1.90	17	64	III−	F	I sometimes keep on at a thing until others lose their patience with me.
1.11	18	67	II+	T	I wish I could be as happy as others seem to be.
2.00, 1.94	19	80	III−, IV−	F	I sometimes tease animals.
1.15	20	86	I+	T	I'm certainly lacking in self-confidence.
1.10	21	88	IV+	F	I usually feel that life is worthwhile.
1.07, 1.87	22	89	II+, IV−	F	It takes a lot of argument to convince most people of the truth.
1.87	23	95	I−	F	I go to church almost every week.
	24	98		F	I believe in the second coming of Christ.
1.95, 1.97	25	104	III−, IV−	T	I don't seem to care what happens to me.
	26	107		F	I am happy most of the time.
1.12	27	122	IV+	F	I seem to be about as capable and smart as most others around me.
1.15, 1.15, 1.10	28	130	I+, III+, IV+	T	I have never vomited blood or coughed up blood.
	29	131		F	I do not worry about catching disease.
1.11	30	138	II+	T	Criticism or scolding hurts me terribly.
1.13, 1.10	31	142	I+, III+	T	I certainly feel useless at times.
1.95, 1.94	32	145	III−, IV−	F	At times I feel like picking a fist fight with someone.
	33	152		F	Most nights I go to sleep without thoughts or ideas bothering me.
	34	153		F	During the past few years I've been well most of the time.

Table 3-3 (continued)

MEAN ITEM SCORE [a]	MMPI ITEM NO.	D SCALE CONSECUTIVE NUMBERING	DEPRESSIVE TYPE	MMPI SCORING	ITEMS VERBATIM
1.12, 1.15	154	35	I+, III+	F	I have never had a fit or convulsion.
	155	36		F	I'm neither gaining nor losing weight.
	158	37		T	I cry easily.
1.15	159	38	III+	T	I cannot understand what I read as well as I used to.
1.90, 1.94	160	39	III-, IV-	F	I have never felt better in my life than I do now.
	178	40		F	My memory seems to be all right.
	182	41		T	I am afraid of losing my mind.
	189	42		T	I feel weak all over much of the time.
	191	43		F	Sometimes when embarrassed, I break out in a sweat which annoys me greatly.
1.10	193	44	III+	T	I do not have spells of hay fever or asthma.
	207	45		F	I enjoy many different kinds of play and recreation.
2.00	208	46		F	I like to flirt.
	233	47	III-	F	I have at times stood in the way of people who were trying to do something, not because it amounted to much but because of the principle of the thing.

1.12, 1.11	48	236	I+, II+	T	I brood a great deal.
1.87	49	241	IV–	F	I dream frequently about things that are best kept to myself.
	50	242		F	I believe that I am no more nervous than most others.
1.94	51	248	IV–	F	Sometimes without any reason or even when things are going wrong I feel excitedly happy, "on top of the world."
	52	259		T	I have difficulty in starting to do things.
	53	263		F	I sweat very easily even on cool days.
	54	270		F	When I leave home I do not worry about whether the door is locked and the windows closed.
1.93, 1.90, 1.90	55	271	I–, III–, IV–	F	I do not blame a person for taking advantage of someone who lays himself open to it.
1.11	56	272	II+	F	At times I am full of energy.
1.02, 1.05	57	285	I+, III+	F	Once in a while I laugh at a dirty joke.
1.95, 1.85, 1.90, 1.97	58	288	I–, II–, III–IV–	T	I am troubled by attacks of nausea and vomiting.
1.11	59	290	II+	T	I work under a great deal of tension.
1.15	60	296	III+	F	I have periods with which I feel unusually cheerful without any special reason.

[a] These means are derived from the "Clusmean" program written in Fortran, which computed the D scale items means and standard deviations for each depressive type. Endorsement values ranging from 1.00 to 1.15 are included in Table 3-3, where total endorsement gave a mean of 1.00; likewise, rejected values ranged from 1.85 to 2.00, where total rejection of items equaled 2.00.

Table 3–4

Depression Items Endorsed on the MMPI,
Four Depressive Types, Where
Endorsement Means Concurring With *D*
Scale Scoring

DEPRESSIVE TYPE	ITEM NUMBERS		ITEM	*D* SCALE SCORE
	MMPI	*D* Scale		
I	2	1	I have a good appetite.	F
	30	6	At times I feel like swearing.	F
	86	20	I'm certainly lacking in self-confidence.	T
II	67	18	I wish I could be as happy as others seem to be.	T
	138	30	Criticism or scolding hurts me terribly.	T
	272	56	At times I'm full of energy	F
	290	59	I work under a great deal of pressure.	T
III	57	15	I'm a good mixer.	F
	159	38	I can't understand what I read as well as I used to.	T
	193	44	I don't have spells of hay fever or asthma.	T
	296	60	I have periods in which I feel unusually cheerful without special reason.	F
IV	88	21	I usually feel life is worthwhile.	F
	122	27	I seem to be about as capable and smart as most others around me.	F

complaints. As one patient said, "If you only knew how miserable I feel." The systems of complaints proffered by Type I patients seem to come before any effort to engage in therapy; it is as if they were saying: "Before we work on my problems, I want you to fully understand how wretched I feel." Sloshing around in these mired-down feelings can act to exacerbate this kind of complaining; yet, touching too lightly on the patient's misery in order to get on with the business of therapy, might turn off the patient and allow him or her to feel misunderstood, dealt with carelessly, or might contribute to similar refractoriness to treatment. If not very careful, the therapist, then, is put in a dilemma vis-à-vis the

Table 3–5
Depression Items Rejected on the MMPI,
Four Depressive Types, Where Rejection
Means Disagree with _D_ Scale Scoring

DEPRESSIVE TYPE	ITEM NUMBER		ITEM	_D_ SCALE SCORE
	MMPI	_D_ Scale		
I	58	16	Everything is turning out just like the prophets of the Bible said.	F
	95	23	I go to Church almost every week.	F
II			None	
III	46	12	My judgment is better than ever.	F
	52	14	I prefer to pass by school friends, or people I know but haven't seen for a long time, unless they speak first.	T
	64	17	I sometimes keep on at a thing until others lose patience with me.	F
	233	47	I have at times stood in the way of people who were trying to do something, not because it amounted to much, but because of the principle of the thing.	F
IV	43	11	My sleep is fitful and disturbed.	T
	241	49	I dream frequently about things that are best kept to myself.	F
	248	51	Sometimes without any reason or even when things are going wrong I feel excitedly happy, "on top of the world."	F

patient—if the therapist is too commiserating, this allows the patient to exacerbate the reported distresses, but if the therapist is too matter-of-fact this may "turn off" the patient and allow for less therapeutic cooperation. The main deficits with this type of patient seem to be not only an absence of social skills in the sense of satisfactory social exhanges with others, but an adamancy against developing such skills; there is an overarching attitude of "What's the use?" which makes for a "difficult" patient in most circumstances.

TYPE II. This group also shows high elevations on _D_ and Pt (mean _D_ scale = 81.74; mean Pt scale = 73.93). With Type II patients' endorsement of such D scale items as 30 and 59, "Criticism or scolding hurts me terribly" and "I work under a great deal of tension," respectively (see Table 3-4), the profile of obsessive reactions is supported. The record, however, illustrates other significant features distinguishing this group from groups of Types I, III, and IV. Among the four types, Type II patients have the largest F–K ratio and in this respect, are the mirror opposite of Type IV patients. With elevated scores on the F, D, Pd, and Sc scales, Type II patients can perhaps most accurately be labeled as "schizoid" in terms of MMPI descriptions. People in Type I can be described as feeling misunderstood and alienated from society in general. F scores in the 65–80 range are indicative of unconventional thinking and frequently appear among the sullen and defiant personalities that suggest schizoid, antisocial, or alienated reactions. These F scale scores typify individuals who are commonly depicted as being restive, unstable, temperamental, discontented, garrulous, and opinionated. F scale scores within the 65–80 standard score range are frequently found in the protocols of young people who report conflicts about their identity and who may resort to unconventional dress and nonconforming values as a means of both identifying (defining) themselves and, at the same time, objecting to standard, alternative social norms. This description seems to adequately characterize Type II depressive cases which, proportionally speaking in our study population, are characterized as having the second largest concentration of young people. In consequence of the identity crisis (or, perhaps, it is a more chronic state), Type II individuals may feel inadequate to function in socially approved roles and therefore may withdraw abrasively. Thought disorders and difficulties in communicating, also characteristic of the schizoid type, undoubtedly compound the young person's feeling of estrangement. In our population, Type II patients' high mean score on Si (79.11) seems to make such a hypothesis credible. These people may not show glaring deficits in social skills, but they tend to repudiate the need for small talk, getting to know people on mutual terms, persevering in relationships, seeking out the company of others without realizing personal gain or ulterior benefits, and so on. Psychotherapeutically they seem to say, "Don't tell me I need more friends or should develop better relationships, when I don't feel such effort is valuable for me." Sometimes, too, a haughty or arrogant attitude is displayed in therapy: "I don't think it is worth my time to try to get to know people on this campus," and other sweeping, negative generalizations of this type. Also, when therapy is successful in getting Type II persons to attempt to act on the social skills they may already have in their repertoires, they may say, in effect: "I tried what you said . . . I went to that party . . . and I talked with people . . . but nothing came of it—it was a washout." These persons expect some greater-than-usual benefit to result from any effort on their part to practice social skills in more or less conventional ways, and thus tend to repudiate the effort when it does not fulfill their considerable expectations.

TYPE III. The patients characterized as being in this group, predominantly women 40 years of age and over, present themselves in a relatively positive light compared with the other three types, as shown by the smallest $F–K$ index among all types. With elevations above 70 on Hysteria (Hs), Depression (D), and Hypochondriasis (Hy) (means 70.75, 77.05, and 73.90, respectively), the profile of Type III patients illustrates the commonly observed "neurotic triad." Individuals in this group are likely to relate to others with meekness, submission, and dependency— behaviors that in turn prompt or seek out nurturent and supportive responses. By their rejection of D scale item 17, "I sometimes keep on at a thing until others lose their patience with me" they appear to be underassertive and willing to go along with others at considerable cost. Their low scores on the Si scale (mean = 54.20), their endorsement of D scale item 15, "I'm a good mixer" (see Table 3-4), and their rejection of item 14, "I prefer to pass by school friends or people I know but have not seen for a long time unless they speak first" (see Table 3-5), on the D scale, suggest that they have a certain facility with some social relationships, but not other, broader relationships. Therefore, their depressive status may be easily missed in clinical assessment and in psychotherapy owing to the less blatant lacks in social skills that they display. Their elevations on the "neurotic triad," however, undermine a characterization of 'social responsiveness" and suggest that Type III individuals' social contacts may be more shallow and immature, selfish and nonsharing. An elevated score on the Hypochondriasis (Hs) scale (mean = 70.75) further describes Type III patients as being querulous, having a (more privately held?) negative outlook on life, and commonly expressing somatic concerns, turning the latter into complaining that seeks compassion, help, sympathy, etc., from others. Many social relationships are, then, not truly sharing ones but hinge on eliciting concern from others around illness, somatic complaints, and pleas for regard for themselves. Type III patients' endorsement of item 38 on the D scale, "I can't understand what I read as well as I used to" (see Table 3-4), also lends support to this description, in that others are then expected to respond with "Oh, my, you don't appear to me to be somebody who has trouble *understanding* things!" or similar replies.

TYPE IV. Unlike Types I, II, and III subjects, Type IV patients attempt to "look good" as indicated by a K score greater than the F score. Mainly composed of older women, Type IV patients tend to minimize disturbances, perhaps proffering a "philosophical" attitude toward distress. They deny sleep difficulties and distressing dreams, reject D scale items 11, "My sleep is fitful and disturbed," and 49, "I dream frequently about things that are best kept to myself" (see Table 3-5). They also express a very positive outlook on life, endorsing D scale item 27, "I seem to be about as capable and smart as most others around" (see Table 3-4). Moderate elevations on K, seen in Type IV persons, are typical of people with multifaceted interests who report being affable, ingenious, and progressive. A moderate elevation on the K scale (mean = 61.42) may indicate good prognosis for recovery—perhaps the best responsiveness to verbally conducted psychotherapy among the four types—since this range of K (44–65, standard score values) suggests adaptiveness and flexibility. This observation is further supported by Type IV patients' scores on the Depression and Psychasthenis scales which, compared to the other three types, are the lowest. Despite the age differences, or perhaps in positive relation to age, these people have a track record of some adaptability in life, react better to stress, and appear to respond to psychotherapy that is based on their already largely adequate social skills and that requires taking further positive steps toward assertiveness, self-help, and forward thrusts to meet issues in life.

Figure 3-6 summarizes in a more pictorial way the itemized results found in Tables 3-3, 3-4, and 3-5. In Figure 3-6 we see at a glance the items uniquely associated with each depressive type and the items that overlap in one or more depressive types.

These findings and those elucidated above support the clinical hunch we started with (at least as far as the MMPI is concerned) that there are different types of depressive reactions other than the endogenous/exogenous classification already well known. These four types may, of course, spill over into the endogenous/exogenous dichotomy; only further research will tell. But as extant measures on the MMPI, the four depressive types appear to ramify widely on the Multiphasic inventory itself, as well as to suggest implications for understanding personality

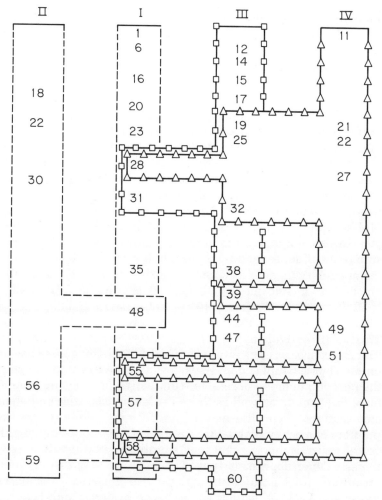

Figure 3-6. Item overlap and uniqueness, four depressed types, based on 34 Depression scale items, MMPI, such items showing highest endorsement/rejection.

better, for possibly improving the prediction and assessment of psychotherapy, and perhaps other issues.

It can be seen from Figure 3-6 that six items are uniquely associated with Type I, with five additional items being shared with other types, with two of the shared items overlapping with two other types. Type II shares only one of six unique items with another type (Type I), giving it considerable distinctness. Types III and IV have several unique items from the D scale, but also share several items with other types. It is these unique and relatively unique items that give the four types their distinctiveness and add substance to the original hunch that such types do exist.

These findings are not only of descriptive significance in understanding depression on the MMPI (we do not, of course, know how well these types would stand up with other measures, or with clinical assessment, of depression) but appear to be of value to the therapist/counselor as he or she looks into the items of the Depression scale and tries to translate their implications into therapeutic tactics and strategies. For example, ramifications of depressive reactions in terms of psychasthenic responses, the looking "bad" versus looking "good" descriptions (the F versus K comparison), and others may carry important implications for psychotherapeutic work. Any additional information on the MMPI about patterns within the Depression scale and among other scales would seem to help break down the more than occasional formidableness with which depression is viewed in therapeutic settings (Beck, 1967a, 1967b; Ekman & Friesen, 1974; Ferster, 1973; Goldsmith & McFall, 1975; Hinschliff, Lancashire, & Roberts, 1971; Lazarus, 1974, 1976; Levitt & Lubin, 1975; Libet & Lewinsohn, 1973; Seitz, 1970; Watson & Friend, 1969; Waxer, 1974; Weisman & Paykel, 1974). Such additional information also suggests ways of approaching therapy more heuristically. For example, depressive reactions with high psychasthenic components—obsessive, ruminative, and cyclic characteristics (Type I), as well as those marked by schizoid and alienated features (Type II)—may require a more carefully detailed program of a behavioral nature and less of the uncovering, highly verbal types of therapy that may simply pry into the depressive morass. Other depressive types (Types III and IV) display more "neurotic" (that is, hypochondriacal and hysterical) responses, especially Type III, which shows more hysteria, and Type IV, which shows more "denial" of disturbances as shown by the endorse–reject items on the D scale and by K scores being greater than F scores. It may be that Types I and II are "submitting" to the depressive condition (posited as these reactions are in this research on the peculiarities of the social skills repertoire), whereas Types III and IV are more actively combating or groping with (or against) depressive feelings and reactions, which characteristic alone may have implications for therapeutic intervention. Therapists interested in researching this problem, either by replicating the present procedures or by different assessment techniques, might examine the success/failure ratio among a number of depressive patients with a view toward determining if these depressive subtypes differentiate themselves on other dimensions and if they appear to hold up among other patient populations.

SOCIAL SKILLS DISCUSSION

More has to be said about the social skills implications of this research. It is the working thesis that social skills underlie pathology, rather than the reverse. However, clear-cut cause and effect dimensions may lie beyond the state of the science at this time, forcing us to argue through parallels, analogies, and a number of bits and pieces of evidence, rather than producing on-the-mark results. That a social deficit may function as a critical element in depression has received theoretical and empirical support. A brief consideration of the evidence that endorses this thesis is therefore appropriate.

Learning theories of depression have stressed its behavioral components rather than the affective properties of the disorder. Notable among these conceptualizations are Ullman and Krasner's notion of inappropriate social role-taking (1969) and the theory of narrowed repertoirial alternatives proposed by Phillips and Wiener (1966). Also from the behavioral framework is Ferster's functional analysis of depression (1973). Because of its ramifications for our own study, Ferster's theory deserves some elaboration.

According to his premise, the loss of social reinforcement precipitates a decrease in the emission of several functional classes of behavior. Other less long-range and less reinforcing classes of behavior, namely escape and avoidance responses, alternatively assume prominence in the absence of the more socially reinforcing responses. Social interaction also decreases as a result of the diminution of social reinforcement, and the person is thus categorized as depressed.

Without the rewarding aspects of social interaction, the frequency of this complex of behaviors continues to deteriorate until the person's interpersonal skill is severely impaired, resulting in the maladaptive behaviors we call psychopathology. Among these maladaptive responses are withdrawal, superstitious behaviors, hostility, excessive complaining, hallucinations, and perhaps self-injury.

Libet and Lewinsohn's proposal (1973) that the withdrawal illustrated in depression is accelerated by the person's loss of facility with social interaction prompted the interest in isolating an instrument that would measure social skills. Although self-administered, self-report measures of social skills have been developed (Goldsmith & McFall, 1975; Watson & Friend, 1969), it is our impression that the Si scale of the MMPI adequately serves this purpose. This scale is empirically constructed along an introversion /extroversion dimension with high scores representing introversive behaviors and extroversive tendencies indicated by low scores. Dahlstrom, Welsh, and Dahlstrom's factor analysis (1972) delineates the following six factor sources of the Si scale: inferiority–discomfort, lack of affiliation, low social excitement, sensitivity, interpersonal trust, and physical, somatic concern. Similar to Ferster's descriptive profile of depressive reactions, these factors further typify the social behavior of the depressed person.

Based on the assumption that the Si scale provides an approximate measure of social skill deficiency, a preliminary investigation (Sowards & Phillips, 1973) was conducted that hypothesized that depressed subjects (Ss), identified by their elevated MMPI D scores ($T < 70$), would score significantly higher on the Si scale than either a normal group or a group of Ss who belonged to diagnostic classifications other than depression. The sample consisted of 120 persons who completed the MMPI at a local psychiatric center ($n = 60$) and at the George Washington University Counseling Center ($n = 60$) at the time of their application for psychotherapy. In order to provide more variety within the sample, two sampling populations were used. Age ranged from 16 to 52 years, with a median age of 24.5 years, for the 75 male Ss and 45 female Ss who comprised the sample.

Group assignment was based on the following criteria. Group A consisted of Ss with elevated D scale scores ($T > 70$), although for some, the MMPI protocol displayed other elevated scale scores as well. To control for the effect that "clinically meaningful" elevations, other than those on D, might have on the Si scale, Group B was selected. Ss in this group had elevated scores ($T > 70$) on MMPI scales other than D and Masculinity-Feminity (Mf).[3] For Group C, there were no elevated ($T > 70$) scores reported on any MMPI scales. Based on these criteria, each group was composed of 20 randomly selected Ss from each of the sampling populations (the psychiatric clinic and the Counseling Center).

Using a simple one-way analysis of variance technique, the mean Si scores of the depressed and nondepressed groups were compared. The study's hypothesis was confirmed in that the Si scores of depressed Ss were significantly different from those of the nondepressed groups. A Tukey test indicated that Group A subjects scored higher on the Si scale than did those in either

---

[3]The Mf scale was excluded because elevations on this scale reliably reflect neither the presence nor the absence of pathology (Drake & Oetting, 1959).

Group B or Group C. Also, there was no significant difference between Groups B and C on the Si scale.

According to the authors, these empirical results corroborate previous conceptualizations (Ferster, 1973; Libet & Lewinsohn, 1973) that emphasized social skills deficit as a crucial element in the clinical assessment and treatment of depression. More empirical data that encourages this discussion of the role that social skills deficit plays in understanding depressive behaviors will be presented in reference to the Mooney Problem Checklist as a set of presenting complaints derived from college student candidates for psychotherapy (chapter 4).

In the present study a good deal of credence can be put on the importance of social skills in relation to depression, to wit:

1. The Social Introversion scale on the MMPI is markedly elevated among Type II depressive cases (mean = 79.11, SD = 17.33), which is a mean score closely approximating the highest D scale mean (81.74), even though the population was selected owing to high D scale scores. The only vitiating factor here is that the dispersion is also marked (SD = 17.33 on the Type II depressives Si scale), but this SD of 17.33 is about average for the range of SDs for Type II cases on all of the MMPI scales (see Table 3-1).

2. Following from this point, it is important to recognize that the Si scale on the MMPI does not automatically equate with lacks in social skills, but it is a rough approximation thereto, and the best measure on the MMPI of any set of behaviors closely resembling a broader definition of social skills (which definition is not clearly extant in the literature on the MMPI, on any other personality measure, or in references to psychotherapy in relation to social competencies).

3. The MMPI Si scale only approximates an elevation in Type I depressive cases (mean = 57.47, SD = 10.19), but this is a somewhat suggestive relationship, enough not to be ignored, since it is the second highest among the four types.

4. In addition to a relationship between the D scale and the Si scale among the four depressive types, we note that Pt (Psychasthenia) and Sc (Schizophrenia) are elevated, above the standard score of 70 among Type I cases. These elevations, however, do have implications (as noted above) for social behavior in that these Type I patients are agitated, self-deprecating, ruminative, self-doubting, none of which are signs of positive or adequate social skills, and may, moreover point directly to social lacks.

5. Similarly, for Type II depressive, where Pt and Sc are again the two most elevated scores (save for Si already noted), but in a relative order opposite to Type I cases. Here, too, the tendencies contradict social skills adequacy or competencies.

6. Type III depressive cases also show elevations on Pt (mean = 69.85) and on Sc (mean = 71.95), bearing out some of the above-cited relationships to social skills, but in addition, Type III cases are more hypochondriacal and hysterical (means are Hs = 70.75 and Hy = 73.90) and thus present social skills deficits in relationship to being complaining, talking about or frequently reporting they have somatic illnesses, being also overly submissive and dependent (in contrast to displaying assertive social skills and competencies). However, in any across-the-board sense, Type III depressive cases offer the least convincing support (after Type IV cases) for the hypothesis relating depression and social skills deficits.

7. Paralleling Type III depressive cases, Type IV cases are the most "normal"-scoring on the MMPI of all depressive types in this population (e.g., no MMPI scale score shows a mean of over 70 standard score, save for Depression); these people also have the lowest Depression and Psychasthenia scale scores among the four depressive types. In the absence, then, of extensive depressive features

comparable to the other types, they also show fewer social skills problems.

8. The F scales on depressive Types I, II, and III all show "moderate elevations" (see Table 3-1), indicating that these populations are prone to present themselves as "looking bad," that is, accentuate their negative feelings and social lacks. Particularly when F is greater than K (as is true to a marked extent in depressive Types I and II, less so but still present in Type III), the outstandingly "negative social presence" is shown to be characteristic of these groups, thus supporting a social skills deficit and depressive relationship fairly convincingly among depressive Types I, II, and III (but note the absence of the F versus K ratio among Type IV cases, again supporting their greater "normalcy" in a general social sense).

9. Qualitatively, in terms of items endorsed and rejected (see Tables 3-3 and 3-4), Type I patients overwhelmingly endorsed "I'm certainly lacking in self-confidence" (in contrast to the other types); Type II patients endorsed two obviously socially related items: "I wish I could be as happy as others," and "Criticism or scolding hurts me terribly" (in contrast to the other types); Type III patients showed no convincing qualitative answers; and Type IV patients endorsed socially positive items (feeling life is usually worthwhile and feeling as capable and smart as others), thus further confirming what was said above about Type IV cases. Rejected items are harder to interpret and to consider supportive of the depression and social skills deficit notion: Type I patients' unique answers reveal no discerning evidence; Type II patients' replies are nonexistent in relation to rejected items; Type III patients' replies are the most revealing, showing three of four unique answers to be related to social attitudes—negative, obstinate, and nonparticipating toward others; and Type IV patients' unique answers are more

subjective in their references and only inferentially related to others (e.g., "My sleep is
fitful and disturbed").

Since this research on the MMPI examined only (1) cases of elevated depression scores, (2) the ramifications of these elevated scores on other MMPI scales, and (3) particularly the relationships between depression and social skills deficits, it cannot be said that other elevated scores from the MMPI profile would not yield similar results. What would happen if one selected first elevated *Pa* (Paranoia) or *Pt* (Psychasthenia) scale cases and then threw the rest of the MMPI into dependent variable relief pivoted on these independently selected measures? One could systematically take each MMPI clinical scale, use it as an independent variable, and observe, in a manner similar to the one employed here, what would be the resultant profile on other clinical scales, and also make strong reference to the *Si* scale in each instance. Doubtlessly such a systematic research (well beyond the capability of the present writers at this time) might bring into far bolder relief not only possible types of hysteria, hypochondriacal, paranoid, or psychasthenic cases, but how each of them might affect or be affected by the Social Introversion scale. In such research, we predict, not only would psychopathology be shown again to be related to broad social skills deficit, we would have a more refined notion of what we now mean by grosser measures of psychopathology (via the various MMPI clinical scales) and also could begin to relate particular social deficits to aggregate collections of items representing the various pathologies or clinical scales. Such research could lead to refined notions of the clinical categories so commonly used and could relate them more specifically to particular social skills deficits, so that psychotherapy (or better, social skills training) could proceed more effectively.

Moving away from the more formal and statistically recorded approach to diagnosis, via the MMPI, attention is turned now to ascertaining the social skills aspects of presenting complaints, those signs of felt and reported distress when the individual first applies for psychotherapy.

4

The last chapter, illustrating types of depression and their relationships to social skills on the MMPI, has shown how this inventory can yield data significant for social skills types of clinical work and research. It is not expected that psychometric devices would be discarded even if the case for social skills training became the dominant treatment modality overnight; which, of course, is not likely. Using psychometric instruments advisedly, insofar as diagnosis is concerned, also suggests that we learn to use the same devices advisedly insofar as social skills objectives are concerned. This chapter goes further into the matter of social skills types of clinical work, derived here from work on the Mooney Problem Checklist.

Looking at human psychological difficulties in terms of presenting complaints—the "up-front" considerations—are what we are examining in this chapter, contrasted with looking at MMPI and other profiles after they have been obtained. The Mooney Checklist provides an immediate leap into social skills assignments. We do not need a diagnostic interlude or any other evaluation; we can use the Mooney as a screening device enabling us to go directly to social skills considerations. The Mooney, being an inventory heavily saturated with social relationships items, permits this direct access to social skills considerations and advances evidence that more or less straight and direct routes to social skills can be obtained from such an inventory.

On Presenting Complaints —The Mooney Problem Checklist and Social Skills

THE MOONEY PROBLEM CHECKLIST RESEARCH

The Mooney Problem Checklist (Mooney & Gordon, 1950) is a collection of 330 items that serve well as a screening measure, as a set of initial or presenting complaints upon admission to a clinic or other psychotherapeutic setting, and as a means of judging what kinds of complaints do, indeed, characterize various populations of patients. In this instance, the Mooney was used in an out-patient psychological clinic setting on a university campus.

Beginning in the fall of 1974, 100 consecutive female and 100 consecutive male applicants for counseling or psychotherapy were given the Mooney. The only exceptions were older people who were mustering out of military or government service, in search of second careers who took educational/vocational batteries of tests and high school students who came for help in making choices about college or other career lines. The mean age of the males was 19.85 years, and for the females the mean age was 19.55 years; the standard deviations for these populations were, 3.91 and 4.15 years, respectively, thus indicating a cluster around the second year of college but including an age range from 17.05 years to 25.44 years for males, and from 16.90 years to 24.88 years for females. None of these students taking the Mooney was in serious mental health status; none was psychotic. All were looking primarily for help with their self-esteem, their relationships with peers and family, and for help with personal development, sexual expression, handling anger, and other (to them) perplexing issues. Ostensibly, all wanted self-improvement in one form or another, a common objective among both youthful students and others seeking psychotherapeutic help.

The Mooney inventory is a collection of brief "complaint statements" about life and relationships in general. The person is asked to indicate if the item applies to him or her by underlining the item; thus, the first item—"Feeling tired much of the time"—will be underlined by pen or pencil if the respondent feels the item applies. If the item is of greater significance (the test directions say of "most concern"), then the person responding also circles the item number. Theoretically one could underline a number of items and circle none, or any combination of under-lined and circled items might be obtained. Generally, in the ex-perience of the psychological clinic where these data were ob-tained, the ratio of the number of items circled (indicating greater concern) compared to the items simply underlined was 1:4.

Data were collected over a single semester's time, from Sep-tember through December. Since every person was applying for psychological help (eliminating strictly educational /vocational cases), there was no known bias in the collection of these data. Furthermore, since the number of men and women of the age group described above and in the setting from which the data were collected was about 50 /50, there was no bias in the direction of sex. No student refused to take the inventory, since it was presented as part of the intake process and was integral and pre-liminary to the assignment of the student for counseling or psy-chotherapy (for either group or individual placement, although the latter disposition covered about 90 % of the applicant's even-tual disposition).

Since there was no delay at the time of intake (the student applying for psychological help at the psychological clinic was seen immediately upon presenting him- or herself), the student's self-report as to acknowledged psychological status was as origi-nal and unbiased as the student could make it. That is, a waiting period or delays of any other type were absent, hence the student had no built-up grudge or disappointment owing to bureaucratic red tape or the like. All students in the 200 person sample (also a 100 % population under the time constraints indicated above) took the complete inventory; none turned it in incompletely done, none refused to respond to the inventory. Most students took about 30–35 minutes to complete the inventory, some longer,

and seldom did anyone complete the inventory in less than 20
minutes.

The Mooney Problem Checklist presents the items as declara-
tive statements, making responding easy (see Table 4-1). If the
item applies, then the first degree of relevance is signified by the
underlining; if the item is of greater importance, as cited above,
the number of the item is encircled. The respondent does not have
to deny the item—that is, say "No, it does not apply to me"—
passing it by signifies that is not relevant to one's self-report.

Items on the Mooney are much more factual than items on
many personality inventories—e.g., item 1: "Feeling tired much
of the time"; item 95: "Needing a philosophy of life"; item 159:
"Trying to combine marriage and a career"; item 259: "Unable to
break a bad habit"; item 301: "Thinking too much about sex matters"; item 329: "Campus lacking in school spirit." None of the
items is an involved statement, with subordinate or dependent
clauses, obscure in meaning, or referring to cultural matters that
are unknown or of no interest to the college student. Frank replies are common; seldom did a question arise about an item's
meaning.

Eleven categories of 30 items each are found on the
Mooney. These include: Health and Physical Development
(HPD); Finances, Living Conditions, and Employment (FLE); So-
cial and Recreational Activities (SRA); Social–Psychological Rela-
tions (SPR); Personal–Psychological Relations (PPR); Courtship,
Sex, and Marriage (CSM); Home and Family (HF); Morals and
Religion (MR); Adjustment to College (School) Work (ACT: ASW);
The Future: Vocational and Educational (FVE); and Curriculum
and Teaching Procedures (CTP). These categories apply to college
and high school students according to the manual (Mooney &
Gordon, 1950).

THE DATA

Data from the 200 cases in terms of the 11 categories are presented
in Table 4-1. It is important to recognize in this table that the totals
are not for the frequency of endorsement of each of the 330 items
in the Mooney, but summarize only the number of items within a
category that were endorsed by an arbitrary criterion of 20% or
more of each, male and female, population. The categories most
commonly endorsed, as categories, based on the 20%-or-more
criterion, are categories that have social relations, social competencies, or social skills implications, viz., Categories III (SRA),
IV (SPR), and V (PDR); these findings were contested only by the

Table 4-1
Based on the Criterion of at Least 20% Endorsement of Any Item (Among 30 Items for Each Category), the Number of Such Item Endorsements Is Presented, for 100 Males and 100 Females, and Total for 200 Cases, for Each of 11 Categories.

CATEGORY (MOONEY)	MALES (N) Circled	MALES (N) Totals	FEMALES (N) Circled	FEMALES (N) Totals	TOTALS (N) Circled	TOTALS (N) Totals
I Health and Physical Development (HPD)	0	0	0	5	0	5
II Finances, Living Conditions, and Employment (FLE)	0	0	0	1	0	1
III Social and Recreational Activities (SRA)	0	6	1	7	1	9
IV Social–Psychological Relations (SPR)	2	4	3	7	3	8
V Personal–Psychological Relations (PPR)	5	8	7	13	10	14
VI Courtship, Sex, and Marriage (CSM)	1	2	0	2	2	3
VII Home and Family (HF)	0	0	1	4	1	4
VIII Morals and Religion (MR)	0	2	0	0	0	2
IX Adjustment to College (School) Work (ACT·ASW)	3	5	0	6	3	6
X The Future: Vocational/Educational (FVE)	3	6	2	9	5	10
XI Curriculum and Teaching Procedures (CTP)	0	2	0	3	0	4

a The totals may or may not coincide with the figures for each sex, as both sexes may have endorsed a given time; if so, that item was counted only once in the total.

findings for Category X, Vocational and Educational Future, which may indirectly bear on assertiveness toward parents in regard to selecting educational/vocational goals and other social matters. Although the exact social skills nature of Categories III, IV, and V are open to discussion, the general intent and implications of many items in these categories are related to social matters and to social skills in asserting oneself, in pursuing social goals, and in coping with social conflicts.

Looking at the Mooney Problem Checklist in another way, i.e., in terms of the number of items endorsed at all (without regard to the 20% criterion) as important or very important in the lives of the 200 respondents, indicates that Categories III, IV, and V again had more items checked from among the 30 items available in each category than any of the other categories except for X (VEF). The total counts (underlined and circled) from among the total of 200 cases are for the following: Category III, 1316 endorsements without regard to the 20% criterion; Category IV, 1434 endorsements; and Category V, 1704 endorsements. The average number of endorsements for the other 8 categories was 1099, including both underlined responses (lowest degree of significance for the person taking the inventory) and circled responses (denoting greater concern for the item). Thus, Category III (Social and Recreational Activities) contained a total of about 17% greater frequency than the rest of the inventory; Category IV (Social–Psychological Relations) was responded to about 25% more frequently than the average of the rest of the categories; and Category V (Personal–Psychological Relations) was responded to about 35% more frequently.

Are III, IV, and V really social-skills-related concerns? A look at the items may throw some light on this question. Some examples of items from Category III are as follows:

> Not living a well-rounded life.
> Wishing to improve myself culturally.
> Awkward in meeting people.
> Awkward in making a date.
> Slow in getting acquainted with people.
> Boring weekends.
> Wanting to learn how to dance.
> Wanting to learn how to entertain.
> Trouble in keeping conversation going.
> Wanting more worthwhile discussions with
>   people.

These items would appear to be strong candidates for social skills consideration. Any one of them could be extracted and made the basis for social skills training, especially in adolescent and young adult populations and, to some extent, even among older persons (see chapter 2 in this regard).

In category IV, items covering the following problems and considerations were noted:

Being timid or shy.
Being too easily embarrassed.
Losing friends.
Wanting to be more popular.
Feeling too easily hurt.
Worrying how I impress people.
Feeling inferior.
Getting into arguments.
Speaking or acting without thinking.
Feeling that no one understands me.

These items as well might easily become the basis for social skills training as all of them either directly relate to overt contacts with others or to personal impressions or the aftermath of unsuccessful interpersonal relations—"Worrying how I impress people," "Feeling too easily hurt," and "Feeling that no one understands me."

Looking at Category V in the same light, we note the following items of interest:

Nervousness.
Too easily discouraged.
Moodiness, "having the blues."
Having memories of an unhappy childhood.
Daydreaming.
Having a certain nervous habit.
Losing my temper.
Lacking in self-confidence.
Can't forget an unpleasant experience.
Too many personal problems.

While the items in Category V do not name others as corespondents, the implications are still strong that others are involved. Items like "nervous" about appearing well, impressing others, making a good start at a relationship, being too easily discouraged would imply that one does not get positive feedback from others; and items like having a temper, displaying nervous habits, and so forth, strongly imply that others' judgments are involved. A social context is the matrix in which these experiences occur. Anything that contributes to unpleasant experiences—embarrassment, awkwardness and the like—have, as well, a social context and imply a lack of skills in relating to others and in evaluating one's contributions to these relationships. Each of the items in the immediately cited list could likewise form the presenting questions for social skills training, probably rephrased as follows—*overcoming* lacks in self-confidence, *controlling* nervous habits, *self-management* in overcoming temper outbursts. The item referring to "Too many personal problems" would doubtlessly have to be broken down into specifics with each, then, forming the basis of some social skills training.

If we approach the data from the Mooney Problem Checklist in another way, i.e., proceed in terms of the frequency of endorsement of specific items regardless of the category they belong to, we note the following results, among the *less serious items:*

ITEM "Moodiness, 'having the blues,' " showing 35% endorsement among the 200 cases (30% endorsement for men, 40% for women); Category V.

ITEM "Feeling too easily hurt," showing 34% endorsement among all cases (22% males, 46% females); Category IV.

ITEM "Feeling tired much of the time," 33% endorsement, all cases (31% males, 35% females); Category I.

ITEM "Not getting enough exercise," 31.5% endorsement, all cases (38% males, 25% females); Category I.

ITEM "Daydreaming," showing 30% overall endorsement (23% males, 37% females); Category I.

ITEM "Wondering if I will be a success in life," endorsed by 28% of all 200 respondents (25% males; and 31% females); Category IX.

Thus, among the six most highly endorsed individual items in terms of stating the item to be somewhat of a problem (not the most serious problem), three of the items referred to social skills areas or their implications, two to exercise and fatigue (suggesting lacks in time /energy management), and one to vocational matters in that the respondents wondered if they would be a "success" in life. The judgment of "success" would not only hinge on their own self-estimates (derived as they are from assessments from others, standard cultural expectations, and the like), but directly judged in terms of income, promotion, status, all of which have a social reference. Broad items such as "success in life . . ." are hard to manage from any conceptual viewpoint—they are not directly identifiable as social skills (or social skills lacks), although indirectly success may pivot a great deal on relationships with others in business or professions that provide for success in terms of promotions, recognition, status, and similar considerations. Sometimes people fail to be as successful in the broader sense because they are lacking not only in acumen and competence but also in social skills and social effectiveness.

Considering the more "serious" items, where endorsement included circling the items, the ones that stand out are the following:

ITEM   "Lacking self-confidence," found endorsement to the most serious degree among 32.5% of the whole population of 200 (males 29%, females 36%), Category V.

ITEM   "Having feelings of extreme loneliness," found 29.5% overall endorsement (males 23%, females 36%); Category IV.

ITEM   "Moodiness, 'having the blues,'" showed 26.5% overall endorsement (males 22%, females 31%); Category V.

ITEM   "Nervousness" and "Finding it difficult to relax," average endorsement 25.5% among the total population (male and female endorsement 20% and 31%, respectively, for "Nervousness" and 25% and 26%, respectively, for "Finding it difficult to relax") Category V.

Thus, among the five most frequently "seriously" endorsed items for the whole populations, all of the items fall into Category IV or V, both ostensibly social-skills-related categories. When left to their own judgments, this relatively youthful population felt that the items in their lives, as surveyed on the Mooney Problem Checklist, that gave them the most problems were those we closely identify with social competence. One item, "Moodiness, 'having the blues,' " also occurred as a frequent item judged to be at a minor degree of seriousness. Thus, a depressive psychological countenance (insofar as "moodiness" is a sign) is both a frequent small problem and a frequent large problem. We have seen earlier how social skills and depression were related on the Minnesota Multiphasic Personality Inventory; evidently, this relationship is present to a noticeable extent on the Mooney.

SEX DIFFERENCES

While the emphasis on presenting complaints as people enter into a psychotherapeutic relationship is common among both sexes, there are some sex differences that need to be mentioned. Women in our society tend to be more "socially conscious" and tend to emphasize social relationships more than men. Women also tend to point to social relationships more than men. Women also tend to point to social relationships—social relationships that are, at base, made up of social skills—as the causes of marital conflict and dissolution more than men. If women are really more socially conscious at the interpersonal level (as contrasted, say, with political/economic types of social consciousness), then we would expect differences on the Mooney Problem Checklist as used in the present study of presenting complaints in a psychological clinic. This expectation is somewhat confirmed, as the following figures show.

The 100 females in this population endorsed a total of 56 items at the higher criterion level of 20%. That is, among the 330 items on the Mooney, setting a significant level of endorsement of an item at 20%, as contrasted with any other percentage of endorsement from zero upward, 56 such items were yielded for the females. Among these 56 items, only 7 were nonsocially related, referring mainly to physical health and exercise, disliking financial dependence on others, and liking to travel more.

Among the 100 males taking the Mooney Problem Checklist at the time of intake and upon checking their presenting complaints, 36 items appeared that were endorsed by 20% or more of the cases. Of these 36 very frequently checked items, only 3 could be said to be unrelated to social skills or social competencies, namely, items referring to financial dependence and wanting to travel (shared with the women respondents), and feeling that grading in school had been unfair in their cases. Men, more than women, endorsed items relating to their vocational decisions with high frequency, but all of these had at least an indirect social reference.

The five most frequently endorsed items at the "more serious" level of concern for females in this study were the following:

ITEM   "Lacking self-confidence," 36% endorsement.

ITEM   "Having feelings of extreme loneliness," 36% endorsement.

ITEM   "Nervousness," 31% endorsement.

ITEM   "Moodiness, 'having the blues,'" 31% endorsement.

ITEM   "Wanting love and affection," 31% endorsement.

The four most frequently endorsed items at the "more serious" level of concern for the males, each of them being in the broad social areas, were the following:

ITEM   "Lacking self-confidence," 29% endorsement.

ITEM   "Having feelings of extreme loneliness," 23% endorsement.

ITEM   "Moodiness, 'having the blues,'" 22% endorsement.

ITEM   "Taking things too seriously," 22% endorsement.

All of these items fall within the categories nominally dealing with social considerations and social skills, since any therapeutic approach to correcting these complaints, as with the female-related complaints above, would entail social skills training and enhancement.

THE MOONEY PROBLEM CHECKLIST
AND SOCIAL SKILLS TRAINING

If the Mooney Problem Checklist lends itself to checking presenting complaints that have social skills implications, as we have
stated to be the case, the next question concerns how the social
skills implications of the Mooney items may be used to advantage.
Several possibilities exist for accepting the items checked on the
Mooney as pivotal points for social skills training.

The first consideration is that the Mooney is a *screening survey* of considerable spread and variety and tells the clinician, at a
glance, what items may be significant for the person applying for
help. Since a total score of a percentile or standard score nature is
not forthcoming on this survey, it is necessary first of all to view
the particular items as potentially significant and also to see
whether the items checked are of minor or major concern and into
which of the 11 broad categories the items fall. Given these bits of
information, the clinician can then interview the patient and gain
some notion as to how therapy or other remedial efforts might
proceed. If most items fall into various socially related categories,
then the probability of some kind of social skills training, at least
parallel to "talking" therapy if not independent of it, might well
follow. There is a more ready translation of the items from the
Mooney into social skills training implications than is likely from
most personality surveys and inventories.

If important items checked on the Mooney refer to shyness,
embarrassment, reluctance in social exchanges, and many feelings of guilt and depression owing to a lack of social "success" as
the person judges this matter, then social skills help is certainly
an economical and straightforward therapeutic modality to pursue. If the applicant for help selects items referring to doubts
about opposite sex relationships, eventual marriage and family
status, sustaining relationships, and so forth, then at least in a
preliminary way social skills help may be called for in that the
applicant may be making unwise judgments about how he affects
others and how they affect him, often leading to ephemeral rather
than lasting relationships.

Another use of the Mooney in determining a social skills
approach to behavior change lies in asking the patient, after he or
she has taken the inventory, to go back and indicate the items
deemed worthy of serious effort or considered to be practical issues
the person would be willing to go to work on immediately. If the
patient selects items that have social bearing on others—

roommates, peers of the same or opposite sex, parents, teachers, employers—these may be reformulated in such a way as to promote social skills training. An example of item selection follows.

A male student selected four items worthy of his immediate attention in a straightforward and deliberate way:

"Getting excited too easily."
"Finding it difficult to relax."
"Being careless."
"Afraid of making mistakes."

The circumstances under which each of these complaints occurred were carefully delineated and a program set up for each one. This person noted that the "Getting excited too easily" occurred as he approached the home of his girl friend when picking her up for a date or even when he dropped in on her casually. More conversation indicated that the young man was very much concerned about his girl friend's overt approval, whether she complimented him on his dress or manner, and other matters; if she did not pay him the proper notice, he felt rejected and depressed. Upon approaching her home, on each occasion, he then went through his "turmoil," as he phrased it, fearing for the worst. On some occasions he deliberated long before approaching her home, walked around the block several times before going up the steps, peered from across the street to see if he could see his paramour or members of her family, and tried other anxiety-allaying (and perhaps also anxiety-provoking) measures. Only after he had been with her for some time did their conversation settle into a normal vein allowing him to relax and enjoy her company and remain fairly calm.

The social skills training consisted in first contesting his expectation that he had to have immediate and total approval, otherwise he meant nothing to her (or to himself!). He practiced with the therapist, vicariously, approaching his girl friend's home, knocking on the door, being greeted by one of the parents, entering into immediate conversation while awaiting his girl friend's appearance, and ways in which he might converse with her with lessened anxiety or without anxiety. He also used a "writing technique" (Phillips, 1977a, 1977b) in which he wrote out in longhand before he approached her home, "I admit that I am anxious and wondering if I will please Jane, but I am going to accept this anxiety, not be deterred, and still go through with this visit as calmly as I can anyhow," and similar comments to himself. This first admission of anxiety helped to reduce the intensity and to turn attention to other behaviors of more social value in the interaction. The practice of the conversational and social approach aspects of his visit to his girl friend's home put him through the actual social paces he needed in the real life situation. He learned from the vicarious practice that "nothing drastic is going to happen to me" and this helped him to think of things to say and do as he interacted with Jane and her parents in the real situation.

This patient's tendency to be tense—"Finding it difficult to relax"—was also noted and related to the visit to Jane's home. Other ways in which he was unable to relax were similarly approached through social skills training, and these pertained to a part-time job in which he had to meet the public and answer questions for them, where he had to converse over the telephone and relay messages, all being circumstances where he was afraid of "getting things mixed up and getting into trouble" as a result.

As the young male patient vicariously practiced these social skills with his therapist, he gained some composure and increased skill in social interaction. Shortly, his confidence grew, and he was able to take on more social responsibilities on the job. He demurred less often in the case of informal situations that came up unexpectedly. His item selection of "Being careless" and "Afraid of making mistakes" were somewhat interrelated and both were worked on in a similar manner, viz., his specific tasks were carefully noted, he saw in detail how he was to complete the tasks, and how he could learn to evaluate his own performance without feeling others would disapprove of him or his work in some vague way.

Developing social skills to cope with such situations as enumerated above in the case of the young male patient, led to the patient himself saying that he realized that his anxieties and tension were due to lacks in social skills, rather than "something being wrong with me in a neurotic or psychotic sense." Beside the approach to specific training in social competence in his therapy, he also took some courses in speech making, in acting, and in dramatics, in which spontaneity was at a premium. These additional skills helped to further increase his confidence. He said at the end of a semester in which he concentrated on developing social skills that all of his past anxieties had arisen out of his own perfectionist expectations (always wanted to be admired, approved of, lauded by others) and, having failed in these expectations, he learned to anticipate the failure and to be anxious as he successively approached what were for him trial situations.

Items from the Mooney Problem Checklist may be gathered together to form a syndrome or interconnected group of anxiety-provoking items, so that an economy in approaching social skills training can be realized. The items people check on the Mooney are seldom unrelated; they tend to form a kind of general approach to social, scholastic, family, and other situations, regardless of the category the items belong to on the inventory itself. People act in generalized ways with respect to anxieties and distressful situations as much as they do in situations in which they are successful, hence it is possible to form clusters of items from the Mooney (or from any other similar checklist) and train for adequacy in coping with many or most of them. Moreover, as one or two items yield to social training efforts, other tend to "fall in line" and become less of a problem, e.g., one student who learned to increase his social skills in connection with dancing and developing some social graces at parties and gatherings also became able, without specific training, to make short speeches in his fraternity to small groups of people where he had previously been anxiety-stricken, and then went on to polish more complex social skills in setting up caucuses and running political training sessions for his favorite political party; the latter coming about "as a bonus," as he phrased it, without specific training or intent on his part at the outset of his social skills improvements. The results of specific skills training, as well as specific problem solving in psychotherapy, often net more generalized improvement. A general rule may be this: Start with specific social skills or training target problems; as these yield to problem-solving efforts, a more generalized effect may be realized. On the other hand, if one always "thinks big" in therapy or in social skills training, the "bigness" may turn out to be unwieldly. Not only will there not be a big change, the small efforts will go unnoticed and the makings of generalized change will go unrealized or will be curtailed.

The Mooney Problem Checklist can serve as a further extension of the ideas presented in the previous chapter on the MMPI, viz., the items in the Mooney inventory can serve as a platform or launching pad for moving rather directly into social skills training.

5

Definitions of complicated and extended processes such as psychopathology, psychotherapy, and even behavior change are not easily found. We know in a common sense way what we mean when we refer to such terms, but to extend these definitions outward, so to speak, and ask for concurrence and a meeting of the minds as to the exact boundaries of the definitions is probably not too likely. We have to work, then, with some common understanding of some of the characteristics of psychopathology or any other complex process we seek to better understand.

The use of the term "psychopathology" goes back many decades. English and English, in their *Dictionary* (1958), define psychopathology as "the systematic investigation of morbid mental conditions." They also say psychopathology is a branch of psychological science and is to be contrasted more with technological considerations, such as the study of clinical psychology and psychiatry.

If abnormal or psychopathological states are to be studied as any other psychological or scientific topic, then our purpose here is to understand what is meant by psychopathology and to conceptualize it in terms of general psychological principles. This implies that psychopathology does not have an independent status with its own laws and principles, but is a study that is embraced within general psychological laws and principles, i.e., within behavioral principles. The position taken here is congruent with this perspective on psychopathology, except the emphasis here is on behavioral, not "mental," states.

If psychopathology is to be studied as a branch of psychology, then we will need to account for the occurrence of psychopathological conditions rather than simply enumerate and

What Is
Psychopathology?

describe these states (i.e., nosological or diagnostic classifications). Our purpose is to account for psychopathology however it may occur—in experimental paradigms, from natural observations among people, or as it is theoretically posited to occur in terms of prevailing clinical theories (e.g., psychoanalytic theory, behavior theory), concentrating on observable behavioral states, not on mentalistic accounts and not on organic lesions or other known (or knowable) neurophysiological conditions of the organism. We are interested, by definition, in *learned*, socially derived and maintained maladaptive behavior. We must account for how this behavior occurs as well as any other behavior we may want to investigate.

A FUNCTIONAL DEFINITION OF PSYCHOPATHOLOGY

For our purposes, a functional definition of psychopathology is as follows:

1. The organism is unable to solve a problem, reach a goal.
2. The organism persists in attempting to solve the problem.
3. The organism lacks the immediate skills or means with which to solve the problem or reach the goal.
4. The persistent or redundant efforts to reach the goal are not adaptive, resourceful, inventive, or effective.
5. The redundant and maladaptive efforts to reach the goal bring about, or are associated with, maladaptive and unsuccessful be-

haviors in other respects, or in other aspects of the organism's repertoire, or in other goal-seeking.

6.   The organism is temporarily unable (under the conditions under
which the above definitional terms are observed, or are observable), in
terms of the existing repertoire, to make the adaptive shifts needed to
solve the problem and therefore requires some means that will increase its adaptability, such as utilizing previously unutilized behaviors, learning new behaviors sufficient to reach the goal, restructuring goal efforts (e.g., redefining or relinquishing the goal), or gaining
the aid of a prosthetic environment in order to attain the goal.

Let us see how these definitional terms apply to various situations. Let us say a person whimsically wants to be able to swim
the English Channel, but is not really seriously bent upon this
quest. A few hours in the water and contact with the fatigue and
risk factors inherent in the effort will convince the aspiring
swimmer that the goal is a futile one, and so he gives up. Each day
all of us may temporarily decide on some goal that turns out to be
unreasonable for one or more reasons (takes too much time, costs
too much, interrupts other activities, seems to lessen in importance
as we temporarily approach the goal, and so on). This kind of
restructuring of goals goes on all the time: We seldom ever pursue
all our goals seriously; we probably drop more than we pursue.
This shows an adaptability, helps us set priorities as to what is
important for our energies and time, and what the various future
"payoffs" might be if we do such-and-such instead of thus-and-so.

Each day, we may whimsically say to ourselves and others
many such passing things: "I'd like to date that girl." "I wish I
could change jobs." "I really wish I had a million dollars." "I'd
like to go to law school but I doubt that I can get in." "I would like
to spend next summer traveling throughout Europe but I'm sure I
won't have the money and besides. . . ." And so on and on.

But, when we seriously pursue goals, that is a different matter. We *have* to have a Grade Point Index (GPI) of such-and-such
before we can graduate or apply to graduate school; we have to
present certain qualifications before we can be considered for a
job; and we have to have acquired many kinds of skills and preliminary qualifications before we can pursue a variety of goals of
importance to ourselves. The conditional or contingent nature of
prior or pivotal conditions sets the terms under which we can
pursue or achieve some goal. Together with the goals as important
objectives, the terms or conditions or contingencies form an
axis that encompasses our behavior: *If* we want *this*, we have to
do *that*.

In experimental paradigms, from the early days of Pavlov and his associates to recent work by Seligman and his associates, the organism is artifically given these contingent conditions: If the organism wants to escape pain or punishment, it must do so-and-so; if the organism is hungry and seeks food (we can observe how the organism behaves and thus can relate its behavior to food, drink, or whatnot, under the experimental conditions we have contrived), it must do certain things; and so on.

However (and this is where the psychopathology comes in), if the person in life, and if the organism in an experimental arrangement, can proceed forthwith to the goal, there is no problem. When one wants to drive into the city, one starts up the car and goes, or takes the bus and arrives fairly soon at one's destination. Failing to use car or bus, one finds another way, rearranges plans, or the like. If one is hungry, one goes to the refrigerator or cupboard and gets or prepares what one wants. Lacking food, one purchases it, eats something else, eats out, or adapts in some way. One's behavior is adequate to the situation; one reaches one's goal in one way or another without complications. However, if the means to the goal are, for any number of reasons, substantially frustrated or blocked, and further, if one persists with strong and unrelenting effort and a failure to regroup the forces to solve the problem, one then enters into a state of "psychopathology." The person is then *learning* maladaptive behaviors, or applying behaviors maladaptively (i.e., one may kick the TV set that won't go on and possibly get it to work—that's maladaptive behavior because, given the nature of TV sets, kicking the apparatus will not long suffice to produce desired results). Applying behaviors maladaptively and persistently can mean continuing to look for something that is not there, for ways to achieve an end that is unproductive (e.g., trying to study when unable to concentrate, trying to play the violin when one is practically tone-deaf, and so on), and not adapting to these limitations.

These illustrations show how we can move either to solve problems or can run into impasses that make up the definition of psychopathology cited above. In experimental paradigms, the animal is put into situations in which it is overtaxed in its problem solving, or so disturbed in time that even though problem solving might be possible, its repertoire is too depleted at the time to afford the means to a solution. In the case of such impasses—and they may be contrived on ground used by Masserman (1943), Maier (1939, 1949), by Pavlov (1941), by Solomon (1964), by Seligman (1973, 1974, 1975), Seligman and Maier (1967), or by others—the organism shows a number of maladaptive behavioral signs that relate to the species itself and also behavioral signs that may be reminiscent of the behavior of humans. While we have not placed human beings in such experimental paradigms as to make them permanently neurotic, we can see in the common human circumstances, viewed from the vantage point of the psychological clinic, a number of similarities with experimental work on "neurosis" in animals, and we can also characterize solutions to human problems based somewhat on what we learn from animal experimentation.

In the experimental work of Masserman, Maier, Pavlov, Solomon, Seligman, and others, there is always some kind of conflict involved. The animal is hungry and is prevented from getting to food and consummatory eating behavior owing to shock that is applied at some juncture along the way toward the food. The prevention is not just passive, such as a wall to climb or a small maze to transgress, it is formidible, perhaps even impossible to overcome in some cases, but the animal is kept hungry and afforded no other solution to finding food. The animal is "boxed in"—a reference many human beings use to describe the feeling of conflict they experience. In such boxed-in arrangements, felt or objectively real, the responding organism—man or animal—is placed in an impasse. Moreover, the impasse is rendered constant by the "need" for food or the desire for relief, escape, or conquest, the latter being examples supplied by human beings who describe their plights. If the "need" for food or escape is constant and the availability of solutions impossible or highly unlikely, then the state of conflict persists, along with all that accompanies intense conflict: maladaptive behaviors, loss of control, perplexity, trying solutions over and over (redundancy), and even bizarre or unusual behavior. These extreme conflict situations exist at a level one can easily observe among human beings or animals, and also are reported on by patients in psychotherapy who are fairly able to account not only for some of the objective circumstances but also for their own private or internal states. Much of the language we use to describe patients (and much of their own subjective descriptions) centers on the feelings of unworthiness, self-abnegation, loss of confidence, and so on, as they continue to confront unsolvable conflict. The objective, independent descriptions, and the reports on internal private states match remarkably well.

Of equal importance is that the chronic impasse or conflict not only results in current behavioral loss and inadequacy (along with personal suffering and self-abnegation in the human case) but also leads to *prolonged behavioral disturbances and self-*

abnegation; in short, neuroticism. Organisms adapt to the persistent conflict in the same sense that they adapt to any fairly constant feature of their environments—they adjust to these circumstances, and this adjustment comes to characterize their lives and their behavior to a considerable extent. Thus, conflict leads to maladaptive behaviors; persistent conflict leads to persistent maladaptive behaviors. This is the stuff of which neuroticism is made.

Another feature of psychopathology is that the conditions maintaining it are always up to date. As the organism "bends" to accommodate environmental pressures, conflicts, and contingencies, this adjustment becomes a more or less permanent feature of the behavior of the organism (man or animal). If the conditions change, the organism may improve in problem-solving ability and in adjustment; however, if the conflict persists, it will become a more or less constant feature of the organism—environmental interactions, and this constancy will keep the organism "bending" to accommodate the prevailing exigencies. The balance between the organism and the environment is, of course, under flux and open to change. How else could therapy or behavior change ever become effective if change were not possible? But the change must also be persistent and consistent for the behavior of the organism (man or animal) to change materially. For change in the organism's behavior to occur, the contingencies must change— the conflict must lessen, the organism must learn new approaches to solving the conflict, the outcome of solving the conflict must lead to the satisfaction of "needs," and so on. If the structure of the conflict changes, then behavior change will follow.

ANXIETY AND PSYCHOPATHOLOGY

If the term "psychopathology" is used often and interchangeably with other terms such as "abnormal," "maladaptive," and the like, then the term "anxiety" has an even wider usage; it is sometimes used so broadly as to defy definition. In this discussion, we will try to limit and define the use of the term "anxiety" and to give it a central role in the understanding of psychopathology.

The use of the concept of anxiety is embedded in conflict theory, somewhat elucidated above. Conflict consists of an approach toward a goal (approach gradient) and avoidance of the same goal area owing to punishment, aversiveness, or untoward circumstances (avoidance gradient). These gradients of approach and avoidance characterize all conflicted goal-directed behaviors. If a goal is nonconflictful, that is, if there are no aversive or punishing aspects, the goal is sought and achieved forthwith. Similarly, if a goal area is wholly aversive or punishing, one avoids this goal area, i.e., avoiding deep, turbulent, and violent streams where one would otherwise swim, avoiding an unreliable elevator and ascending or descending the heights by steps, and so on throughout a myriad of circumstances.

Experimental evidence shows that approach gradients tend to be gradual and lacking in the steepness of avoidance gradients. Approach is less critical, avoidance more dramatic and hurried. However, in both cases, as Figure 5-1 shows, as the goal area is approached or receded from (avoided), the behavior is "stronger," more probable, and more resistent to extinction. Often patients report how it feels to be caught "high" on the approach–avoidance gradient, that is, near the goal area, e.g., how a young man feels as he approaches, with trepidation, the actual time and place where he is to pick up his "date," or the anxiety one shows prior to an important interview, and the apprehension as well as the desire associated with these conditions, being a time when the conflict is highest. Or how much "pro" and "con" one feels as he or she approaches a subject of strong concern and mixed feelings about oneself in discussion with the therapist—the embarrassment of admitting masturbation, hair-pulling, petty thievery, or the like, against the "pro" of getting things stated, admitting and changing unwanted behaviors, and feeling better about oneself. In popular parlance, conflict situations may be called "Catch 22."

As one moves into the conflict arena—up the approach gradient towards some goal area that is nonetheless frought with aversive, negative, and punitive consequences—one gets bodily and other signals that there is "danger" ahead: the uncertainty as to whether one will prejudice his or her case in the minds of other persons, if one pursues the matter, whether it is better to "shut up, go away, and let the matter drop," or similar avoidance tactics. This uncertainty, these trepidations (shown bodily and in one's subjective [private] states as apprehension, heaviness in the pit of the stomach, parched throat, indecisiveness in manner and verbal delivery, and so on almost in an unlimited way) are all *anxiety* manifestations. Anxiety is the bodily, motoric, subjective manifestation of tension, of equivocation, of grappling with both strong positive and negative tendencies. *Anxiety means conflict.*

Without conflict there would be no anxiety. With conflict there is always some anxiety, more or less severe, depending on where one is placed in regard to approach and avoidance features,

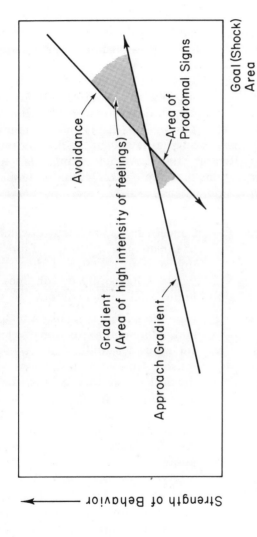

Figure 5-1. The more gradual nature of the approach gradient and the steeper avoidance gradient; the gradients were based empirically on the pull of animals in harnesses as they approached or avoided the goal (or shock) area. Adapted from Miller (1944, 1951).

and on what the conflict situation means to the person (an important interview that tells whether one gets the job, a matter of impressing one of the opposite sex favorably, a speech in which one's intelligence and competence will presumably be judged, a musical rendition on which hangs a scholarship). Even when anxieties seem to pop up unexpectedly, there is some kind of conflict present, some "trial" or "test" the person is precipitously going through, some mixed feelings about staying-in-there-and-facing-up" versus "leaving-the-darned-place-as-soon-as-possible."

Anxiety, then, occurs in a conflict context. It would be interesting to try to think of anxiety being elicited without conflict; it is doubtful if such an effort would prove fruitful. But having said that anxiety is integral to conflict (that is, more than minor or passing conflict), there is more to say about the manner in which anxiety operates (Rycroft, 1971). Anxiety brings into focus a number of considerations that impinge on the individual and include the following non-exhaustive list:

APPREHENSION	Concern lest something unwelcome or threatening will occur; a foreboding without specific or discernible features, hence the person does not know what to prepare for.
ALERTNESS	Here there is some focus on the general nature of the situation one faces, such as an examination, a championship athletic contest, playing at a musical recital, being called before an inquiry board, and so on. One becomes alert to the situation and is somewhat prepared, although the specific nature of the test is not fully known.
THE FUTURE	Anxiety concerns future events, or how past events may be forecasted, together with concern that one handle the future events well. If one has been anxious in the past and has not settled the anxiety, one will likely be as anxious in similar situations in the future.

**PREPARATION
FOR ACTION**

One prepares for the future as best he or she can, hence, preparation implies future action; but the anxiety is felt early on, far before the critical tests occur, as if the tests were at hand. Among measures attempting to control anxiety is relaxation training, where the patient focuses first on any minor feature of an (anticipated) anxiety-provoking situation that causes concern, then is progressively desensitized on that first step, then measurably in later steps, until the whole situation is brought under control—thereby preparing the person for later effective action rather than yielding to the earlier anxiousness that preceded the learning of adequate behavior.

**FLIGHT OR
FIGHT**

Anxiety, like fear, prepares one for an emergency—to stay and fight, or to run. If one is to fight, the whole body is prepared; muscles are tensed, the blood rushes adrenalin to parts of the body, breathing becomes light and shallow, eyes enlarge, and hundreds of other supporting emergencies of a neurophysiological nature are put into action. Felt anxiety, as subjectively reported but also discernible with proper observations and instrumentation, may record these various body conditions as we are closely in touch with our bodily processes at such times. If one chooses to run, or if the battle is called off for some reason, one feels the reverbations of these physiological conditions for some time to come and may be confused as to why there is such discomfort. Chronic states of anxiety tend to produce chronic states of alertness, exhaustion from the physiological preparation for flight or fight, and may render the person somewhat incapable of concentrating on things other than the emergency.

SIGNALS

Signals are signs that something untoward is about to happen. Signal-anxiety is a brief sign that a larger situation is about to occur that provokes anxiety: A light signaling to the animal that an electric shock will be administered; a child seeing the presence of his or her parent as he or she attempts to take money from the parent's purse; a student becoming anxious as he or she observes the professor calling on students alphabetically, approaching the anxious student's name. If the untoward event does not occur, the anxiety diminishes (unless the signal remains); the signal-anxiety is a sign that the person has learned to be anxious about something on cue from a small part of a larger situation. (One could teach him- or herself to diminish signal-anxiety by systematically presenting the cue a number of times but not having to face the "real situation"—a matter of extinction.)

VIGILANCE

Vigilance is more or less prolonged signal-anxiety—a stealing for something that might happen in a generally dangerous situation: An animal stealthily finding its way through the domain of predators; a person finding his or her way through the dark in unfamiliar terrain; a person choosing words with extreme care lest he or she be "shot down" by criticism; a general awareness that something might happen, with the preparation foreseen and the nature of the danger somewhat comprehended. Vigilance is a preparatory state for flight or fight. Some have called this state an "investigatory reflex" or a "What is it?" reflex (Rycroft, 1971, p. 11).

It is important to know that anxiety, as used here, is not the same as fear. Fear is defined by English and English (1958) as "an emotion of violent agitation or fright in the presence (actual or anticipated) of danger or pain. It is marked by extensive organic changes and behaviors of flight or concealment" (p. 204). A further differentiation between fear and phobia by English and English indicates that the latter refers to ". . . persistent and irrational specific fears" (p. 204). Fear would lead to fight or flight; the organism would cope as well as it could with the fear-provoking situation (most likely a predatory animal of a more powerful bearing) and would either fight-it-out or escape through some cunning, swiftness, or deployment. Anxiety, then, appears to be a subclass of fear, a subclass of events where the danger is either not present or not reacted to in the more forthright way that fear is. Anxiety may be thought of as ineffectual fear-responding, as a case of prolonged or chronic reactions that transcend the specific situation that elicits fear. If a fear is discriminated and reacted to by the organism—either by leaving the fear-ridden situation or by conquering it—then the matter drops summarily (as soon as the physiological processes have settled back to a state of equilibrium or homeostasis), and the organism returns to its customary behavior. In contrast, anxiety may persist far beyond the actual "danger," may be aroused and persist in the face of only cues or signals (with no independent indication of danger or threat), and may form such a prolonged and common feature of the organism's behavior as to render it wholly out of keeping with the situation in comparison to itself or to other organisms without the anxiety. Presumably, all organisms of a given species would react similarly with fear to a given and known danger; organisms showing anxiety, on the other hand, would react quite differently and would not "drop the matter" once the fear or anxiety provocation had passed and, especially in the case of humans, the anxiety reactions might increase out of all proportion to the actual danger (or construed danger).

While anxiety and fear may share many common features at the level of eliciting the respective reactions (all the bodily mechanisms supporting flight or fight), the *consequences* of anxiety and fear are considerably different at the time of danger and particularly in the longer range passage of time, anxiety being a more persevering condition, disrupting the organism's other (nonanxiety-ridden) behavior, and becoming easily conditioned (cued) to only very slight or non-danger-provoking situations.

IS ANXIETY A SYMPTOM OF PSYCHOPATHOLOGY?

In the lexicon of traditional thinking about anxiety (May, 1977), anxiety is regarded as a symptom of a "deeper" problem, along with other symptoms such as those reported in diagnostic, therapeutic, and psychometric evaluations of patients or in descriptions of animal behavior under experimental neurosis regimens (Masserman, 1943; Seligman, 1974; Solomon, 1964). This kind of theorizing about psychopathology, abnormal psychology, and psychiatry is often referred to as the "medical model" (Ullman & Krasner, 1975), in which it is posited that symptoms signify and are defenses against more basic and less accessible problems. The symptom is not the problem, but in analogy with physical medicine, the symptom (or collection of symptoms called syndromes) is a sign of some more profound problem not as immediately available as the symptom. Phylogenetically, the symptom is a signal or sign that some distress is present and acts as a warning to the organism to adapt in some way (rest, cool off in languid waters, avoid interacting, climb a tree, hide in a bush, hibernate momentarily, and so on).

The medical model construction of the meaning of symptoms has been adapted by many students of traditional personality theory. It fits well with psychoanalytic and other psychodynamic formulations of personality, human motivation, and social functioning. All of the so-called defense mechanisms are guard posts, as it were, protecting the basic problem from asserting itself and getting into the arena of other human functioning. In this more traditional formulation, anxiety is a more or less persistent effort on the part of the organism to keep repressed matters repressed, lest they disturb the conscious, overt, and socially functioning features of one's behavior. In this light, then, anxiety is a sign of "another problem" removed from the arena of immediate observation.

As anxiety is understood here, it operates as a signal or sign of distress or threat of some kind, not due to repressed or hidden forces "within" the psyche, *but in anticipation of environmental danger ahead*, similar to the way a yellow traffic light is a warning that the red light will shortly appear. Anxiety is first of all a conditioned stimulus, a cue, that more stress is (likely) ahead in time, space, or in some interaction sequence the organism is about to enter, much the same as the "click" of the food-dispensing magazine is a signal that food is about to appear. As the latter case is not a conflict-ridden one, the resulting "anticipatory" behavior is not ordinarily anxiety-ridden.

The reason the anxiety-cued behavior is different from behavior that is cued prior to the delivery of food (a signal that the organism or person is responding "correctly" and is followed by reinforcement in the form of food, a token, praise, etc.) is that anxiety-cued behavior is part of a conflict situation: The organism is *approaching* some positive goal, while at the same time there are *avoidance* features. The approach and avoidance features increase alertness and produce cue-sensitivity. As long as the organism is in a conflict situation, the cue-sensitivity or vigilance remains high, hence conditioned anxiety may occur to any of a large collection of stimuli present in the conflict situation. A person or animal proceeding forward in an approach way to some positive reinforcement (food, conviviality, sex, praise, etc.) without conflict present is in a more bland and less intense situation, where alertness, vigilance, and readiness to fight or flee are essentially nonexistent.

Under a state of high-readiness for conditioning to (or learning of) cues in the conflict situation, the organism may engage in a lot of behaviors that have been conditioned to the anxiety aroused by the conflict, some of which may turn out to be functional (that is, stay close to a tree so the frightened animal can thereby escape; or, in the case of a person feeling "closed-in" in groups, the individual may sit close to an exit in a crowded room so as to provide for escape) and some of which may be idiosyncratic, bizarre, or superstitious behaviors. The common ones reoccur, by definition, among large numbers of people in common anxiety-arousing situations, and hence, are included in personality and adjustment questionnaires; the less common ones may be written up as unusual, bizarre, or as posing some kind of important question for personality theory (Phillips, 1977a). However, it is hypothesized that they all come from a common base: conflict-conditioned cues—fight or escape (see Figure 5-2).

Anxiety, then, has several roles to play in what we usually term psychopathology:

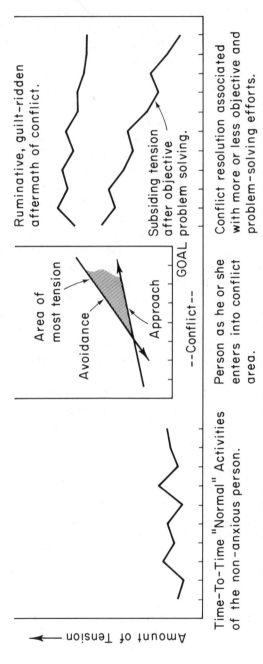

Figure 5-2. Hypothetical account of how a person is first relaxed and comfortable in a nonstressful way; an introduction to conflict with accompanying tension and distress; and two possible sets of solutions (more objective, less objective) to the conflict situation.

114

1. As an outgrowth of conflict, anxiety signifies a state of alertness, vigilance, stress (with physiological, behavioral, and covert/private aspects), and many other equivalent terms denoting a high state of "readiness" or "What-is-it?" reaction.

2. Given this state of alertness, the environmental stimuli or cues present at the time become conditioned to the anxiety and reoccur when anxiety states are elicited on subsequent occasions, hence, the collection of common and uncommon "symptoms" noted clinically and psychometrically. Since the organism does not yet know how to solve the conflict, there is both variety among various persons and/or animals in anxiety-cue-conditioned behaviors (commonly called symptoms), and redundancy, inasmuch as under repeated conditions, the organism tends to fall into a "rut" with some behaviors being selected because they may assuage tension somewhat (e.g., more physically vigorous activities, such as pacing, wringing hands, and other hyperactive behaviors, may reduce tension more than others). Further, with autonomic nervous system arousal, this heightened state that prepares the organism for fight or flight may further fuel the fires of particular responses (e.g., skeletal muscle activities and gross bodily movements may predominate).

3. Anxiety is reduced by escape behaviors (or, where the danger can be appropriately anticipated, by avoidance behaviors), then whatever behaviors are occurring at the time of escape from danger will more probably occur under similar circumstances at later times, in short, they are reinforced. Anxiety *reduction* is reinforcing. This is, of course, known as negative reinforcement, which is the turning point of a noxious or aversive stimulus or circumstance.

4. In the instance of human anxieties, as written about and often intensely studied in psycho-

therapy, the immediate anxiety may be re-.duced by escape and/or avoidance, but the long-range consequences of escape and avoidance do not lead to problem solving, hence therapy has to reverse this tendency to escape or avoid in order to reduce the pathology and to prepare for longer range solutions. The immediate reduction of stress by avoidance, as cited above, leads to two consequences: the avoidance or escape again on similar subsequent occasions, and the increase in other concerns (lower self-worth, feelings of guilt, failure and resignation owing to not solving long-range problems), both of which keep the pathology active. Thus, anxiety may act to promote the continued occurrence of conditioned behaviors (symptoms) on the immediate or momentary level, *and* to keep alive the psychopathology (all symptoms, syndromes) owing to reinforcing escape and avoidance behaviors that assuage anxiety.

5. Anxiety also functions, in a way corollary to role 4, to make readjustment or relearning difficult, since new learning depends on some reactivation of the conflict paradigm, thereby increasing both the avoidance and the approach gradients. At this juncture— relearning or learning more adequate behavior—theories of psychotherapy split into two relatively opposing camps: those that say the anxiety has to be relieved, reduced first before new learning can be accomplished (a kind of "subtractive" theory), and those that say that relearning and restructuring can take place upon the occurrence of graduated tasks, redefinition of the goal or task, and problem solving based on successive approximations where anxiety reduction is utilized in that it *follows the occurrence of more successful behaviors.*

Elaborating on the latter point, those theorists and therapists who hold that anxiety must first be reduced through examining one's history (find the meaning of the anxieties, the occasions when they occurred in interpersonal relationships, etc.) are described as *depth* therapists. They hold, further, that the anxieties are symptoms, as well as being signals, of the earlier distress (Freud, 1936; Korchin, 1976) and that anxiety acts as a kind of guard against those earlier (now repressed) events lest they be reactivated and cause more trouble. In the depth theories, anxiety is reactivated in the security of the therapy (transference, for example), but this step must precede the allaying of anxiety, in a more general sense, and the acquisition of more mature behaviors as well.

On the other hand, the anxiety-is-learned-and-can-be-unlearned, non-depth approach states that no matter how the anxiety was learned, it now acts to deter new learning because it is not handled in judicious ways (i.e., in terms of successive approximations or in selecting the appropriate target behaviors that are reinforced) and that it is the by-product of skill deficits which, of course, act to deter new skill acquisition. Anxiety, from this viewpoint, acts to discourage skill acquisition—the person is reinforced by and through escape and avoidance, allowing the anxiety to remain unchallenged. But anxiety can be directly approached and reduced through appropriate means and by observing that it is the other side of the coin of skill adequacy. Following this viewpoint, teaching social skills will simultaneously deal with the anxiety (in graduated amounts) *and* reduce the likelihood of anxiety reoccurrence in formerly anxiety-provoking situations. The emphasis is then put on social skills, and anxiety takes a secondary, or derived, position; it is "treated" primarily through social skills development. This does not preclude teaching the patient to "understand" what he or she will be doing in learning social skills or in relating lacks in self-confidence (hence anxiety) in common social situations to feelings of discomfort, wanting to escape, and the like; but it does recognize simultaneously that the anxiety is due primarily to deficits in social skills and to seeing that these skills have to be taught on a gradual basis in order to assuage anxiety. This is clearly an alternative to defining anxiety as *the* independent problem.

HOW SOCIAL SKILLS DEVELOPMENT FITS THE PRESENT ANXIETY THEORY

Following an essentially Freudian "depth" model in handling anxiety (Freud, 1936; Korchin, 1976), the clinician and patient would work to find out more about the history and meaning of the anxiety and would center primarily on the anxiety feeling and responding itself. The issue would be reducing the anxiety so that with later opportunities, the person would presumably function better and more satisfyingly. From the traditional viewpoint, the clinician would not encourage the person to develop social competencies, since the latter would be assumed to follow logically from anxiety reduction. They would be conceptualized as unrelated—or at least not integrally related—problems. Appropriate to this point, Wachtel (1977) says,

> ... the therapist might note that since the patient is deprived of chances to learn, he's left with the feeling that *all he can do* is get people sorry for him and hope they help. This further perpetuates the cycle. As long as he succeeds in eliciting help, he continues to *need* help. (p. 50; emphasis original)*

And further,

> Yet unless a *great deal* of attention is paid to ongoing interpersonal process, such processes are not likely to seem sufficient to account for the phenomena analysts observe. Only a detailed examination of the subtleties of interaction can provide a convincing alternative to the traditional psychoanalytic emphasis on the past. The Freudian tradition does not point inquiry in that direction. (p. 50; emphasis original)*

In this connection, Wachtel and others have observed that not only does the traditional Freudian or depth therapist avoid teaching social skills or intervening in this way in the patient's life, but such action is *contraindicated* on grounds that it will vitiate the patient–therapist relationship, hinder the transference, and put an emphasis on data that does not relate directly to the patient's expressed anxiety.

Wachtel (1977) grapples further with this problem when he writes about additional observations and an enlarged data-base for treatment:

> Despite the limitations, however, direct observation of the patient in his life setting can at times be a way for the clinician to observe aspects of the patient that would otherwise remain obscure. Though used infrequently by the behavior therapist who is engaged in an office practice with adult outpatients, it nonetheless remains an option for him that gives him added flexibility in his work. Moreover, it is on a continuum with less expensive methods such as role-playing life situations and enlisting the *patient's* participation as a behavioral observer by record-keeping and making charts or lists. Use of all these adjuncts to interviewing ... enables the behavior therapist to notice a variety of contingencies and relation-

ships between problems and life events that might be overlooked in
traditional clinical practice. (p. 112; emphasis original)*

Returning to the conflict paradigm and concern for the
approach /avoidance gradients, it is useful to observe that both
avoidance and *approach* tendencies can be dealt with in *direct* or
indirect ways. In the case of reducing the avoidance gradient (typical as it is of escaping and other non-coping tendencies), the
therapy can proceed in traditional ways, trusting that the avoidance and reluctance aspects of the patient's makeup, with respect to a particular problem and /or perhaps more generally, will
gradually diminish when the patient understands, accepts, and
otherwise sees his or her plight more clearly. This is, of course, an
indirect way of handling anxiety described in gradient terms and
characterizes the more traditional depth approach to therapy, as
we have noted.

A more *direct* way of reducing the avoidance behavior and
related anxiety is to use some of the behavioral and biofeedback
techniques that pointedly attack the anxiety (Lazarus, 1971, 1972;
Phillips, 1977b; Wickramasekera, 1976). There are a large number
of techniques applicable in such a case: relaxation and desensitization, verbal confrontation, reconditioning (e.g., with a phobia),
flooding, hypnosis, implosion, in some cases role playing, and
other techniques (Phillips, 1977b). All of these direct techniques
would take the anxiety at its manifest level and attempt to reduce
it through a variety of means. There would not be much concern
in such techniques with how the anxiety got started (perhaps in
many cases the eliciting stimuli would be noted but not studied
extensively) and an emphasis would be placed on reported relief
of the anxiety and behavioral evidence of same. These direct approaches would select specific situations in which some particularly paralyzing anxiety was present—fear of elevators, anxiety in
the face of public speaking demands, "free-floating" anxiety at the
beginning of the day, and so on.

In the case of the traditional depth therapy patient, approach
behaviors would be elicited through indirect means. It would be
assumed that as the avoidance characteristics diminished, the patient would then move forward toward previously anxiety-ridden
situations, simply out of better understanding, improved self-
confidence, and an increased motivation to assert his or herself.
As stated above, it would be largely unthinkable in traditional

* Reprinted with permission from *Psychoanalysis and Behavior Therapy: Toward an Integration,* by Paul L. Wachtel, pp. 50, 112, © 1977 by Paul L.
Wachtel, Basic Books, Inc., Publishers, New York.

modes of therapy to try to bring about these changes as direct, purposeful objectives—the patient would move in these improved directions when and as he or she felt like it. The therapy would wait for these events to occur. We note in our own behavior common examples of doing things "when we get ready," and we all balk at being reminded too often or too explicitly about our deficiencies. However, small changes in behavior of this type, based on some subtle preparation when there has been no formidable opposition to the behavior, are quite different from the more clinical instances of foreboding anxiety and reluctance to do that which the person avows he or she wants to do but cannot perform owing to the anxiety inhibition and aversiveness.

Direct approach behaviors are taught more explicitly among the behavior therapies proffered by such clinicians as Wolpe and Lazarus, (1966), Ellis (1962), Phillips (1977a), Nay (1976), and others. These would include the most cogent examples of social skills training, where the emphasis would be placed on getting started in small ways toward assertiveness, contacting others, social problem solving, and the many varieties of social skills noted in chapter 1. In such direct approach cases, the motivation to achieve, to relate socially to people (usually extant in many ways in the patient's life already, which can serve as models of applying the learning to new situations) is capitalized on in gradual, incremental ways that help build confidence as the person moves more surely toward his or her goals. *The anxiety is taken into account in limited, controlled amounts.* Anxiety is seen as the derivative of the skill level of the person and is not allowed to get out of hand and deter or inhibit the person. If the anxiety level is raised too much or too quickly in a social skills, direct-approach method, the person and /or the therapist have to fall back on a less challenging level, solidify progress, then later move on toward more assertiveness judiciously. Anxiety in such instances is used as a sign that the social skills training has not yet "taken hold," hence the training has to proceed with caution.

CLINICAL EXAMPLES UTILIZING
APPROACH–AVOIDANCE GRADIENTS

It is useful to cite clinical examples of each of these four ways of dealing with the approach–avoidance bases of anxiety. Taking anxiety, then, as the derivative or product of approach–avoidance conflict, the first case, that of a person in traditional "depth" therapy, is shown as an indirect approach to reducing the avoidance gradient.

Therapist A, a psychoanalytically trained therapist, was treating and reporting on a case of a 20-year-old college male student who had been in, and summarily quit, four schools during the previous four semesters, following high school graduation. This young man was seen three times per week. The theory was that the youth wanted to fail, was aggressing against his parents in this way, and becoming very obsessed at times with his life, his lack of school progress (although he "wanted to fail," this was "unconscious" and not fully recognized by the patient), and what would finally become of him if he continued on his failure course. The psychoanalytic therapist felt that attention to study matters, picking courses more judiciously (he had failed calculus three successive semesters owing to leaving school but had accumulated a failing record in each case prior to quitting school), and developing social skills of value in his leisure time would be unproductive in therapy. The patient was an only child of relatively old parents and had been "waited on" and cared for by a maid in the home throughout his childhood. The analysis of the therapy, which had been in progress 6 months at the time of the report cited here, indicated that "Paul" was speaking mostly of his sense of failure, his feeling not liked by girls, and his inability to concentrate. The actual therapeutic effort was aimed at uncovering the reasons and occasions in his childhood wherein these tendencies developed. The therapist considered "Paul" to have been a rejected child, to have repressed his anger and resentment at his parents for their treatment of him, and to be acting out his hostility toward them in his trail of failures in college. During discussion Paul's case with other clinicians, Paul's therapist disclaimed any value that might be associated with more attention to the patient's actual school work, study methods, concentration ability, or social life, saying "All these matters are superficial, not the real problem—Paul knows how to study, he's bright, he knows how to talk with girls, but he lacks a sense of self that makes these matters come to life—he can't be successful because he wants to punish his parents and he cannot do this any other way." Upon questioning, the depth therapist also denied that any value would be associated with consulting with the parents, on any level whatsoever, and the therapist discouraged Paul's talking with his parents at all about his (Paul's) feelings toward them. "He'll have to settle this *first* for himself—with himself—and then later, maybe, with his parents."

The depth approach to a fairly common set of problems among young adults—both male and female at the college level (the high school level, also)—is to be viewed as an instance of trying to reduce the *avoidance* gradient through *indirect* means, eschewing any direct approach techniques, such as relaxation and desensitization, teaching Paul how to cope with examinations, or encouraging him to attend even minor social functions. "All those things you suggested," the depth therapist averred, "would only keep him from relating deeply to me—he would then see me as a teacher and *not as a therapist*. It would destroy the transference relationship and replace it with—well, with nothing, if I might be that bold!"

When four possibilities exist for broad approaches to treatment—direct and indirect avoidance gradient reduction and direct and indirect approach gradient increase—to use only one of them (in the case of Paul above, the therapist used only an indirect approach to reducing the avoidance gradient) is to overlook common and useful therapeutic resources. The depth viewpoint, as expressed by Paul's psychoanalytically trained therapist, considered the "psychoanalytic reduction of anxiety" to be the sine qua non of therapy. "Even if I accepted any other technique," the therapist said, "I would not use them myself—I mean, I would refer the patient at some later time to another worker who might help him with his school work or in some ways suggest improving his social contacts, or the like—that would be *after* he understood himself, *after* we analyzed his reasons for behaving in his anxiety-ridden manner, and certainly not beforehand, and certainly not by me."

The more direct coping with the anxiety condition by avoidance gradient reduction would come from a therapist (many or most with a behavioral persuasion) who would be willing to tackle the anxiety as a kind of blocking or inhibiting condition that had to be confronted forcefully. A therapist utilizing Stampfl's position (Stampfl & Lewis, 1967) reported a case conference of a young woman in therapy, where a direct avoidance gradient reduction technique was followed.

Mary was a 25-year-old married woman working part-time as a secretary. She had been married 5 years, but the couple was childless owing largely to Mary's unwillingness to have intercourse except on rare occasions. She came to therapy because her husband was about to leave her if she did not at least try to overcome her problem. She was very self-protective in attempts at lovemaking, often failing or refusing to uncross her legs even when sexually aroused, according to her report. She was treated in therapy in a manner suggested by Stampfl and Lewis, in that she imagined scenes relating to sexual intercourse and was verbally induced by the therapist to relive sexually stimulating occasions with her husband, then, later, those relating to earlier "dating" instances of sexual arousal and/or attempts at intercourse. She was a markedly inhibited person, very "proper" in her social behavior, and usually underassertive about common matters such as asking for food at the table with guests or finding and using the bathroom in a host's home. The therapy zeroed in verbally on her sexual reluctance, getting her to say aloud sexual words that were aversive or that aroused her, getting her to talk about sexual activity in common language (in place of saying "when you do that . . ." referring to intercourse), and helping her to relax through deep breathing coupled with statements about her willingness to learn more about sex and to participate in sex when aroused. As she uttered the words related to sex more and more willingly and upon the therapist's demand during the therapy sessions, she relaxed a great deal and began to feel better, she reported. She cited some instances of asserting herself more fully: "I took those apples right back to the store after I got home and upon unpacking them, realized how nearly rotten they were—I *never* would have done *that* before," she stated with great emphasis, the reporting therapist quoted her from his therapy notes. She also reported she was able to laugh at jokes about sex without feeling embarrassed. Within a few weeks time, based on two or three sessions per week with implosive therapy, she began to engage in sexual intercourse with her husband, first very tentatively, later more often and with greater pleasure on her part.

It can be noted readily that as the avoidance gradient is reduced in the manner described here briefly, the alternative to no sex naturally becomes sexual participation. As the sexual willingness increases, skill in sexual intercourse (willingness to approach and be approached sexually, sharing activities and feelings with her husband about what is arousing sexually, and willingness to experiment with intercourse positions, and so forth) increases, and what was originally primarily a reduction of the avoidance gradient now also becomes a matter of approach behaviors. This is a more or less clear-cut case of direct anxiety reduction that leads forthwith into approach behaviors, as they are the natural alternatives to inhibition and avoidance behaviors. Of course, skilled participation in sexual intercourse has to be learned in order to maximize mutual pleasures, but willingness to be aroused and to begin to act on arousal are fairly readily exhibited and require no great preparation once one has an acceptable partner. In Mary's case, the primary therapeutic technique was that of reducing the avoidance conditions and behaviors related to sexual activity, but this melded readily into skill acquisition and execution. This direct approach, contrasted with the first case (Paul) in which a long-term indirect approach to reducing the avoidance gradient was utilized, leads quickly into approach behaviors and allows for their reinforcement in real life situations. The direct avoidance gradient reduction engages quickly and decisively with approach behaviors (the avoidance gradient reduction, while of paramount importance in this case and with implosive types of confrontation, is not an end in and of itself) and develops a broader base for therapeutic change and anxiety reduction. The vast differences, then, between the indirect approach to reducing the avoidance gradient (the case of Paul) and the direct approach (the case of Mary) are at once apparent (see Figure 5-3). The direct reduction of the avoidance gradient from conflict theory is more resourceful, i.e., feeds into more alternatives to anxiety for the patient, gets to the problem sooner, invites more active participation by the patient, sets specific objectives to be attained, and can be tested fairly easily and quickly by the therapist and his or her patient, so that if a change in therapeutic tactic is called for, it can be recognized early and other methods can be tried.

The *indirect* method of dealing with strengthening the *approach* gradient refers back to the indirect method of reducing the avoidance gradient. The two therapeutic positions regarding anxiety reduction, viewed from the standpoint of conflict theory, are closely similar, and most instances of indirect approach gradient increases are theorized to come from indirect avoidance gradient reduction. Thus, the depth theories stemming from psychoanalysis view approach behaviors (as in the case of Paul) as coming along gradually as the avoidance conditions are better understood. This position has some validity in general life situations where people "get around to doing something when they feel like it," as one therapist put it, and "there is very little you can do to accelerate the process."

In primarily verbal therapy, as practiced by most out-patient psychotherapists in mental hygiene clinics, counseling centers and in private practice settings, the verbal reconstruction of the problems presented by the patient and ways to work on the problems do arise in connection with indirect references to the problems. That is, rarely does the therapist visit the classroom where the student is anxious, rarely does the private practice psychologist or psychiatrist go into the home of the adolescent who is a reluctant and rebellious student to see first-hand what is going on in the family. The therapy setting constitutes an indirect approach to the problems presented by the patient; the therapeutic setting is, in a way, a minor (but sometimes powerful) realignment of the patient's environment, even though we often fail to see that therapy is, itself, a kind of environmental manipulation, a kind of miniature social reorganization of the patient's life. But this rearrangement of the patient's social milieu is indirect and is

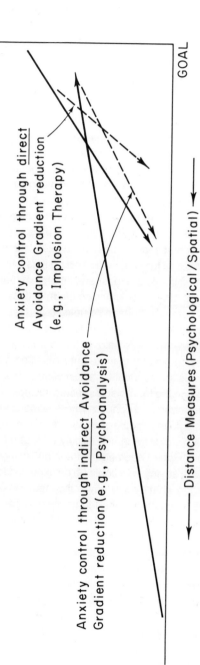

Anxiety control through direct Avoidance Gradient reduction (e.g., Implosion Therapy)

Anxiety control through indirect Avoidance Gradient reduction (e.g., Psychoanalysis)

⟶ Distance Measures (Psychological / Spatial) ⟶

GOAL

Figure 5-3. How the avoidance gradient in conflict is hypothetically reduced through *direct* means (implosion therapy, for example) and through *indirect* means (e.g., psychoanalytic/psychodynamic therapies) as ways of handling anxiety. Often, the therapist posits "underlying causes" but seldom posits conflict as basic to the therapeutic handling of anxiety. In behavioral formulations, anxiety arises in the conflict between goal-seeking and avoiding aversiveness, and not as a symptom of any cause other than the features described in relation to approach–avoidance conflict.

based on a small sample of the patient's out-of-therapy behavior (Phillips, 1977a).

Given that the therapy setting, constituted as it usually is, remains a generally indirect way of teaching and exploring how to *increase the approach gradient,* we need to know more about how this operation is influenced. The case of "Robert" will help in this connection.

Robert was a 35-year-old married male with two children. He was well educated, having practiced law 10 years since receiving a law degree at age 25. He was moderately successful in his agency practice of law but was irresponsible in his social relationships, in his duties at home with his wife and children, and in meeting debts and other obligations with the "outside" world. He readily admitted his "incorrigibility" as he put it, in most matters impinging on him outside his office law practice. His irresponsible attitude at home was a constant problem to his wife—children not cared for, fed, put to bed on time when the wife was attending an evening class, bills not paid, letters not mailed when they contained important checks or other communications, and many instances of lack of care with household upkeep and repair. "He seems to sluff off on everything he's obliged to do, except to go to work and do a fairly good job there," his wife said. In the therapy with Robert there was no willingness on his part to try to put himself on a schedule or to accept specific goals as reasonable. "I just want to talk about things," he said, and of course the therapist respected this position. The talking centered around Robert's childhood where almost everything was done for him by a doting mother; where the father had died when Robert was 4 years old, leaving him largely without a father-model to observe and follow. Robert seemed to "trade on" this fact that he had no father after age 4, saying how could he be expected to be different if he had never learned what he was now supposed to know. In classical parlance, he resisted change. Although he liked to talk about himself, much of his talking was a kind of rambling, and little of it in his unstructured therapy came to bear on his daily life where his most serious problems were noted. After 2 years of therapy at the rate of 3 times a week, it was apparent that Robert would change very little unless, as his wife put it, "somebody builds a fire under him and keeps it hot!" His wife was a school teacher and as part of her additional training she had heard seminar reports on therapeutic work with persons she deemed similar to her husband. She decided (after Robert's 2 years "of *intend*-sive therapy—I don't know what it was *intending,* but it has not produced much," she averred) that she would try to help him get into a more practical kind of therapy, and she volunteered to go with him and participate with him, if Robert agreed. Robert demurred, said he didn't want to change therapists, said he was "making progress" and did not want any change of course. He said, in his own behalf, that he had done better with the children at home, had cared for them more reliably when his wife was away, and had "done some work around the house." The wife agreed that there had been a modicum of progress, and the therapist felt "Robert needs more time to come to grips with his problems—don't rush him, he'll make it." The wife countered, "But his progress is so slow and so painful for me—I just don't know if I can wait and wait for these piddling little changes to occur—I just don't know how long I can go on regardless of the progress Robert *thinks* he is making. I don't see why we can't set some goals and work together on them—his therapy is so far off, so distant, so uninvolved with me, my life, the children, and our social life. It is just all for him in some ruminative and even selfish way. I just wonder what it all adds up to." The therapy did continue in its traditional vein, however, and the wife simply put up with matters of daily life and was still doing so at the time of the report on this case.

It was assumed by Robert's therapist that Robert would, in due time, evolve ways of living more fruitfully with his family. The whole therapeutic approach was an indirect one—not so much based on the psychoanalytic model of uncovering, but more a kind of "cognitive restructuring"—that had to go on with Robert before his behavior in other ways could change. The therapist explained a strong dichotomy between feelings and emotions on the one hand, and behavior on the other. He contended that the restructuring had to come about cognitively (inside Robert, so to speak) and could not be accelerated by any planful means. This therapist did not think that setting plans and objectives would destroy the transference, or the therapist–patient relationship, or play into obsessive or other undesirable personality tendencies; rather, the cognitive restructuring therapist felt that cognitive change had to come first, and that verbal, talking-it-out, restructuring efforts were preliminary to overt behavior change in Robert's relationships with his wife and children. The therapeutic theory here was one of "cognitive matters first—behavior change later." As these hypothesized cognitive changes took place, Robert would then "see the relevance of behavior change in some ways, entirely up to him, and not for us to determine in advance or from our vantage points."

While there is merit in turning over as much change responsibility to the patient as possible, and as early as possible, there may be a number of ways in which the therapist can do this. The therapist's role in the case of Robert was a very passive, unstructuring one, based not on depth notions of personality and human motivation but on cognitive restructuring. The restructuring was supposed to take place in and around Robert's expression of feelings and emotions about his life and on the results of this restructuring as it would possibly lead to overt social behavior change. If no change came, then that was Robert's option, and his wife would have to deal with the consequences; the therapist would not participate in this aspect of Robert's life, or in the therapy if it intended to bring about specifiable results. Robert was apparently not able, in the context of this therapy, at least, to actually "set goals" for himself (one sets goals even if one does not explicitly specify them, the goals being set by default or by continuing with an already established precedence) in the usual sense of specifying changes he desired. Robert's goals were, so to say, to be left alone, to handle everything as he saw fit, as if he were acting in isolation, not in concert with his family.

There are, of course, many far-reaching conceptual and philosophical problems that can be raised in connection with Robert's case. Is the patient entirely responsible for his or her own therapy goals? Is no input in the way of suggesting goals, priorities, and means of working on goals and priorities possible from the therapist without damaging the patient's self-determination? Is the individual patient in therapy solely and entirely as an individual, or is he an individual-in-relationship-to-others who also have a right to their interest in the relationships shared with Robert? Is Robert an individual or is he a "contexted individual"?

In the light of individual preferences and rights associated with Robert's therapy, where are the rights of the wife and the children? If they were in therapy, would they, too, have the right to preclude or eschew changes that impinge forcefully on others? Where do Robert's rights and privileges begin and end in relation to those of his wife and children? Is being in therapy tantamount to creating some preferential domain that one insulates oneself in and says, in effect, "I am in therapy, therefore I have the right to complete self-determination and any abrogation of this right is an injustice to me." Is psychotherapy a hiatus, or is it a relationship that bears importantly on the patient's other relationships? Would Robert have been more cogently dealt with had he been in group therapy in contrast with, or in addition to, individual therapy? Does individual therapy, more than group therapy, promote a kind of psychological isolationism? These and many more problems of technical, ethical, and philosophical natures have to be confronted when therapeutic stances are taken; the therapy is responsible to more than the patient—it is also responsible to the matrix of relationships in which the patient is involved, including the interests of society. In studying psychotherapy and its efforts to overcome the constricting anxieties and conflicts of the person, the fact that these anxieties and conflicts are part of a social context and that that context can never be dismissed out of hand must never be overlooked.

Therapies, then, derived as they are from conflict theory and from the manner they purport to handle anxieties, are large-scale choices made by therapists (and indirectly by patients); their value and their scientific/humanistic impact are matters for everyone to see and judge, not the province alone of the therapist or the patient.

The last type of therapy, as it purports to deal with anxiety derived from conflict, is one that seeks *directly* to *increase the approach gradient*. What does "direct" mean in the context of other therapeutic strategies that cope with conflict in other ways (by indirection, by working more on the avoidance gradient)? Does "direct" mean that the therapist takes over for the patient, that patient self-determination is minimized or abrogated, that the therapist knows more than the patient and that the therapist's goals and ideas should supervene? Certainly not. The therapist is the servant of the patient in all types of therapy. The differences in therapy outlook are a function of how the conflict resolution and anxiety reduction tasks are undertaking. Therapeutic roles are largely structured by the therapy that takes off in one way or another in its efforts to reduce conflict and anxiety for the patient in his or her life. The often repeated charges that behavioral methods are superficial, take over from the patient, look only at the behavior as the therapist sees it, and exclude the role of the patient are simply misconceptions and myths about how direct behavioral therapeutic methods work (Phillips, 1977a).

The therapeutic choice to increase the approach gradient by direct means and by as many means as possible is a natural and logical choice. Actually, the person in conflict *wants* to approach certain goals (give public speeches, be successful, be accepted socially by particular others, and so on); the motivation is already present. If there were no positive movement toward the conflicted goals, then the individual would abandon them, and the problem would be solved. The conflict between wanting and fearing, between seeking and doubting, between positive and negative expectations is the heart of the matter. If the ultimate end of therapy is to permit, encourage, and facilitate the patient's arrival at his or her goals, then capitalizing on the approach toward these ends is a worthwhile and heuristic objective. The objective of the therapy is to be as inventive and resourceful as we can in assisting the patient in these undertakings.

The following is a case in which *direct approach* toward the patient's goal was implemented, keeping in mind the importance of the patient's reluctances and withdrawal (avoidance) tendencies at times.

"Bill" was a 30-year-old office administrator who had supervisory responsibilities for about 10 clerical staff. He reported several times per week to his superior on how his department was working in filling mail orders, answering questions, and solving delivery problems related to the company's products. He was thus on the spot all of the time in coordinating the work of others to achieve his department's output, with both of these requirements. Whenever his department failed in its output, even for a day, he became irate, scolded his subordinates in front of others, tried to take over menial jobs himself "in order to make things go right," and otherwise put pressures on himself and others to perform immediately and flawlessly. He described himself as "perfectionistic to a flaw," as a kind of play on words, but it aptly described at least some aspects of his daily functioning. Bill came to therapy at the point where he couldn't sleep nights because of worry over his daily activities, which included not only the objective problems related to turning out the work needed, but his reactions to his frustrations. Despite his frustrations and many interpersonal problems, his department had increased its output over the past year before Bill entered therapy, and there were objective signs that in many ways he did well on the job. However, he felt he did less well than others in his company and was ambitious to receive coveted promotions. His daily impact on his subordinates was often seen as a challenge to his own future, as well as a threat to daily output of work. The therapy concentrated on Bill's desire to "do well" but took that objective not as a given but as a goal to work toward, based on daily efforts that Bill could learn to improve upon. Bill was helped to set his daily goals, not alone in his own thinking but to make them extant so that all the supervisees could share them. He was helped to interact on a personal level each day with each subordinate, not only in terms of work to be accomplished but in non-work-related activities as well—sports, family matters, and the like. Bill kept a running log of his interactions with each of his ten supervisees on a daily basis; these were discussed in his therapy. He also kept a log of his temper outbursts and what provoked them (as far as he could tell), plus what the outcome was of each temper display. These activities gave Bill an opportunity to work directly on the main sources of friction in his daily work—his "perfectionism" and "accounts" of how he actually interacted with his charges, as he described his log-keeping efforts—and to see each day how his efforts paid off. The whole matter was reviewed twice weekly in his therapy, along with other matters, such as how he was sleeping, how he had had past frictions with others over his perfectionistic inclinations, and how much these matters led him into bouts of worry and rumination. He saw fairly readily that specific target behaviors dealing with his daily routine with his work not only helped improve these extant problems, but gave him a better feeling of his own worth and led to more composure, better sleep, and more enjoyment in interacting with others on the job. He added, "You know, when I have to put down what I've done on the charts and logs each day, I am really on-the-stick to perform *realistically,* not just in a fantasy way, and to see how I impact others in the process—it is very helpful."

Examples of Bill's daily chart on interacting with his supervisees and his log are presented in Figure 5-4. These entrees were the basis for some of the twice-weekly therapy sessions and took up most of the discussion during the first 2 months of therapy. After that, the log and the interaction chart grew more sparse, and Bill spoke more of how he felt about his life and his therapy, discussed changing his job, and held many discussions with his wife (whom he had not disclosed much to in the way of personal feelings before) about most aspects of his life. An interview with his wife disclosed that Bill was much improved but still had a way to go. Their sex life was better, and although he blew up at her less often and seemed better on the job, there were still topics he was more intractible about than was desirable. Bill moved at this point (after 3 months) to a once-a-week therapy regimen and felt this was adequate, a pace that was continued until he ended therapy about 7 months later (somewhat less than a year in therapy, and a total of about 50 interviews).

Looking at the results of Bill's therapy in terms of implementing the approach gradient, several tentative generalizations can be made.

1. Bill's anxieties and anger outbursts were reduced gradually over the first 3 months of therapy (as per his log) as he refined and moved more surely toward his job objectives.

2. His original objectives to improve his job-related behaviors (pretty well under way by the end of 3 months) gave way in time to im-

Names	Interactions
Aaron	"Talked with him about weekend and his new car; Praised him for help with big mailing"
Cathy	"Out Mon/Tu. but talked with her on phone; still has a fever — work being done by M."
Claude	"He helped me — reluctantly with a messed-up order; I told him I appreciated it."
Debby	"asked me if I was taking tranquilizers — I seemed better. Shared a joke.
Lou	"Was angry with me over my criticizing him last week; a good worker, tho."
Marsha	"Always willing to pitch-in - see ref. to Cathy. I complimented her."
Nan	"May leave job, move away — unhappy in job, and home life — only 18."
Opel	"A real steady person — helps me with Nan. Gave her time off."
Paul	"He and I have the most friction and his temper is like mine; most difficult!"
Ralph	"Very new — don't know him yet. Talks more than he works; seems volatile — be careful!"

10-3 Slept better last few nights — Liz says I'm better. Talked about Xmas vacation plans — I held temper.

10-4 Xmas plans came up again — we didn't agree — I lost my cool; she cried, said I was "hopeless."

10-5 Liz feeling better toward me, but I worked late, lost sleep last night, felt lousy today; work heavy.

10-6 Orders got out late — 2 people out sick — not my fault — worried less. Didn't blow up at Lou or Ralph.

10-7 Feel better at times; not on even keel yet, tho. Some improvement here and there.

Figure 5-4. Notes on Bill's relationships with fellow employees and subordinates and his daily log; both were recorded daily for therapy sessions.

proving his relationships with his wife and with his employees, all in more specific ways.

3. He saw that the data-keeping on his own behavior was not only important for the therapy hours, per se, but also enabled him to get a grip on himself, led to increased confidence,

and to asserting himself with his employees
without anger and recrimination.

4. His active approach toward solving his anger
    and anxiety problems at the outset led to con-
    fidence that his problems were not so "deep
    seated, like my wife said they were, that I
    would need *years* to overcome them."
    Specific problems on specific occasions did
    indeed improve "right before my very eyes—I
    could hardly believe I was acting differently."

5. At first his anger was uncontrolled; as he ac-
    tively tried, through the therapy, to control
    his anger, he often became very anxious, thus
    showing conflict between wanting to vent
    feelings when he felt provoked, yet knowing
    that caution and other tactics would be bet-
    ter for all concerned. "The more I held my
    tongue, the more anxious I became and that
    puzzled me because I thought for a while I
    was getting worse—not better—and that I was
    doing something unnatural for me when I
    didn't blow up at somebody." As the results
    of his better controlled and more assertive be-
    havior toward others became observable to
    him and to others (more objectively centered
    on job activities and job plans), he realized
    how much his anxiety had signalled conflict
    between immediate impulsivity and more
    reasoned diplomacy. He then discerned how
    he could bring about his own more efficient
    job performance and that of his supervisees
    with less tension between all of them and less
    anxiety and anger on his part.

6. By indirection, or by emphasizing the avoid-
    ance gradient reduction, the same or com-
    parable results might have been achieved in
    time; but it is seriously doubted that the re-
    sults would have been as fast or as fully integ-
    rated into his job setting. The improvement in
    home-based and wife-related relationships,
    while not an original objective, was a sort of
    "bonus" for him. Once he improved notice-
    ably on his job, he then turned more attention

to other aspects of his life (a kind of indirect approach gradient benefit) and felt increasingly more confident about solving other problems gainfully.

7. Once a person begins to solve problems (and we are illustrating here the advantages of the direct approach to overcoming anxiety via increasing the effectiveness of the approach gradient), then other means of handling anxiety may come into focus. That is, a success pattern via approach gradient efforts can lead to thoughts and actions that may illustrate indirect approach gradient efforts and indirect avoidance gradient reduction. The conflict that was paralyzing may be weakened so much by direct success and the reinforcement it affords that any and all means of anxiety and conflict reduction may become operative. If this is true, and it has been observed often, the person may then launch into a "success pattern" to replace the old "failure pattern"; where the individual formerly felt hopeless and constrained, he or she will now feel on top of problems, will display a more versatile repertoire, and consequently will learn to deal with anxiety by a variety of means. Social reinforcement will become more broadly based.

8. There is no sure route to overcoming conflict, but the theoretical prediction here is that direct approach gradient efforts will, simultaneously, cover the conflict and anxiety-reduction problem with greater efficiency and more readily give rise to testable therapeutic approaches. The great abundance of extant therapeutic persuasions (Parloff, 1977) testifies not so much to real differences in therapies but to the great likelihood that all therapies are utilizing, in unknown and unrecognized ways, combinations of all of the four means of conflict and anxiety reduction, possibly without discerning the similarities and differences involved, and without being

explicitly concerned with efficiency and effectiveness or results or parsimonious conceptions of their efforts.

The discussion of the four ways of resolving approach–
avoidance conflict and the related anxiety problems are summarized in Figure 5-5. This figure shows at a glance how the
direct and indirect approach and avoidance gradient manipula-
tions are conceptualized. It would be useful to think of how the
various therapeutic persuasions deal with the conflict/anxiety
paradigm proferred here. For example, is Ellis's therapy (1962)
primarily one of *direct* avoidance gradient reduction, with direct
approach gradient increase a secondary but important feature? Is
not classical psychoanalysis primarily a method of *indirect*
avoidance gradient reduction with the additional assumption that
not only does the approach gradient increase escape notice (in
contrast to Ellis), but attention to it is not recommended as it may
thereby contaminate the therapeutic relationship? Is Gestalt
therapy a general therapeutic method for direct avoidance gradient reduction and direct approach gradient increase, with a
mixture of the two that is not well clarified? Are most of the newer
therapies (Harper, 1975) mixtures and blends that purport to teach
the individual to assert him- or herself (approach gradient increase) but, unlike Wolpe (1958, 1969), do not provide clear
means for dealing with avoidance gradient tendencies and do not
recognize the role of anxiety as a derivative of conflict? All
therapies use, as they probably should, mixtures of ways for dealing with approach–avoidance conflict. The issue here is not so
much the inventiveness (if it is genuine inventiveness) of
therapies as it is a matter of clarity of purpose, parsimony, a recognition of the important role of approach–avoidance conflict in
all psychopathology and psychotherapy, and how anxiety is understood and dealt with in both practical and theoretical ways.

PREVENTION

As an outgrowth of the discussion of psychopathology in terms of
conflict theory and the relationship of anxiety to conflict, immediate questions arise: Is preventive work more likely to follow
on a social skills version of psychopathology, in contrast to one
based on a more traditional nosological system? If social skills are
basic to most or all forms of functional psychopathology, does this
viewpoint suggest that there are explicit social skills that the child

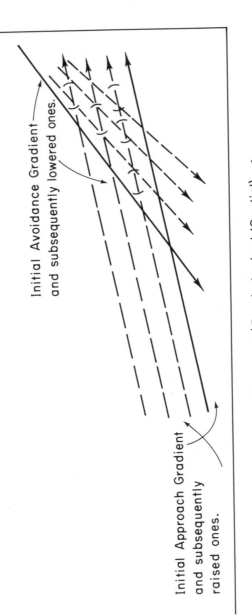

Initial Avoidance Gradient
and subsequently lowered ones.

Initial Approach Gradient
and subsequently
raised ones.

◀— Distance Measures (Psychological/Spatial) —▶

Figure 5-5.   The original avoidance gradient and original approach gradient (solid lines) change as a function of conflict (anxiety) reduction via social skills training, which constitutes a *direct* method of therapy. Although the primary thrust is direct, many indirect changes occur in both the avoidance and the approach gradients. The area of intersection is where the "therapeutic battles" are won (parentheses at intersections of dotted approach–avoidance gradients). Skill applications help resolve these conflict areas that may be spun off from the larger conflictful issues. Social reinforcement comes from winning these hypothetical battles, and approach behaviors and personal confidence ensue.

and adult can be taught as part of his or her social /emotional development? If we have good corrective measures for psychopathology, do we, perforce, have good preventive measures at hand as well?

We must be careful to view prevention in the right light. It is not prevention in the sense of an inevitable connection between the past and present. Apropos of attempts to find "first causes" or initial developmental conditions, in contrast to looking at here and now social conditions and social skills, it is important to realize that throughout the last few decades there have been theories and various avenues of research purporting to tie childhood experiences to later personality characteristics or abnormalities (Orlansky, 1949). Orlansky's review of the relationship between childhood experiences and training and later personality characteristics showed tenuous interconnections at best. More recently, Sameroff (1977) has concluded that constitutional variables and later personality or developmental outcomes do not have proven interconnection. Sameroff (1977) says,

> There has yet to be demonstrated a causal connection between a constitutional variable and any personality or intellectual developmental outcome. This may sound like a strong statement, but it characterizes the developmental data from myriads of longitudinal studies. Whenever retrospective research has indicated a variable thought to be causal to some adverse behavioral outcome, prospective research has shown that individuals with exactly the same characteristics or experiences have not had the adverse outcome. (p. 60)*

Garmezy (1974), in his studies of children at risk, has reached the same conclusion. Sameroff (1977) adds the following:

> Why is it, then, that in the face of these negative indications we continue to believe that premature children, difficult children, or handicapped children will all have poor developmental outcomes? I would suggest it is because we do not have the necessary developmental perspective. As long as we believe that labels are received rather than given, we will be confronted with the problem. Only when we come to see that the label is not only something we have attributed to the child but also the initial ingredient in a self-fulfilling prophecy, will we come to the heart of primary prevention. (p. 60)*

As well as the above evidence, a recent summary of the role

---

* Reprinted with permisson from Sameroff AJ. Concepts of humanity in primary prevention. In Albee, & J.M. Jaffee (Eds.). *Primary Prevention of Psychopathology*. Hanover, N.H.: University Press of New England, 1977.

of early experiences in later development has been systematically reviewed by Clark and Clark (1977). Indications are that the general psychotherapeutic preoccupation with early childhood experiences as the chief subject matter of personality change may be misplaced and that more emphasis should be placed on the here-and-now, on the social matrix in which anxiety is elicited and maintained, and less on retrospective analysis of one's life as the prerequisite to contemporary change.

In the field of nutrition, there are preventive measures in the form of proposing a balanced and nutritious diet. It is known that rickets comes from certain deficiencies in the form of calcium and vitamin D, and as a result, corrective diets or general nutritional care can be used to overcome or prevent the malnutrition underlying rickets. In nutritional areas, and perhaps in some forms of health care, the environmental, dietary, or other conditions that will prevent, as well as overcome, deficiencies can be specified. But the specifics, even in physical medicine do not go too far— there is no exercise regimen that will *prevent* low back strain. One has to be careful not to strain one's skeletal and musculature system; prevention is based on general exercise, care, and alertness, not nearly so specific as in the instance of preventing or correcting rickets. Perhaps it is not known exactly what will prevent any given illness or infirmity, even though it may be known after-the-fact how to correct the malady. Raising questions concerning prevention of psychopathology by drawing attention to the importance of social skills interpretations of psychopathology does not necessarily provide us with easy preventive measures. In a later chapter we will discuss the problem of a social curriculum, which will discuss some principles of value in functioning well as a social human being, but this posture will be a broad and general one, not a set of "musts" that are developmentally given or irrevocably true or valid. We must, then, turn attention to the social setting, to skills learned in meaningful social contexts, if we are to come to grips with this problem.

At present, the best indicator of the social skills of the individual (child, adolescent, or adult) is the ability of the person to develop his or her own potential in a social context with others in ways that do not hamper the development or relatively smooth functioning of either the individual or his or her social reference group. Because a person's social reference groups are always in flux and even change markedly from time to time, and since adaptability is called for in such changes by way of employing functionally adequate social skills, the shifting locus of control and means of adaptability lead to a very complex situation for which there are no ready answers or descriptions. At the level of correcting already deficient social skills, there are potentially encouraging ways and means to accomplish this; but these ways and means cannot now be extended *backward* in time to earlier developmental stages or crises to identify the *particular* social deficits that led to the present disturbances. The situation with social skills is perhaps somewhat like the situation with physical exercise and proper health measures. Today, we cannot correct very many maladies on the basis of a specific lack in the person's health history; more likely, we can correct *today's maladies with today's remedies*, because it is only the present context that affords a proper definition of both the individual's status (as to health, exercise, and physical strength, social skills, or whatnot) and the demands of the situations in which he or she now lives and moves.

An example of the latter point appears in a brief account of a 25-year-old male, "Cecil."

Cecil was a college-trained foreign language expert who, upon taking a job, soon found that he was not able to satisfactorily contact the women in the job setting in terms of simple social skills (having coffee with them, carrying on conversations that displayed some interest in the other person even for a brief period of time, "passing the time of day," and other minor social encounters). Because of, or in relation to, these felt inadequacies, Cecil began to stay more to himself, felt he was liked only by males, and began to wonder if he had "homosexual tendencies of an underlying nature." An intensive resumé of his social life history showed that he functioned only marginally with the opposite sex in high school and college, rarely "dating," but more likely going to mixed parties and social gatherings related to his school work where he was mainly an onlooker and had no specific or important social role to play (i.e., he was not the chairperson of a committee to put on a party, nor was he a member of a social clique that instigated social activities for themselves or larger groups). Further study and interviewing showed that Cecil lacked simple conversational skills, that he considered anything he said or felt to be of no interest to others (because his ideas were not great enough, or his feelings profoundly enough revealed by references to poetry or literature), and so, "Why should I participate?" His social awkwardness was shown by his continually laughing or snickering for no socially adequate reason, accompanied by a failure to laugh more wholeheartedly when a good joke was told or when some especially humorous situation developed in the office. It was learned early on that Cecil always felt somewhat awkward as a child and adolescent in social situations unless accompanied by his slightly older brother. When the brother, some 15 months his elder, was present and acted to structure the social requirements, the patient seemed to get along fairly well. The older brother's social monitoring appeared to protect the patient during his high school and college years, but when the patient took a job in another city, leaving his older brother and the rest of his family behind, he began to perceive the stated social ineptitude and presented himself for psychotherapy, thinking that he had primarily a sexual problem. He did have problems with all kinds of intimacies, including sexual ones, but the springboard of his difficulty was considered to be his social skills deficits, and these were the primary thrust of his therapy, which began to produce some positive dividends within a few months' time.

Cecil's therapy was centered around finding the most appropriate social skills development and training opportunities in the here and now, knowing full well that what he was currently obliged to learn he should have learned between the ages of 10 and 20, or perhaps even earlier. The therapist could not go back in time and teach social skills at the level of the 10-, 12-, or 15-year-old; the training had to be at Cecil's current level; sometimes this was painstakingly simple and obvious, yet he had to learn it "from scratch." The myriad of social skills lacks were so extensive that he would be learning them for the rest of his life, not simply the modifications or corrections or refinements placed on all of us, but more basic social adequacies that would need some attention throughout his social functioning.

What could Cecil have been taught earlier? To speak directly to others when spoken to; to initiate social contact, not always wait for others; to carry on a conversation, not simply fall back on yes or no or other one-word replies; to express gratitude toward others; to let another person walk before one in passing through a door; to wait until one is served something, even in an open social encounter (even more importantly at the table); and to thank others, to say "please," to share, and all the other elementary interactions we begin to teach children from age 2 onward. These are all elementary indeed, but they were not skills that Cecil had learned. In his social situations as an adult, he felt awkward because he not only failed to say and do the correct and acceptable things under prescribed conditions, but he had a prevailing anxiety that he could not function at all. Socially speaking, Cecil felt that it was better for him to withdraw than to constantly err. Each social situation was an anxiety-provoking one, placed high on the intersection of the approach and avoidance gradients. As a result, he was socially paralyzed.

Preventive experiences would have been for him to have learned, at least to a modicum of efficiency, the social skills he lacked. These skills were his "social vitamins," and without them he was undernourished in a social sense. Unlike vitamins, social competencies could not be fed to him—he had to acquire them slowly and often painfully. As he learned social adequacies, he was preventing himself from remaining socially incompetent; the preventive work and the remedial work became one and the same. Perhaps this is the real role of prevention at any juncture in one's life—the needed social skills have to be learned at the time (for optimal functioning), and if they are not learned, current problems will remain and later ones will be more likely to develop or become exacerbated. As and when the social skills are learned, at whatever time in life, they are a basis for present adequacy and prevention of future inadequacy.

Prevention is a succession of "nows" and "laters," with each being important in its own right and at its own time. Correcting present social skills deficits means only that they are currently regarded as social lacks, and although these lacks go backward in continuous ways in time, there is likely no one critical event of the type described by Sameroff (1977) that precipitated matters. Today's social skills lacks require a turnaround, a kind of "affirmative action" that will redress previous deficits; the emphasis is shifted from the past to the here-and-now by teaching social competency, regardless of how the deficits were learned.

It will be possible in time, as we learn more about human development and become more precise in our teaching and correction of social skills, to fortify the person with social skills competencies from the earliest age onward, so that at each juncture, the social competencies will be found to be relevant and adequate, with these adequacies boding well (but not incontrovertibly) for the future. In order to accomplish a high level of social skills relevance, *mankind will have to invent a social curriculum*—a curriculum that only exists now in more or less vague form, like a trail through a forest that appears and disappears through the underbrush with no clear outcome and many opportunities to be lost along the way.

6

Training and /or education have long been equated with therapy. Many would say that no matter what psychotherapeutic persuasion one holds to, the therapist is simply educating or training the client or patient in better ways of living or problem solving. There is nothing that goes on in psychotherapy that does not go on, more or less, in education as we ordinarily understand it, or in training as it is usually practiced. Pupils often show "resistance" to the teacher's or school's requirements (at least they have their own ideas about what is important, and these may often not coincide with the standard fare) and there are struggles with learning, such as problems in concentration, memory, and conflict in values. Paying attention to the process of acquiring information and to evaluating it go on in therapy and education alike. Therapy and education are both conducted individually and in groups, large and small; and special target objectives and general "open" formats are found in each. The similarities are legion. What of the differences between therapy on the one hand and education or training on the other?

Therapists who hold to a repression model of human problems, such as is found among more traditional Freudian thinkers, would likely argue that therapy has to do with the "unconscious," whereas education does not. The depth therapist would hold that making the unconscious conscious would be a task differentiating the therapist from the educator or trainer. The plethora of unconscious factors, such as resistance, transference, countertransference, repression, displacement, the defense mechanisms, etc., would all be offered as essentially distinguishing characteristics

Training as a Therapeutic Modality: Implications for Social Skills

of therapy, seldom if ever found in educational and training pursuits.

However, a non-depth, or an interpersonal, model of human functioning, which located the significant variables in the environment–person(s) interaction, would drop the notions of the unconscious, defense, and so forth, and would replace them with concepts describing behavioral tendencies that conflict with other behavioral tendencies. Posed against others are the tendencies of the person ("I'd rather not be in school," or "I wish I had this job done," or "I wish she would act differently toward me," and so on), or other preferences that conflict with those put forth by schools, institutions, society, and other important people or organizations. Even when one seems to have an intrapsychic conflict, this is understood as conflicting behaviors the person has had separately reinforced from time to time, which, if kept apart, may not conflict. However, inevitably there will be a point or time of reckoning, such as the end of the semester, when the *requirement* to study conflicts with one's having wasted time and not studied, when the *incompleted job* will conflict with the boss's demands, and when the *preferences* of the other person will conflict with one's own, perhaps showing an incapacity to change either preference readily.

If we view any task, conflict, learning opportunity, challenge, or whatnot as a set of conditions having approach characteristics, and likely avoidance ones as well, we can approach any of life's problems or demands, whether set in the clinic, the home, the school, in business, or in society at large, under the same 143 general set of principles. As stated earlier, the issues related to therapy and human problem resolution arise from conditions of conflict; the conflict, in turn, stems from tendencies to both approach and avoid—to feel or act two opposing ways about something or someone or oneself—and it is this condition of conflict that gives rise to problems encountered in all manner of human interactions. There is nothing unique about the clinic in discovering or posing problems; the school, the home, the office—everywhere there are in principle similar problems to be found. We could, likewise, place clinical skills in a school or in an office or elsewhere, or apply the skills at large to society and still confront the same kinds of problems, requiring more or less the same techniques, with essentially similar types of outcomes. Put another way, psychotherapy, behavior change, attitude change, social conflict resolution, and so on, are based on data-gathering procedures and processes of a similar nature, best known by the consequences of their problem-solving actions and all viewable from a homogeneous perspective.

If then, there are no hard and fast problem differences between educational or training settings and therapeutic ones (save some semantic problems we often fail to recognize), we are able to review some interesting developments in the area of research and application referred to as *training*. The studies of training may instruct us further in how to regard traditional problems of therapy and psychopathology in more heuristic ways. If training is an alternative therapeutic modality, it can be shown to embrace many concepts and practices of importance to a social skills view of psychopathology.

SOME BACKGROUND FACTORS

Some people can more readily accept new ideas or emphases if they can be shown that Freud or some early psychoanalyst thought of, used, or at least mentioned in passing the "same" idea current today. While Freud and members of his early coterie did not utilize training as a therapeutic modality or emphasize social skills as we think of them now, one can loosely interpret Freud's words of advice to the father of "Little Hans," in the child's interest, as a form of training (Freud, 1959). If training and behavioral therapy and other direct methods of handling problems are considered to be 20th century matters, the following quotation will show otherwise:

... if your child shrieks and runs away at the sight of a frog let another catch it, and lay it down at a good distance from him; at first accustom him to look upon it; when he can do that, to come nearer to it, and see it leap without emotion, then to touch it slightly, when it is held fast in another's hand; and so on until he can come to handle it as confidently as a butterfly or a sparrow. (Locke, 1693)

How perceptive of Locke to have written this and to have anticipated many aspects of today's training as a therapeutic modality suggesting a case of desensitization or successive approximations. The Ansbachers (Ansbacher & Ansbacher, 1956) report on Adler's early work which can be construed as training parents, teachers, and others in the development of therapeutic postures toward children. Blatz and Bott (1927), Campbell (1933), Hamilton (1947), Hooker (1931), Furman (1950), Fuchs (1957), and Bonnard (1950) wrote even earlier about using parents effectively in the treatment of the emotional problems of their children, as did Phillips and Haring (1959). Acting in part on the basis of a study of the similarities in parent–child personality disturbances, Phillips (1951) went on to investigate short-term parent–child psychotherapy (Phillips, 1956; Phillips & Johnston, 1954,) and to show ways of utilizing the teacher as an adjunct therapist in child guidance work (Phillips, 1957).

Early experimental work on modifying reticent and uncooperative behaviors among preschool children was reviewed several decades ago by Murphy, Murphy, and Newcomb (1937). This review includes the still earlier study by Jack (1934), in which overly submissive children (we would call them "underassertive" today) were taught to be more ascendant by way of learning social skills in the preschool (making designs with colored blocks, learning a story from a picture book, and assembling a picture puzzle). Testing situations and observational ratings found these children to show increases in ascendent behavior and in self-confidence. Control children who did not receive the ascendent behavior training through social skills practice did not show any increases in this critical behavior. In a similar kind of study attempting to overcome a social deficit or an unwelcome or unwholesome attitude, Updegraff and Keister (1937) helped children overcome school failure and to learn to handle failure constructively. Children were exposed to failure in three situations: being unable to solve a puzzle, facing an unsolvable challenge to physical strength, and facing a social obstacle. The children were trained to overcome the derived sense of failure by introducing them to graduated tasks, seeing their progress and success, and learning to persevere in the face of difficulty. Murphy, Murphy, and Newcomb (1937) generalize from this study as follows:

> The trained group showed remarkable improvement in many ways. Sulking and crying dropped out entirely, and interest and attempts to solve problems alone increased significantly. After training, the child usually tried longer, showed more interest, solved problems unassisted, and completely eliminated emotional behavior (p. 435).*

These are very convincing early studies of modifying emotional and social behaviors under experimentally derived and controlled situations; they serve as models, even today, for behavioral intervention. As ways to develop social skills, and as programs of social skills intervention to correct many personality and emotional problems, they command attention.

More recent work from a more explicit behavior modification viewpoint is that of Walder, Cohen, Breiter, et al. (1971). They systematically instructed parents in handling their disturbed and disturbing children by teaching parents operant methods for understanding their own behavior and the behavior of their children. Among other techniques, parents set agendas for group discussion, charted progress in the child's target behaviors, and used systematic reinforcement techniques to foster behavior change. McLaughlin and Lalaby (1975) went even further and trained elementary school children as behavioral engineers. Siegel and Steinman (1975) taught one child in the classroom to function as an agent of change, via reinforcement principles, toward another child in the same classroom. Long and Madsen (1975) were able to use 5-year-olds as trainers and reinforcers for controlling the behavior of younger children during story, snack, and art periods in a day-care center. There is, then, considerable evidence that training as a therapeutic procedure has been more or less systematically used for decades and that the present day rationale for training is now being vigorously discussed and extended to ever wider settings (Ramp & Semb, 1975).

Training can be construed as having two approaches: the training of surrogate therapists, or "significant others" as Carkhuff (1971) expresses it, and the training of the patients or clients themselves. Both approaches are based on the same principles, some of which stem from Rogerian therapy stressing acceptance, responding to the emotional content of the other person's behavior, and some based on behavioral principles where rein-

---

* Reprinted with permission from Murphy, G., Murphy, L.B., and Newcomb, T.M. *Experimental Social Psychology.* New York: Harper & Row, Publishers, Inc., 1937.

forcement contingencies, self-observation and self-management loom large. In the studies under Carkhuff's stimulation (Bergman & Doland, 1974; Carkhuff, 1969, 1971; Carkhuff & Berenson, 1967; Carkhuff & Bierman, 1970; Carkhuff & Truax, 1965b; Vitalo, 1969) we find a behavioral orientation posited which is not only suggestive of many ways of proceeding with training, but which also has given rigor to outcome studies and encouragement to carry out other training programs that are capable of replacing conventional therapy. According to Carkhuff (1971):

> The behavioral modification approaches are simple, direct and concrete.They require no understanding of complex causes and psychodynamics. In these respects, they are ideally suited for training non-credentialed personnel and their implementation. Applications in training significant others are, therefore, natural extensions of the behavior modification approaches. (p. 125)

A study by Minuchin, Chamberlain, and Graubard (1967) illustrates some ways in which a behavior approach nets specific target behaviors to study among disturbed or delinquent children, where the social skills training was focused directly on the children. These youngsters had problems in school with concentrating, communicating effectively with others, and with teachers. A special curriculum to overcome these deficits was devised that emphasized several social skills, viz., listening skills, taking turns, learning how to stay on an (educational) topic, telling simple then longer stories, and so on. It is reported that progress was made by these disturbed children through a direct approach in regard to their attention to subject matter, in communicating with peers and teachers, and in intellectual or cognitive ability. Whether researchers or clinicians take the indirect route to training surrogate therapists or train the patients or clients directly seems to hinge more on practical matters and not on the kind of client, the nature of the problem situation, or on diagnostic studies. A general conclusion reached by Carkhuff (1971) is that training is an effective mode of therapy if it offers a truly helping relationship and an effective helping program, with some benefits arising out of either a relationship or a program alone, but with better results emanating from both (pp. 126–127).

Not only are training procedures targeted at clients or patients (both children and adults) but they may also be used to train counselors and therapists (Carkhuff & Truax, 1965b). These authors see the issue in training quasiprofessionals as based on a scientific–didactic–intellectual approach by utilizing behavioral principles, as well as on an experiential approach that attends less to actual counseling skills but more to interpersonal relations, emotional empathy, matters relating to feeling, and the like. Collingwood (1971) trained 40 undergraduate psychology students, under a 10-hour regimen (some in small groups, some in a group of 20 subjects) to respond more effectively to affective content by studying taped interviews of therapy. The training objectives were to assess how well the trainees responded to examples of empathy, respect, genuineness, and concreteness in the tapes. The students trained in small groups tended to respond better to such affective (therapeutic) training in the Rogerian modality and to retain their discriminative skills better over time. This and other studies show that noncredentialed but capable persons, such as carefully selected undergraduates, can be trained in a manner similar to therapists to respond to the emotional content of recorded therapy sessions and thereby simulate to an extent the usual role of a therapist. This does not mean, of course, that lay persons can learn quickly to do *all* the things that therapists do, but under limited circumstances, the nonprofessional can sometimes function remarkably well in simulating therapeutic activities, perhaps even in carrying them out in clinical settings.

Writing therapy (Phillips, 1977a; Phillips, Gershenson, & Lyons, 1977; Phillips & Wiener, 1966) may be considered as a training method. In this approach to therapy, the client or patient writes for 1 hour about his or her concerns at an appointed time (just as the person would appear for a face-to-face therapy hour) and the notebook in which the person writes is kept in a confidential file between writing sessions. The therapist reads the protocol and replies also in writing; the therapist and client never see each other in person and usually do not even know each other's name. Research findings indicate that not only do clients like and respond well to writing therapy, but objective psychometric results and independent ratings show that gains associated with brief writing therapy periods (usually about 10 sessions) are reliable and tend to fall into the following areas: better self-management, improved ability to relate assertively to others, and less introspection and ruminative self-abnegation (Phillips, Gershenson, & Lyons, 1977). Carkhuff's statement that training modalities that substitute for psychotherapy are best when both effective helping relations and effective helping programs are combined may be challenged through the results of writing therapy in which presumably only effective training programs are present (although a kind of relationship is advanced through the writing, it appears to be most unlike that arising from face-to-face encounter). Studies are yet to be done comparing a variety of training modalities with each other, with writing therapy, or with conventional face-to-face therapies. As therapists admit a larger variety of therapeutic modalities into their repertoires, instead of assuming that therapy deals primarily with psychopathology, research and clinical findings will contribute to and gradually develop a broader basis for therapeutic work. The more inventive one can be in therapeutic work, the more one will learn about human behavior and the greater the benefits will be to clients and patients in all settings.

Rioch and associates (Rioch, 1966; Rioch, 1967; Rioch, Elkes, Flint, et al., 1963) set out to train lay psychotherapists not only to demonstrate effectiveness in training social skills or finding training modalities to substitute for more conventional therapy, but they actually trained lay therapists who later engaged in additional professional training and were admitted into full professional status.

There are problems recognized by Rioch (1966) in regard to training lay persons to do therapeutic work. One problem would be the apparent differences between lay persons doing therapy (usually younger, and in this case women) and older, often male, therapists. Status factors in even an out-patient clinic, not to mention a hospital setting, would tend to differentiate between accredited therapists (addressed by staff as "Doctor") and those in a lay role. Sometimes, too, patients would have had previous therapy, and their knowledge of therapeutic practice and theory, who had written what books about psychotherapy, and a variety of subtle factors, might well differentiate between experienced and untrained therapists. Despite these and other differences, and concentrating wholly on the actual therapeutic interaction, it is difficult to show that trained therapists were significantly different in skills and in therapeutic outcomes from lay therapists who had had ample preparation and were of stable character and personality, and equally serious about their training and performance.

If lay persons could do many therapeutic tasks as well as professionals, what then for professionals? Rioch (1966) says that the "system" of training, accreditation, and long-range schooling should be modified to take in the lay persons and to reserve for the professionally trained more expert roles in regard to training, to research, and to the advancement of knowledge. Many previously competent therapists may, in time, "burn out" and lose the zest for therapy, yet remain excellent trainers, researchers, and supervisors for novice therapists. The very work of training lay persons is an important educational, clinical, and research undertaking; it should be upgraded as an important aspect of being a clinician, and should not be thought of as a way of putting the older clinician "on the shelf" or relegating the experienced therapist to minor roles where the young, zestful, but lay-trained, could compete directly. Too many experienced and highly trained clinicians, especially psychotherapists, tend to regard the training of lay persons as direct competition, whereas the role of the latter is entirely supplementary and supportive and in need of some of the supervisory roles of the better-trained clinician. The fully experienced clinician can enhance his or her effectiveness by passing the skills on to young students, lay therapists, and other peer-type helpers, thereby enhancing the value of mental health work. The experienced therapist cannot gainsay the therapeutic value of the lay therapists (Carkhuff & Truax, 1965a). Not to roll-with-the-punches when lay workers can be shown to do effective therapy is to belittle the lay workers and preserve a sanctimonious attitude among professionals that is not only unbecoming but is also injurious to the public, which is so much in need of mental health services of all kinds, especially psychotherapy.

Not only have lay therapists been trained in the sense of Rioch's programs (Rioch, 1966; Rioch, 1967; Rioch et al. 1963), but younger, less mature and less highly selected college students have been trained for therapeutic roles with excellent encouragement. Bergman & Doland (1974) used "case aides" (college students) to work with chronic hospitalized patients. From a larger list of patients, 26 were randomly selected to become patients of the case aides, and 26 other patients served as controls, matched on the basis of sex, age, education, hospital tenure, and so on. The aides worked with their patients for 12 consecutive weeks. Results showed that not only did the hospitalized patients benefit, so did the case aides, as each population (the older hospitalized patients and the younger college-level aides) was reinforced through a personal and friendly relationship with the others. The emphasis, appropriate to training objectives among lay persons and to the importance of emphasizing social skills, was found to be on the case aides taking an attitude of constructive social support toward the patients, ignoring bizarre or psychopathological behavior, being honest and open about expressing feelings, and reinforcing social efforts and successes among the patient group.

The important generalization suggested here, aside from the profit to the patients observed in all the above-mentioned training programs, was also the profit to the lay persons themselves. Very convincingly and almost overwhelmingly the findings presented in all the training programs attest to the value of developing practical social skills, offering direct encouragement and reinforcement to the patients in their efforts to relate better and to solve interpersonal problems. The whole rationale was that of taking fairly specific segments of patient behavior and working toward changing them in order to help solve current problems and also to generalize these changes to other life situations outside the hospital, clinic, or training setting. If an emphasis had not been placed on a social skills training model, or if a more traditional view of psychopathology had been followed, not only would the results of this training have been missed, there would have arisen no reason for training lay or peer groups in the first place and no understanding of how simple therapeutic skills may become viable methods of personality and behavior change for patients and for nonprofessionals alike.

RELATIONSHIP BETWEEN TRAINING AND SOCIAL SKILLS AS ALTERNATIVE WAYS OF VIEWING CONVENTIONAL PSYCHOTHERAPY AND PSYCHOPATHOLOGY

This chapter has illustrated a number of ways in which training has been used as an alternative psychotherapeutic modality. Training measures have been used among many populations: patients, teachers, college undergraduates, hospitalized patients and counseling center clients, and among other lay persons; and the purposes of the training have ranged from developing some relatively minor problem-solving skill to the use of lay counselors and therapists to function fairly independently of credentialed professionals (although the latter still hold the final responsibility). Social skills methods have accumulated an equally versatile set of results covering almost every kind of presenting or chronic problem among patient populations and utilizing an extremely large number of actual skill development procedures. How are these approaches to mental health or behavior problems similar and different, and what can we learn from these findings?

Training and social skills approaches are similar in that they both identify fairly well-defined target behaviors to be changed or, in some cases, to be learned. Both procedures pivot their methodology on a limited number of steps or interim measures to reach the targeted goal; both are usually carefully time-limited in that a specified number of contact sessions or hours, spread over a definite number of weeks or months, are decided on in advance. Both procedures utilize specific ways of measuring progress in terms of charting frequencies of given behaviors (more related to social skills) and/or psychometric and rating methods (more related to a training modality); quantitative results, based on statistical or probabilistic figures, or on baseline and reinforcement contingency schedules, are offered as evidence of change. Training and social methods have often but not always collected follow-up data to investigate how well the learned changes have persisted. Both training and social skills methodologies have conceptualized their findings in terms of a teaching and learning model essentially devoid of theories of psychodynamics, psychopathology, or conventional psychotherapeutic theory.

Some ways in which training and social skills behavior modification are different should be enumerated. Training modalities are often based in part on Rogerian or relationship theory, where the "helping relationship" is thought of as covering such concepts and therapeutic practices as warmth, emotional acceptance, empathy, genuineness, and a "trying to get inside the head of the client" approach; the social skills approach more often emphasizes the end product (some specified behavior change), based on a rapport between the "teacher" and the "learner" in which the interim, progressive approximation steps are successfully utilized with reinforcement contingencies being followed. The process of change in the training model is more cognizant of personal and emotional concerns; the behavioral social skills model does not deny or overlook the personal aspects but asserts they are under the control of the reinforcement contingencies, not separate considerations in their own right. The training model tends to use less precise measures of change, relying more on ratings and psychometric results, whereas the social skills model uses the same data-base throughout the change process from the baseline measure (how often a given social skill occurs with a particular person under a given set of conditions) through reinforcement contingency changes to the final criterion measure of change. The social skills or behavior change model appears to have a tighter grip on the changes that are demonstrated in that this model can provide for "reversals" of the reinforcement contingencies and can put the client back where he or she was previously with respect to a given behavior change; whereas the training model has thus far gone in only one direction, viz., toward the targeted objective without regard to how the reinforcement contingencies are operative. In fact, the training model does not conceptualize change in terms of reinforcement contingencies (although some researchers may recognize that contingencies are, indeed, involved) but more in terms of setting up a kind of inviting, stimulating situation (a kind of broad-based "stimulus control" in the behavior modification sense) based on acceptance, warmth, positive regard, which is conceptualized more as an initial motivating condition than one related explicitly to reinforcement contingencies. A concluding, but not exhaustive, difference between the training and social skills methods is that the former is based on what is often called an "experiential component," which is more cognitively and motivationally oriented than is true of the behavioral and social skills approach to altering behavior.

In spite of the differences between the two approaches, the similarities are compelling from a scientific viewpoint—they both illustrate viable attempts to engage in modifying behavior or personality without basing their efforts on the traditional views of depth psychology and psychopathology—and all levels of complexity have been shown to be economical, heuristic and stimulating. In terms of the overall orientation of this book, the training model and the social skills model each contribute materially to the view that these practices constitute practical alternatives to personality and behavior change.

7

It has been a strong tradition in the study of human behavior to locate causal or explanatory conditions "inside" the person. Many words are used that strike a familiar ring in this case: the *will*, the *self*, our inner person, the true self, the *mind*, the *psyche*, *élan vital*, how we feel about something, and so on. These notions have derived partly from philosophy, partly from folklore. They have been continued by psychologists or other students of human behavior, with minor changes here and there, throughout the ages. There is a kind of face validity in the use of terms that locate causes for our behavior inside us—we say we "decide" to go someplace, we "feel" that we are uncomfortable and have to change our position, we note that we are hungry and seek food. Momentarily we do note a feeling or make a decision, when physiological or environmental conditions stimulate us to do so. What we "decide" does not reside within us, independent of our relationship with the environment (internal and external), but what we refer to as *ourself* is in constant interaction with the environment. Most interactions that promote changes are cyclic, such as recurrent needs for food, rest, and activity.

There is no homunculus inside us, no "little man" independent of our activities and relationships with the environment that "tells us when to do something" (Skinner, 1974). What we call our "self" is a momentary distillation of many facts and feelings and conditions that make up and encompass our behavior. Likewise,

The "Inner" Problem: Feelings, Locus of Control, Biofeedback, and Crisis Intervention

what we loosely call the "mind" is a complex set of sensory and memory stimuli in contact with the environment. For example, we're looking for someone's home in a largely unfamiliar neighborhood, we try to sense whether the curve in the road is one we remember from a previous trip, we make a turn to the right because we orient our friend's house "off to the right someplace," and upon turning note in the large yard a marble plaque in front of a church, *then* we "remember" (take in new stimuli that help us discriminate better) that our friend's house is the third one beyond the church. "That's where John lives," we say, and then proceed to check out the impression. In the case of finding a friend's home in an unfamiliar neighborhood, we make explicit as many items of experience as we can: the turn in the road, the road narrowing, the church sitting back from the road, the big yard with a marble plaque in front, and so forth.

Usually, however, we arrive at decisions to act in various ways without the explicit steps being taken: doing "mental arithmetic," for example; recalling a person's name upon passing him or her in the street; recalling that we have to pick up our laundry when we see someone coming along the street carrying a bag from the cleaners. Most of our "mental activity" takes place in such rapid, smooth succession that we do not note how much it depends on current environmental stimulation. We know how to solve problems in regard to momentary memory lapses, in regard   155 to vaguely understood or remembered directions, by calling up related stimuli that are available to us in the environment; we learn to cue ourselves in appropriate ways (cues are environmental stimuli more or less under control and available).

To seriously suggest that any behavior takes place without such stimulation, however subtle, places an enormous burden of explanation on one to say how obvious stimulation (hurrying to avoid an oncoming car) is different from less easily discerned stimulation. In the interest of parsimony and predictability, we have to say that stimulation in and from the environment impinges on us all of the time, and that stimulation varies in its importance and immediacies.

Stimuli from inside the organism as well as from the external environment are also important and should not be overlooked. If the internal and external environments are unusually calm or steady for a period of time, we tend to reduce our overt behavior and become drowsy or bored. Changes from inside the skin or outside of it are all of one general class—stimuli that impinge upon us in some observable or measurable way. If some changes in the environment, external or internal, are of no importance (the falling of a leaf, an itch, or belch) we discount them and they mean nothing; they do not influence our behavior in important ways. The way we tell if stimuli are of importance is to assess the consequences they have on our behavior, knowing that the consequences may sometimes be immediate but may also be delayed, e.g., when nutritional lacks in our diet result in certain diseases such as scurvy or pellegra.

Dichotomizing the organism into inside and outside events, even though a common practice, is of only minor practical importance and may even be misleading if we are carelessly ascribing causality to certain events. Folklore has it that inside events, such as our thinking, are necessarily the causes of our behavior—we think, then we act. Actually, we may act as often prior to thinking as we do the opposite, especially when our behavior in some sequence becomes fairly routine—the violinist notices his instrument is out-of-tune after he bows the strings, as he cannot tell before that. The runner knows, upon running, that his stride is not right and he then has to act to remedy the matter. The stutterer does not always know until he has stuttered just what words will be the most inhibitory for him; and so on through countless examples. Even when we "think things out first," we do so on the basis of prior experience, e.g., we can tell how may feet of rug to lay on the dining room floor by multiplying the width by the length "in our heads," but we first have had to learn the multiplication tables, initially a rote and thoughtless matter, the importance of which becomes evident to us only later in life.

Stressing the inside problems of human behavior has led to many problems throughout the ages. We have punished people for "thinking bad," even though the so-called bad thoughts did not lead to unwelcome behavior. We chastize ourselves, feel guilt and remorse, and vitiate our efforts at times when we become burdened by "ill feelings" and "nasty thoughts" toward others. We tend to consider the thought as father to the deed, when there are, in actuality, thousands of thoughts that never lead anywhere for every one that seems to lead to some overt act.

Throughout the study of psychology as a formal discipline, say, from the late 19th century to the present, students have studied the "inside" problems in various ways and from a variety of vantage points, some of them productive and others not. Among the many "inside" problems studied more or less scientifically (that is, with objective and repeatable experimentation) are images, sensations, cognitions, thoughts, feelings, and memories. Sometimes these experiences are broken down into constituent parts and studied by way of verbal reports and various discriminations (telling the differences through matching techniques, between tastes, smells, location of feeling sensations on the surface of the body, and the like). Verbal reports on sensory experiences (smelling, tasting, seeing) tend to produce more reliable information than reports on feelings and emotions. However, feelings and emotions are very important in human affairs, especially in areas such as personality theory, motivation, psychotherapy, and other clinical studies.

Recent developments in what we refer to as the "inside problem" have resulted in a number of developments in *cognitive* psychology. Cognitive study has to do with a variety of developmental and other aspects of the living organism that relate to intellectual functioning, solving abstract problems, and using verbal and symbolic skills of many kinds.

"Cognitive" also refers to "mediational processes" that are said to go on inside the head in ways that are not immediately and directly open to observation, where one knows about the person's thinking only from the product or outcome (that is, whether or not the article was assembled correctly, the "mental" arithmetic problem solved accurately, disparate elements aligned properly) with the thinking process emphasized more than the product.

Cognitive explanations have been proffered more frequently in recent years to account for difficult to explain results from behavior change efforts (Bandura, 1977; Mahoney, 1974; Michenbaum, 1977). One way of illustrating the problem of presumed cognitive mediational process and reinforcement is to note that reinforcement is often subtle and elusive—we do not always know what is reinforcing for complex human actions, whereas we can pretty well show that small sips of "Coke" or a spoonful of ice cream is verifiably reinforcing for autistic or retarded children. Facing problems in regard to the subtlety of reinforcement has led to the positing of many dichotomies of the mental /physical type, such as "covert /overt" and "inside /outside" references to explain complex human behavior. We will now examine these further.

It can be asserted here that the covert /overt or inside /outside problem is considered to be spurious. What we lack data on at the moment (it may be, at best, elusive and hard to pin down objectively or we may be less searching than is necessary) we tend to regard as covert or as residing inside the organism (usually in a mentalistic way). The basic problem in this area of behavioral study is whether events are private or public.

We are all privy to private events. The problem arises when we consider our private events to be different from others' private events. The private physical event of a toothache is not momentarily shared by another person, but on other occasions, given enough time, we all have, or have had, toothaches. It is not as important to assert that a toothache is a private event as it is to learn how to control or prevent toothaches. The private event is a momentarily physiologically registered event that the dentist can verify through x-rays or other means and thereby describe far more adequately than can the person who is registering the private event. Moreover, the dentist with his scientific technology, knows how to relieve the toothache, which most of us do not, no matter how thoroughly we might be driven through pain to remedy the distress. It might be possible to describe the history of medicine and dentistry, in part, as technological progress along the lines of making private (those particularly painful or even fatal) events public by and through special detection (diagnostic) and remedial (therapeutic) techniques. In the life sciences, progress consists of making private events of some consequence into public ones so that intervention and control are possible.

It is the same with private "mental" events, some authors to the contrary notwithstanding (Bandura, 1977; Lazarus, 1976; Mahoney, 1974). The cognitive movement can be characterized not so much as making new discoveries as in putting forth "cognitive explanations" for behaviors that are sometimes admittedly subtle and hard to identify, or as applying to behaviors that have not been properly analyzed concerning what their reinforcement contingencies are. Part of the problem is in discovering ever more searching techniques for probing the person as a physiologically functioning organism as well as a verbally and socially functioning one, and trying to synchronize these two aspects more fully. Fortunately, as biofeedback and other probing techniques are developed, the realm of the private is forced to recede. Biofeedback research and clinical applications (we will address them more below) afford opportunities to give better data about subtle physiological events and to bring these events through various feedback devices under deliberate control. Some events so private that they are not even registered in the person's verbal schema or awareness can be brought under deliberate control—events related to high blood pressure, skin sensitivity, and the like. When previous states of unawareness can be made more aware, they can be followed by self-control measures that may reduce tension and suffering, as well as give us more scientific information. More will be said on this topic when biofeedback control is discussed below.

Another aspect of the problem of private events is that probing techniques, which attempt to find out what the person is thinking or feeling and the basis for same source, are ways of *enlarging the data-base*. This is an empirical matter. If electrodes inserted into or on the surface of the body can give information on bodily functioning, and ultimately on one's health status, these ventures are to be encouraged. If these empirical probes can also be related to one's verbal commands over oneself (one's physiological functioning), such as reducing tension or relieving anguish, the basic scientific data can then be directly applied to clinical use. However, many problems cannot be directly solved through clinical applications; many cannot be directly relieved or prevented (insofar as we know), although many theories exist in most human science domains that try to take up the lacks in empirical knowledge. Clinical help and scientific understanding will wait upon more accurate probing techniques which, once functionally available, can then be put to practical services. It is strongly apparent that the proffers of many cognitive therapists are pointing to the importance of enlarging the data-base. In some cases, their efforts have been educational, such as emphasizing the importance of feelings (Phillips & Ferster, 1976) in psychotherapy and behavior change—which, when empirically supported, no one can gainsay.[1] However, cognitive explanations are

---

[1]Phillips and Ferster (1976) suggested that the place of feelings in a behavioral matrix is one of regarding feelings as part of the behavioral stream, where feelings, per se, might be now discriminative stimuli, now reinforcers, or serve other behavioral functions. To regard feelings as nonbehavioral is not only clinically confusing and unproductive, but appears scientifically inaccurate.

often at odds with an empirical and objective view of human behavior and appear to be hasty excursions into "mentalistic explanations" that may not advance either knowledge or clinical skill (Mahoney, 1977; Michenbaum, 1977; Williams, 1977; Nay, 1976).

Therapists do, however, take the "private events route" (to give the matter a name) and ask the patient, or arrange in terms of biofeedback or other means, for the patient to come into contact with the private events that may be germaine to the solution of a problem. Therapists try to make the facts and circumstances of private events explicit. It is assumed that these events relate to behavior, or to physiological events that are not yet fully discerned. Revealing private events so they can be "seen" to operate in some functional way in the person's behavioral economy is an important step in changing behavior. This is a way of enlarging the data-base for the patient, with the help of the therapist who may know more about what to look for in the way of private events than the patient does.

CONFLICT THEORY WIDENS THE DATA-BASE

All therapists have the experience on occasion of saying to the patient that his or her impasse is due to conflictful tendencies about someone, or something, of importance in the patient's life; and that some resultant emotional response, perhaps anger (wanting to please another, but resenting the fact that the pleasing came on the other person's terms, not on the patient's terms), is part of the conflict (see also chapters 2 and 5 dealing more explicitly with conflict theory). As we have seen earlier, tension aroused by conflict distracts one from problem solving; therapy helps to focus on the events (some of them private, some very public) that make up the conflict so that solutions are possible. The role of the therapist is that of discovering with the patient what the public or private events may be. The emphasis among the new cognitive behavior therapists is on the private events, as such; events that are subtle and, of course, not at first as open as public events. But some private events are actually more "open" to the therapist (due to his or her experience) than to the patient. The therapist must conjecture that some events are important and probe to get them stated and conceptualized and ultimately tested by the patient in vivo. The privacy of the event is, momentarily, of little or no value to the patient—it is like the physiological states that relate to hypertension or high blood pressure—the physician has to probe and bring the matter into the open, since the patient cannot do it. In time, however, the patient learns to discern more carefully and readily these private events (when and as they are demonstrably important) and thereby brings them under progressive control.[2]

The issues relating to the inner world of the person are not just recesses or entities as our natural language inclines us to believe, but data-base areas that need to be probed by whatever means might be available at the time, with a scientific view that says our acumen depends on enlarging the data-base and with a clinical view that asserts that the enlarged data-base will likely prove heuristic therapeutically. It is not a matter of cognitive variables being different from behavioral variables, we have only behavior to work with. It is not a matter of different universes of discourse, different laws or principles. (We can, of course, challenge any laws or principles, if we have the data to do so, then confront our selves if new laws or altered principles are needed.) As it now stands, the "inner world," by whatever name, is just another example of the need for better probing techniques and for enlarged empirical vantage points, not a matter of nonbehavioral information or newly discovered cognitive principles. We shall shortly go on to discuss this matter further by including more detail in regard to locus of control, biofeedback, and crisis intervention.

The reason for selecting these four topics (feelings, locus of control, biofeedback, and crisis intervention) when other topics might have been discussed is that they align themselves along a continuum from the "inside" to the "outside" and progressively move toward more objective study of subtle events that affect behavior. Furthermore, each of these four topics is a current area of much research activity and theorizing, and each is relevant to clinical practice and psychotherapy. Take, for example, *feelings*, which are the least objectively defined of these four topics. They are subtle and appear to reside inside the person, and even to mysteriously affect behavior. The traditional role of feelings is that they are wholly covert, nonbehavioral phenomena (Phillips,

---

[2]The impression should not be gained that this discussion is obliquely in agreement with the classical notion of the unconscious, or that the important therapeutic work is that of making the unconscious conscious. Actually, most clinical work is based on observable behavior, or on behavior which is potentially observable; it is only the very occasionally subtle or elusive events that are referred to in this section, the more private ones that have to be discerned and conceptualized to fit the person's prevailing behavioral tendencies (Phillips, 1956, 1977b).

1977a) and that they are largely eschewed in scientific psychology, save in the case of emotion-centered psychotherapies. The viewpoint here about feelings is that feelings are behavior and their importance, subtle or not, arises from the use that can be made of them in behavioral change efforts. Feelings, being behavior, are no more the "cause" of behavior than any other stimulating condition; their subtlety only entices us into using them as explanatory or causal concepts because we are less careful than we might be in delineating their role. Feelings act as motivators, as reinforcers, as anticipatory of aversive or pleasant consequences, as broad stamps of approval or disapproval of our own and others' behavior. They generally fit in with any other item of behavior that we might want to focus on. Feelings are not a world apart, subject to other laws and considerations, nor are they the first or final matter in understanding behavior, clinical or otherwise.

In the case of *locus of control,* we observe a concept that has attracted interest in the last decade or so (Phares & Lamiell, 1974, 1977). It represents a movement along the continuum from subjectivity to objectivity in studying "inner" events by converting the concept of internality/externality (I-E) as the locus of control of reinforcement into objective, psychometric instruments with known or knowable reliability and intercorrelations with other personality dimensions. The move toward locus of control of reinforcement, while it may not fulfill the empirical definition of reinforcement, does help to objectify a consideration of importance in changing behavior, viz., whether one discerns that he or she is responsible, capable, and likely to exercise certain self-control issues in life or "beg off" and attribute them to unknown or uncontrollable conditions. While the range of items in locus of control of I-E events is relatively narrow, many social, political, economic, and consumer issues (Barmash, 1976; Maccoby, 1976) are not addressed, and technical issues that are demonstrably outside the pale of individual control are omitted; sometimes individuals "perceive" issues to be under their control which facts do not support. Clark (1975) suggests that locus of control may differentiate between degrees of internality/externality on the basis of the amount of control people feel they have over *the behavior itself,* not the events the inventory items refer to. People often think they have an amount of control over events, know what to do in principle, etc. (e.g., returning a faulty object to the store where it was purchased), only to find that their confidence is shaken in trying to remedy the frustrating situation which, itself, is remarkably different from the way they theorized. If people think they can remedy a situation, they see the control as a matter of their own initiative or skill; but if the resolution is very refractory or wholly frustrating, the control is not theirs, but lies elsewhere. Nevertheless, many of the personal happenings of everyday life may be changed to constructive ends by the person acknowledging that he or she can wrestle with these means–ends relationships to influence outcome, rather than passively or hostilely ascribing causality to chance or to wholly impersonal influences.

Thus, the locus of control of internal/external events deals with subjectively reported events, presumably located "in" the person but somewhat objectified by way of a questionnaire capable of some independent scientific tests, and an opportunity to study how people ascribe self-control to various matters in their lives. The characteristic of I-E of locus of control is probably not that of truly locating reinforcement contingencies but can better be thought of as a variable allowing the person to identify his or her *confidence* in self-control in regard to a variety of daily life considerations. It is a step forward nonetheless toward objectifying subtle events that influence behavior.

Biofeedback, on the other hand, seems to combine all the necessary criteria for a scientific study of "internal" events: the probing techniques are fully described; the source of internal (physiological) data are partly understood and amply described operationally (Schwartz & Beatty, 1977); the procedures for objectifying internal events (i.e., making these events public and measuring and controlling them) are known and described; the use of the probing results, i.e., the use of the data that are fed back to the person, are described and made available to the person. The clinical and scientific values associated with biofeedback go hand-in-hand, i.e., the more scientific information obtained, the more likely the information can be put to some useful clinical purposes. The present applications of biofeedback can be demonstrated clinically in dealing with a variety of complaints and conditions; the person is taught how to discern subtle, internal, physiological events and to bring them under control; their therapeutic value is clear to the individual. The results of biofeedback can be related to other substantive areas of knowledge, such as physiological functioning, disease processes, and functional or psychological disturbances, citing the role of operant processes in modifying these fed-back events. Biofeedback affords comparisons with therapeutic outcomes from other methods of therapy for the same problems; it teaches a kind of self-knowledge and self-control set of skills closely parallel to social skills. It may be a precursor to, an assist toward, or a reinforcer of, general social skills whose effectiveness is based on progressive anxiety reduction in conflict situations.

Biofeedback is apparently the link between inner process and outer measures of control and regulation. However, biofeedback has a definite physiological bias; it is not an externalizer of thoughts, images, feelings, etc., other than when these states are shown to be offshots of physiological and behavioral events. Perhaps the answer to the covert/overt, internal/external dichotomies is through a set of procedures that explicitly link them together in ways that provide for knowledge, measurement, and control of subtle events that we have heretofore mostly speculated about.

Crisis intervention, while not a substantive body of knowledge like biofeedback, is, in principle, one kind of application of the implications of social skills and their relevance for the solution of personal problems. The whole vantage point of crisis intervention is posited on encouraging, teaching, and reinforcing social skills—on the part of the crisis worker, who needs certain functional interactive and clinical skills, devoid of the usual depth notions of human difficulties, and on the part of the caller (patient or client) who is in need of social skills help. Some of the social skills deficits on the part of the recipients of crisis help are synonymous with those of others who ask for help at hospital emergency or out-patient settings, in out-patient mental health centers, in university and college counseling and psychological centers, in social and welfare agencies, and in the private practices of psychologists, social workers, and psychiatrists.

The crisis intervention center is a relatively new type of facility that essentially ignores conventional psychopathological formulations (at least in its practical posture) and attempts through brief, skills-centered, problem-solving, practical measures to move on, through preventive work and relieving distress, to helping the person mobilize self-directed energies. The latter may involve selected referral to community agencies (health, legal, social) so that these agencies may be utilized by the person for further problem-solving efforts.

The crisis center does not say that people's problems are superficial or transitory, but that whatever the problems are, they must be addressed here and now by mobilizing potential individual and social resourcefulness pointed toward a limited goal, all of which are best understood as social skills in operation under specific conditions.

We move on now to further details in regard to these interesting internal /external concepts and practices with a view toward resolving these dichotomized differences and making some whole cloth out of them.

VIEWS REGARDING FEELINGS

Some would hold that feelings are an *experiential* ("inner") *state* that may be caused or brought on by behavioral events, e.g., feeling anger (the inner event) when provoked by somebody, and that feelings may cause, or be part of, a causal chain of consequences such as redressing the grievance by fighting back or ignoring the person. Similarly, physiological measures, as afforded by biofeedback, are measures of internal physiological processes, and are not measures of feelings, per se; but these physiological events may tap into many subtle stimulating antecedent conditions that give rise to particular feelings (tension, vague unrest, a sense of foreboding, etc.) and that result in overt stress, reports of headaches, a feeling of emptiness in the pit of the stomach, and similarly reported experiences.

In this construction of the role of feelings, they would be preceded and followed by behavior; a chain of such events (provocation by another, a feeling of anger followed by fighting back, escalating into another provocation by the offended, and so on and on) would be noted and experienced. But at each juncture of a "feeling event," the behavior would be interrupted, since the feeling as defined here is not a behavior as such. A plot of such a series of events would be: behavior—feeling—behavior—feeling, etc. This is not hard to grasp except for the fact that feelings are considered to be nonbehavioral in this viewpoint, so the theorist proffering such an account would be obliged to account for the switch from behavior to feelings and back again in a presumably unending chain. Also, such a theory would have to account for feelings causing feelings without any behavioral interruption, or chains of behavioral cause–effect relationships without any interposed feeling states. Since feelings seem so omnipresent in human affairs, so integrally related to behavior, whether we attempt to separate feelings and behavior or not in a conceptual sense, a theory posing a major, qualitative difference has to account for this difference in neurophysiological and behavioral terms. This might not be a fruitful undertaking. Certainly there is little evidence available today to support such a set of notions. The findings from biofeedback seem to suggest the opposite, viz., that feelings are intimately related to certain kinds of behavioral events, such as those that challenge the organism's equilibrium or safety: We feel more when we are in danger, discomforted, threatened, or perhaps chronically disturbed.

The theory that separates feelings and behavior in a qualitative way seems to be carrying another message as well. This is the familiar "surplus meaning" notion, viz., that there is "something more" to feelings than behavior. We meet this surplus meaning or "something more" notion in all human affairs: There is more to X than one ascribes to X, there is more to almost anything than the words, concepts, measurements, etc., which we use to describe or understand the phenomenon. There is more to intelligence than what the test measures; there is more to personality than what we see in poetry, literature, science, and experimental methods of describing personality. All this may well be, as no science, no account of one's life or of any phenomenon whatsoever can hold out to be complete; there is always more we can say. However, in science, we must go with what we can objectively assess, replicate, have confirmed or disconfirmed by others with comparable skills, and so on. Even if there is more to the stars than the astronomers say, even if there is more to anything than we usually admit, the surplus meanings, the additional considerations must either be admitted and sought after, or dismissed as possible obstructions to understanding. We cannot forever hold out that anything we do in science or in practical affairs always leaves something more—usually of a mysterious nature—to be discovered, revered, or awed by. There are practical, useful rounding off points in our knowledge of anything, including the experiential basis for the "something more" theory, which do not preclude further study and investigation (no man or woman of science or philosophy feels he or she has the final word on anything). One could humorously imagine a group of "something more" theorists all going each other one better, using their own experiential bases for this kind of "one-upmanship," and never being able to pin down just what the something more is, or might be, or how one might seriously try to find out what the surplus matters are.

Alternatively, we can regard feelings as part of behavior or as an example of behavioral phenomena in several ways. Take, for example, the psychotherapy situation (Phillips, 1977a) in which the therapist hears about or observes directly the patient's excursions into his feelings. There are three vantage points, or databases, from which the therapist can operate to understand the patient's feelings in a behavioral way. First, the patient *verbally reports* his or her feelings, telling of disturbing events, emotional or feeling states, and a long series of consequences, some of which are the reasons the person is in therapy in the first place. The patient labels these feeling events as best he or she can, often erring in the sense of calling anger or resentment by other names. (Fear is often reported when anger is the issue; as we have seen in chapter 5, fear is understood to elicit primarily avoidance behaviors, whereas anger may promote repeated attacks on the adversary, an unwillingness to retreat from the aversive situation, and many pro and con approach and avoidance reactions.) But, people also may not like to report or self-apply many feelings because they regard these feelings as socially objectionable (e.g., feeling left out of social situations, feeling angry, feeling misunderstood) and often their unrealistic or self-modeling ideals will conflict with honest reporting on themselves. Contrary then, to many notions about feelings and their importance in psychotherapy, feelings are not always "up front" and many efforts are exerted by patients (and all of us at times) to avoid feelings in order to "look good" or avoid "looking bad." Raw feelings are sometimes pretty objectionable on social desirability grounds. Thus, feelings as reported by patients may be either directly referred to, or they may be handled in indirect ways; their relevance and their relationship to the stream of behavior may be moot, and they may not often be a clear road to the root of the problem.

A second stance afforded by the psychotherapy situation as far as feelings are concerned is that *nonverbal behavior* (motor expressions, facial gestures, and like movements) may reveal feelings not reported verbally and /or may conflict with reported feelings, thus calling for resolution. We often say in common parlance "feelings will out," meaning that we cannot successfully hide them; we may give ourselves away not only by some slip of the tongue but in overt behavioral slips. The well-trained therapist is skilled in observing these behaviors and in relating them forward and backward in time to the patient's problems and to his or her verbal behavior as well. Observing overt, expressive, "body language" behavior (which has received a new and popular interest today) has, in fact, been in the lexicon of psychology for many decades. Nonverbal behavior may be closely related to feelings, as shown in various measures of depression, in emotional perplexity, in forgetful behavior arising from brain damage, and in hysterical behavior.

Third, one may learn about a patient's feelings through references to *behavior outside of the clinical setting:* "I felt so depressed I did not go to work for a week," or "I feel so angry at him I am going to turn in my resignation as soon as I can do so." While behavior outside the therapy hour is less reliably understood—

and a therapist wishes to relate as much as possible of the person's out-of-therapy behavior to the therapy discussion itself—some events occur outside of therapy that may never occur in therapy (e.g., sexual impotence, suicidal attempts, fights with another person). Out-of-therapy behavior presents a fairly patterned way of looking at the person and is subject to verification from the reports of others important in the patient's life, such as parents, teachers (especially true in the case of children), spouses, employers, and so on. One may act very badly according to personal standards when upset in the out-of-therapy world, but under the confines of an accepting therapeutic relationship, may appear very "cool." No matter, then, how one may appear in therapy, data are gathered in therapy that may give rise to many examples of feelings–dominated behavior located elsewhere in the patient's environment, and may help fill out the impressions one may have of the person's difficulties, the potential for change, and other important matters.

Following the reasoning that places feelings naturally among other behaviors and contends that feelings are not a separate, qualitatively different category, is the recognition that feelings may be summary statements, distillations of experience or the like, where feelings are wrapped up verbally and expressed in some way: "I felt good about how the examination went," or "I feel badly that things with her are going so poorly." Feeling states, verbally expressed, are in such cases shorthand for a large number of antecedent and consequent conditions, a kind of stamp of approval or disapproval on a series of events or interactions. In such cases, one could easily substitute another word for feelings—one could simply say "I think . . . " and get by with equal clarity in reporting on one's experiences. One might try an experiment on him- or herself: Instead of using the frequent references to feelings in interaction with others, one could use the word "think" and then see if meaning were lost, clarity gained or lost, or if there were, indeed, no difference.

Statements about feelings also form a kind of metalanguage (a statement about a statement) where the reported feeling is supposed to carry another statement to the person one is interacting with: A person who is expected to get ready for a social evening says, "I have such a splitting headache" to her spouse, where the message about the headache carried the implied meaning: "You can't expect me to go out with you when I feel so badly," or "You are pressuring me too much—leave me alone," or similar implied meanings. Thus, many classes of feelings verbally reported may carry the hidden agenda items of: "You're supposed to indulge me," "You're supposed to understand and accept me," and the like. When we talk about feelings in these ways, we are talking about several levels of interacting: direct interaction, implied states, expectations of certain actions from others, implied or inferred criticism or felt criticism, and so on. Our natural language is rich in such meanings and that is why we easily gain the impression that feeling states are much more than behavior—they are simply about a lot of different behaviors, sometimes pyramided on each other, sometimes comprising conflictful messages, and they may additionally refer backward in time or forward in time to expected states of affairs ("If I go with you and begin to have some fun, you'll want to come home early").

The point is simple: Whether statements or actions about one's feelings, or about others' feelings occur, they are all references to behavior. We know the meaning of the feeling states better by knowing the antecedent and consequent behaviors associated therewith, just as we know and understand any other behavior in terms of its antecedent and consequent conditions.

Finally, sometimes students of human behavior have asserted that feelings are a potential for behavior, a kind of "potential energy" situation as exists in the cases of force or energy exerted when an object is dropped from a height or gasoline is burned to create energy, and so on. In this case, the feelings seem to fuel behavior, push behavior here or there, or elicit or excite energy. This view gives feelings an exclusive stimulus value without recognizing that stimuli may act as reinforcers or consequences to other behaviors in an unending chain.

LOCUS OF CONTROL

Among the many interesting problems that tend to center attention "inside" the organism is one termed locus of control (Lefcourt, 1966, 1976; Phares, 1976; Rotter, 1954, 1966, 1975; Strickland, 1977). Is it true that reinforcement can come either from "internal" or "external" sources, and that whether the person "perceives" that the reinforcement is located inside or outside of him or her makes a difference in the consequences of the reinforcement? More formally stated, "I-E refers to the degree to which an individual perceives that the events that happen to him or her are dependent on his or her own behavior or are the results of fate, luck, chance, or powers beyond one's personal control and understanding" (Strickland, 1977, pp. 219–220).

The I-E dimension grew out of Rotter's social learning theory

(1954, 1966) and has stimulated research and thinking in a number of directions that have to do with personality theory, clinical psychology, psychotherapy, and the understanding of psychopathology. Some of the directions into which I-E, locus of control, has branched out and its relationship to the social skills issue will be addressed below.

When subjects dealt with tasks that required skill, and perceived (or suspected) that their success at the task depended on their own skill and ingenuity, they used their own past success / failure record, made judgments, and were said to display an internal locus of control (that is, the information important to them was based on judgments about their past experiences). If, on the other hand, directions were vague or seemingly a matter of chance, or somehow outside their control, the subjects responded like "gamblers" by acting as if their success lay beyond them or their efforts to control it (Phares, 1957). Investigators observed that persons predicted success for their undertakings (skill efforts, problem solving, etc.) according to whether they saw the task as dependent on their own control, as contrasted with uncontrolled or capricious factors. When persons saw themselves in a determining role (making appropriate judgments based on past experience and prevailing directions) they saw their efforts as affecting the results; contrariwise, when directions and self-control factors in task solving were lost or in jeopardy, the persons made judgments without relating them to their own previous performance. The control in the former case was in their hands, but in the latter case, control was out of their hands. Hence, the locus of control was internal (within the person's control based on the judgments available) or external (outside one's control, not understood, not available).

Since the locus of control slides immediately into common uses of reinforcement, it is important to understand that locus of control means "control of reinforcement." Just how important the addition of the concept of reinforcement is in this context is not always clear, but the proponents of I-E have called extensively on the use of reinforcement (since it is the results of the person's behavior that is reinforcing or not) and, say, in the words of Strickland (1977),

> The importance of all these studies has to do with the fact that human learning and /or performance appears not only to be a function of reinforcement but also is dependent on the individual's perception of locus of control of reinforcement.

As Rotter (1966) defines the matter:

> When a reinforcement is perceived by the subject as following some
> action of his own but not being entirely contingent upon his action,
> then, in our culture, it is typically perceived as the result of luck,
> chance, fate, as under the control of powerful others, or as unpre-
> dictable because of the great complexity of the forces surrounding
> him. When the event is interpreted in this way by an individual, we
> have labeled this a belief in *external control*. If the person perceives
> that the event is contingent upon his own behavior or his relatively
> permanent characteristics, we have termed this a belief in *internal
> control*. (p. 1; italics original)

In this scheme of things, reinforcement is, in turn, contingent
not upon whether the behavior that is presumably reinforced is
more likely to occur under similar circumstances, but on whether
the person perceives (locates causality) as being under his internal
(already learned, already demonstrated) control or whether it is
perceived (understood) to be due to external circumstances
which, by implication, have not yet come under the person's control (or, indeed, may not be amenable to the individual's control).

I-E research has covered a large number of related problems:
Assessment (whether persons tend to hold to generalized notions
about locus of control) where the instrument is composed of a
series of forced-choice items ("Whether or not I get to be a leader
depends upon my ability") commonly used in personality and
attitude questionnaires; relationship to *conformity* and *social per-
suasiveness or influence*; relationship to *task performance* and
problem-solving methods (cues used to respond to tasks, care, and
decision making in solving problems, time taken to solve problems, and the like); relationship to *achievement*; attitudes and
characteristics related to *physical care* and *physical health*, as
well as *psychological adjustment*; *social aspects* (socioeconomic
characteristics and cultural factors); and so on. Children, adolescents, and old people have been studied, as well as social offenders, the incarcerated, and members of other cultures in various
walks of life. Almost no extant interest group has been omitted in
studies of I-E.

Some generalizations about locus of control (I-E) may be
proffered, and they may be of use in understanding how behavior
is modified, how social skills may play a role in behavior change,
and related problems of psychopathology. These generalizations
are not hard-and-fast rules but broad trends from research
findings.

1. Individuals differ as to how important information about successful reinforcement in various undertakings is to them. The athlete cares more about "winning," the musician about a musically skilled performance (whether or not he or she "wins over" another).

2. I-E measures may refer to generalized attitudes (e.g., common themes in I-E) or to specific situations (e.g., school achievement or making money).

3. Some persons consider positive results to be their own doing, but negative results to be beyond them; others may feel the opposite: tragic or untoward events are their "fault" or responsibility, but good results are fortuitous. People, then, do not necessarily ascribe the same meaning to internal or external events, either positive or negative.

4. "Externals" tend to be more compliant (more dependent on external demands, instructions, etc.), whereas, "internals" decide more for themselves, less influenced by outside factors.

5. "Internals" and "externals" may use different strategies to arrive at decisions, process information differently, assign credence differently to information received, etc.

6. I-E differences carry with them different assignments of causality in ascribing meaning to the behavior of others, e.g., internals explain others' behavior on the basis of choice and meaningfulness of the others' behavior; externals see people more as victims or pawns.

7. Internal or external locus of control is by no means a "pure" dimension; it is, in turn, complicated by attribution of conditions that influence behavior ("just" or "unjust" conditions) (Lerner, 1974; Steiner, 1970).

8. Internals appear to be more achievement-

centered, more striving, more goal-oriented (Collins et al. 1976).

9. Internals may be more willing to delay gratification, appear less impulsive, more able to plan gainfully.

10. There appears to be less "social distance" between internals and others than between externals and others, as the former seem to more easily approach others they do not know.

11. Internals are more likely to follow and commit themselves to political and social action beliefs.

12. Externals in some societies and social groups may, indeed, reflect reality, as some social aggregates do not exert control over their destinies but are more victims of social and economic forces (e.g., in more authoritarian societies).

13. Although the point is moot, externals may be more likely to be clinically depressive cases.

14. Counseling and psychotherapy results tend to show that internals may respond better to mental health measures. Having an attitude comparable to internals may bode well for the development of counseling skills (although such findings may, in turn, hinge very much on the kinds of therapy or counseling offered).

Despite some of the relatively restricted generalizations cited above, locus of control research has produced inconsistent results. Some of these results, representative of larger areas of research may be summarized as follows.

Bellack (1972) found that when subjects were trained on a verbal discrimination test, with the experimenter initially reinforcing correct responses, internals and externals were not later different in their self-reinforcement or in the correctness of the reinforcement. Reinforcement contingencies were not easily established in some task situations; the implications for originally receiving reinforcement from an "external" source (the experimenter) did not "internalize" readily. Bellack (1975) later found that internals were more prone to self-evaluation and to locating control within themselves, and that externals had more problems in differentiating their own roles in self-reinforcement.

Cultural and sex differences in locus of control were examined by Bhanthumnavin (1974), who found that females in different countries studied (Australia, Japan, New Zealand, Sweden, and the U.S.A.) tended to believe in external control more than males. Swedish subjects (male and female) also scored highest in external control beliefs. Perhaps cultures that are more avant-garde in their social policies, as is possibly the case with Sweden, may locate the responsibility for change and control more in society at large (attribute importance to external conditions).

Bolen (1976) studied the effects of locus of control, social conditions, and sex on creative thinking among 537 randomly selected subjects. Results showed that those scoring higher in external locus of control were found to be significantly more creative. Creativity, as defined in some experimental situations, may depend more on new information provided the subjects and less on knowledge or skill already attained; hence new ventures into creativity may depend on assimilating and using cues from the environment, which is to say the ventures are more dependent on external circumstances.

Several studies have been conducted in order to relate locus of control to depression and other mental health issues. These studies show varied and inconsistent results. For example, Calhoun, Cheney, and Dawes (1974) found that externality among males was related to mild and enduring symptoms of depression in a nonpsychiatric population, but that females failed to show a similar reliable relationship. Anxiety and locus of control were examined by Cash and Stack (1973) among various hospitalized patients; psychotics tended to be more external in their responses to locus of control measures; neurotic groups and a sample of prisoners did not differ in this respect. Paranoids, as might be expected, tended to be more external in their notion of locus of control than other psychotic or severely disturbed groups. Anxiety and locus of control were studied in more than 200 undergraduates by Himle and Barch (1975); among subjects who were overtly anxious (as assessed by self-reports on autonomic anxiety, feelings of insecurity, and striated muscle tension), those who were more subjectively insecure with high levels of autonomic activity saw control as being more external, while those with lower levels of reported autonomic activity and insecurity saw control as being more internal. Degrees of expressed or reported discomfort may tell us much about whether persons attribute their distress to so-called external or internal circumstances, and corresponding control over same. In a wide-ranging set of measures, Jacobs (1976) found that perceived external locus of control was related to higher neuroticism /psychoticism scores, whereas the more internal person (among college students) is likely to show academic and leadership traits. A serious mental health consideration—suicide in relation to locus of control—was examined in a literature review by Lester (1973) in which he failed to find any consistency between predicted and actual internal orientation of the suicidal individual, or any demonstrable shift in locus of control preceding a suicidal death. Hopefulness and powerlessness have been studied in relation to locus of control. Prociuk and Breen (1974) and Procuik, Breen, and Lussier (1976) examined these topics on locus of control among more than 100 undergraduates and found the more hopeless and depressed viewing control as external in their lives. Wilkins' study (1975) of powerlessness and locus of control compared studies carried out originally in 1964 and 10 years later with a population of about 100 subjects having an average age of 39 years and demonstrated no sense of personal control change over this span of time. Wilkins observed that locus of control is a multidimensional measure; this multidimensionality, it may be added, may obfuscate cross-sectional studies, studies depicting trends in attitude change, and the like.

Is life stress related to locus of control and does it promote active seeking of therapy among undergraduates (Manuck, Hinrichsen, & Ross, 1975)? These authors studied 129 undergraduates, divided into internals and externals, and found that low-stressed externals were somewhat more likely to seek therapy, but that there was no difference between internals and externals under reported high stress conditions.

Among studies that showed equivocal results in attempting to differentiate between internal and external locus of control, a variety of subjects were used and a range of tasks or conditions were employed:

> No significant differences occurred in counseling skills among undergraduates being trained in guidance and counseling (Childers, 1975).
> Locus of control was unrelated to behaviors predictive of goal-directed efforts among equal

employment opportunity candidates enrolled in an upward mobility program (Collins, Taylor, & Burger, 1976).

I-E locus of control was unrelated to the effects of intrinsic/extrinsic motivation, under contingent and noncontingent reinforcement conditions, among 120 undergraduate subjects (Clark, 1975).

The perception of locus of interpersonal control among undergraduate subjects working on tasks similar to those found in the Raven Progressive Matrices failed to show reliable I-E differences where the expectance of generalized interpersonal control was at issue (Goldberg, 1972).

Among psychotherapy patients where client awareness of the need for internal control and orientation was stressed, contrasted with therapy not so oriented, the results showed no post-therapy group differences on the I-E measure (Hayden, 1975).

No significant reduction in rate of speech anxiety by internals or externals, under two treatment modalities (rational-emotive therapy and a modified version of same), was observed among 30 public speaking phobic cases (Morley & Watkins, 1974).

Multiple measures of academic risks and life change potential examined among college freshmen failed to reveal any relationship between locus of control and various combinations of academic risk, goal preferences, and life change (Schuette, 1976).

No relationship was found among 82 college students between Embedded Figure Test performance and dimensions of the I-E Scale (Strahan & Huth, 1975).

The I-E factor may turn out to be yet another measure, or another continuum, much like any other personality variable such as introversion–extraversion, ascendance–submission, or the like, and may not pave the way to a broader or more cogent interpretation of reinforcement. After a comprehensive summary of I-E control studies, Strickland (1977) says,

Purists may wish to argue that the locus of control dimension, as it has been assessed, is tapping only a Horatio Alger-like, ideological orientation that has little to with consistent beliefs about contingencies of reinforcement. Perhaps this is so. Certainly, clarifying the definition and meaning of locus of control beliefs has been and remains a major problem in I-E research. Confusion about I-E arises both from difficulties of definition and problems as to the assumptions about the uni- versus multidimensionality of the various assessment instruments. It is crucially important to delineate further the complex interactive effects of differing I-E expectancies on behavior. Moreover, there are obviously interactive effects of I-E with other personality variables which should be explored and explained. (p. 262)[3]

If the various dimensions of personality, such as introversion–extraversion, internal–external locus of control, ascendence–submission, neuroticism–normalcy, and so forth, have been learned (acquired in one's social environment), these variables are then the products of reinforcement. The *results* of the contingencies of reinforcement are embodied, as it were, in these various polar dimensions. How, then, can we argue that the dimensions themselves (especially I-E locus of control) are a more basic contingency, that reinforcement *depends on* locus of control? It might appear that our logic is not straight in such instances.

Like all other polar dimensions of personality, I-E is made up of a number of parts; there is nothing more basic about I-E than about introversion–extraversion, ascendence–submission, or any other such continuum. I-E is a function of already learned (already contingently reinforced) styles of thinking and acting, already acquired social attitudes, and so forth; these are abundantly present in the correlations between I-E and other variables (Strickland, 1977). I-E would then appear to be neither "basic" nor unidimensional, but simply a way of capturing *some* of the conditions that are part of knowing what-is-reinforcing-what in human behavior. Perhaps the best example of how to analyze behavior in order to know more about locus of control (what-is-reinforcing-what) is a brief clinical example of the parents of a 10-year-old boy who had been a chronic behavior problem in school, and how the parental attitudes were changed when a more detailed analysis of the child's behavior was forthcoming.

---

[3] Reprinted with permission from Strickland, B.R. Internal-external control of reinforcement. In T. Blass (ed.). *Personality variables in social behavior.* Hillsdale, N.J.: Lawrence Erlbaum Associates, 1977.

Duane was 10 and in the fourth grade when referred with his parents for therapy and consultation. The school authorities had been trying for over 2 years to get the parents involved in some home-based constructive help for Duane, who was prone to push and pinch other children, take their possessions, usurp the ball or other play equipment on the school grounds, and in other ways keep up a barrage of attacks on classroom and school-ground composure. The school had told the parents of Duane's problems but the parents refused to seek help, saying that if he did all these things at school (he did not do them at home), it was the school's responsibility to control the child's behavior. Where was the classroom teacher, the physical education teacher, the parents asked, when these misbehaviors were going on? Why tell the parents about these matters if they occurred only at school? There was a considerable standoff as a result, until finally, more or less by chance, the school psychologist pointed out that Duane was "insecure" and lacking in self-confidence and self-assurance, which seemed to propel him to do these socially destructive things. Well, if the child was "insecure" (if the difficulty was located *in the child*) that was a different matter the parents said, and the parents were then convinced (as much as they temporarily could be until they got another opinion) that something should be done about Duane's "insecurity." The social behaviors at school, then took on a different perspective, and the locus of the problem—mainly a semantic issue—was transferred from the school ("Why don't you make him behave at school?") to the parents via a characteristic or trait or cause that was "in" the child, namely his insecurity.

Actually, it made no difference at first how the child's behavior was explained or from what vantage point the description of his misbehavior was offered, as long as some constructive help resulted. Fortunately, the therapist took not only the parent's perspective into consideration (assessing how and under what conditions the boy was selfish, ungiving, demanding, forcing his way, etc., even at home, with neighboring peers, etc.) but worked with the school to help overcome the problems there (teacher attention to Duane's misbehavior was changed into overlooking many small misbehaviors and reinforcing him well when he achieved and conformed reasonably well). The problem was at a standstill because the parental theory about the child's behavior was too limiting; their ascription of causality was meaningless, insofar as understanding and changing the child's behavior was concerned, but it was meaningful in determining whether or not they would initially cooperate and be moved to promote a broad change plan around the child. Ascribing causality to "inner" conditions (e.g., "internal locus of control"—the child's "inner insecurity") fits nicely with Duane's parents' behavior and with some interpretations of social behavior theory that do not differentiate between what has already been learned (and thereby exerts a controlling influence on current behavior), and analyzing the social conditions under which the observed (desirable or undesirable) behavior occurs.

Research has shown that internal locus of control is correlated with social desirability measures (Cone, 1971; Strickland, 1977; Vuchinich & Bass, 1974). Duane's parents displayed their "social desirability" biases by responding to descriptions of their child that located the problem "in" the child (it is undesirable for a child to be insecure), and hence were able to take constructive measures that approached a problem with wide ramifications at home, at school, and in the neighborhood. Other than finding the "right" words for some behavioral descriptions, other than appealing to peoples' semantic preferences (which, of course, are initially important and have to be considered), and other than locating a problem initially in a matrix that invites inquiry and change, what have we accomplished by locating reinforcement contingencies "in" the person? Science is not based on such prejudices. We may begin with semantic leads and use them as best we can, but in the larger picture, in the larger effort to delineate objective descriptions of the behavior we are interested in, we have to have an analysis of behavior that locates variables where they can be studied, manipulated, and explained. The inner locus of control is simply the distillation of theories, generalizations, biases, truly objective observations, hits and misses that we all harbour about our own and others' behavior; the locus of control in "inner" terms is not an explanatory principle but simply a starting point for a more complete behavioral analysis.

BIOFEEDBACK AND CONTROL

The term "biofeedback" comes from the more general term "feedback" and applies specifically to bodily processes. Feedback is defined as a condition where information is fed back to some regulator, where the information comes from the activity of the things, person, or animal that is being regulated or controlled. Thus, the steering wheel of a car gives feedback to the driver on where he or she is driving, the condition of the road, whether the car is drifting off course, and so on. The thermostat on a furnace feeds back information to the electrical circuits governing the furnace, "telling it" whether to put "on" or cut "off" the heat. One of the first examples of a feedback mechanisms is seen in Watt's steam engine (DeLatil, 1956).

Biofeedback is the application of feedback to biological processes, or to sensory and other internal processes of the animal or
human being (Schwartz & Beatty, 1977). Biofeedback also consists
of a number of methods for training persons to discern and possibly to (voluntarily) control bodily or physiological processes,
such as blood pressure, cardiovascular responses, alpha brain
waves, heart rate, skin conductivity, etc.

Biofeedback consists of an external sensor that can be "read"
in some way (a dial, a light, etc.) that tells the person observing
the sensor that an internal physiological process is varying and
that this variation can be measured or controlled by the observing
person, thereby allowing the person to control the particular bodily process, which in turn, controls some "felt" condition (e.g.,
headaches, bodily tension).

One reason biofeedback is important is that it is an excellent
example from experimental psychology as to how an internal process can be brought under external control. It reaches inside the
person, so to speak, and renders more available, makes more objective, data on the internal process (blood pressure, for example),
allowing the individual to regulate these processes by increasing
or decreasing them, or by maintaining some condition of relative
constancy—e.g., learning how to relax and prolong relaxation.

Broadly concerned, biofeedback is a technique (perhaps better, a scientific tool) for studying physiological processes. In a
more narrow clinical sense, however, biofeedback is a therapeutic
measure or procedure that can help teach the patient, or person,
how to reduce tension, to know one's body better so that control of
processes, otherwise out of control, can be achieved. Biofeedback
is an example of a scientific and experimental procedure that can
readily be put to clinical use—that is, for immediate, personal
benefit as can be realized by helping a person to relax and sleep
better, overcome headaches or high blood pressure, or the like. It
helps a person to be able to say, "I believe I can control that
tension if I want to do so," although the person exercising such
control may not know all the mechanisms underlying this control
(Brenner, 1977).

Until recently, it was considered that the autonomic nervous
system was not subject to deliberate or "voluntary" control
(Schwartz, 1973). This was, as we now know, a dichotomous view
of how the nervous system worked. This view tended to support
the notion that the skeletal muscular system was under voluntary
control (you can move your hand whenever you "will" it), but that
the autonomic nervous system was not under "conscious" control
although it conversely controlled emotions, the "animal side" of

human behavior, with the two not meeting rationally in one's behavior. Thus, many notions of why and how emotions were hard to control were related to the supposition that they were "autonomic nervous system activity only." As a result, it was often considered impossible to "control emotions" directly in psychotherapy; one had to go back in time with the therapist to relive and ventilate the previously suppressed and unavailable emotional conflicts and trauma that were thought to be basic to the present emotional (or irrational) beliefs, practices, and behavior. This split in the presumed functioning of internal, irrational, emotional processes versus rational or intellectual processes made it difficult to understand just how therapy could tackle the more refractory problems included in a patient's history and could revise them in a way that provided for more satisfactory and rewarding living in the present.

The development of biofeedback has, in a very real sense, provided a bridge, if not an answer, to the age-old notion of the split between the central and autonomic nervous system activities on the one hand, and the corresponding split between intellectual understanding and controlling one's life through rational, deliberate process versus having to give in to irrational, emotional, internal processes on the other hand. If there is no longer an immutable dichotomy between the autonomic and the central nervous sysems (that is, if the autonomic system can be "taught" through biofeedback to do what the central nervous system can readily be called on to do), the solution of human emotional problems, the reduction of tension, the gaining of knowledge about internal processes need no longer be regarded as a puzzlement way beyond our "conscious" control and management. Biofeedback is a tool that goes a long way toward unifying the body and what is loosely called the "mind." It is a tool for bringing subtle, internal processes under the same kind of control that we now exercise when we dress ourselves, drive a car, sit in a chair, and the like. This is not to say that the bridge is complete and easily accessible, for there are many problems inherent in biofeedback control that the first blush of success has brought to light (Schwartz & Beatty, 1977). It is not necessary to go into details about biofeedback from the standpoint of intricate, physiological functioning. But, it is important to see what some of the benefits and limitations of biofeedback are and to apply these to our present problem of unifying what goes on "inside" the organism with what goes on via the external world, unifying the inside and outside as one set of processes, not two separate and irrevocable worlds.

Biofeedback can not only be thought of as a therapeutic modality (Black, Cott & Pavloski, 1977; Lazarus & Rosen, 1976; Rosen, 1977), but it can be regarded as a skill, perhaps a social skill, or at least as underlying and closely related to social skills. Thus, a person who overcomes sexual tensions and performance problems can feel more confident and have better commerce in social situations because he or she is not plagued with inadequacies in the sexual realm. A person who can learn to relax through biofeedback training can also sleep better, be more alert in social situations, be more able to control the tensions that heretofore caused him or her to escape from or avoid social interaction. Anything that an individual can learn in the way of self-control, at whatever level (social, interpersonal, individual, physiological), can accumulate an advantage for the person, as the self-control helps individuals to negotiate in commerce with the social world. The "payoff" is usually, if not always, in the social exchange between the individual and others, no matter whether the beginning stages of self-control consisted of biofeedback examples of tension headache control, sexual performance improvement, or other areas in the individual's behavioral economy.

In biofeedback training, the individual gains information from some signal system (a meter, a light, a bell) that tells whether he or she is relaxing or responding in some other way than is desired. The individual could report that he or she felt relaxed or not, but useful as this might be, the basic physiological measurement would still be required, because that is all that is reliable and open to observation. Aside from the reading of the signal, is there any voluntary or willful or awareness process going on that controls or assists the effectiveness of the physiological feedback? Some authors say yes to this query (Lazarus, 1976); others feel that either awareness is not needed or its presence is doubtful (Black, Cott, & Pavloski, 1977). The issue is an important one for the study of the internal processes and for better understanding of how self-control can be achieved by whatever means (physiological control of bodily states, skill in social situations, confidence in one's performance and oneself).

Psychologists who feel that there is an important cognitive element in biofeedback assert that the emotions we want to control have at least three aspects: subjective, physiological, and expressive or overt or instrumental. The first is felt subjectively, the second goes on internally via physiological changes, and the last is overtly executed (e.g., a person escaping some danger, avoiding a social gathering because of tension, or going to sleep to combat a tension headache). Changes in the emotions are not possible, these psychologists assert, unless there is some "cognitive mediational" process—a kind of choice the person makes consciously or a meaning attached to the experience of trying to control tension or discomfort. The biofeedback procedure is not simply an in–out procedure (something done to the internal organs through an outside procedure). There is an internal, mediational, or cognitive process that puts meaning and relevance into the biofeedback operation, a kind of awareness of what's going on, and permission or approval associated therewith.

It is further noted that these three aspects of emotional processes are not highly correlated with one another—one cannot push a physiological button, so to speak, and get either a specific overt response or a subjectively felt condition. These three aspects are not a single dimension, but are all aspects of a larger process. One might report no subjective distress (e.g., associated with hypertension), yet show strong physiological signs of hypertension; or one might "feel anger," but due to social factors inhibit any overt impulse to act angrily or aggressively toward the provoking person or situation.

In therapy, when we try to help a person overcome his or her penchant for angry outbursts toward others, it is often a complex process of teaching the person that there are certain antecedent conditions that are not "read" correctly which provoke angry outbursts, and that if these signs can be noted sooner, the person can bring the propensity to anger under control. Both bodily and social signs can be noted (discerned, discriminated) sooner: (1) a sinking feeling in the pit of the stomach, a feeling of the throat tightening with the associated feeling of the mouth being dry, as physiological signs; and (2) a "certain look" as a social message given by another person, body postures, verbal comments, and elevated voice volume as social signs. In therapy, we try to combine and interrelate these various aspects of emotion, since all of them have to be brought under control for a complete behavior change to be made: we cannot simply say, "Be still my heart," as the poet did, or "control your anger," as moral sanctions indicate; the whole matter has to be interrelated in all of its aspects for there to be reliable change. If there were no internal, perceived, cognitive aspects, these psychologists say, we could just train people to switch their feelings off and on (or control of same) and let it go at that; it would be a simple matter. Yet, as people have to "want to change" their behavior, it is not under the control of an outside person or condition handing out change like someone turning on and off a light switch (The wiring mechanism is the internal physiological aspect, so to say, and the light going on or off is the overt, observable change, comparable to some action-oriented change in behavior.)

The cognitive process is not simple either. What we call awareness or cognitive control is not an easy explanation for what is going on in biofeedback change or in any other behavior change for that matter. For example, among animals, rats can be trained to elevate their heart rate. The animal is first given food to the extent that maintains 80% of normal body weight (the animal is continually hungry to some extent, hence is prepared for experimental supply of food contingent on some physiolog cal or behavioral change). Once a baseline of body weight is estal lished, the animal is placed in an experimental situation in whicl heart rate is measured. In addition to the two conditions cited—weight maintenance below normal and heart rate measures—a tone is sounded periodically. Further, the average heart rate remains fairly constant around a given average (say, 450 beats per minute, but this will vary slightly from animal to animal even under the same experimental conditions) during and between the sounding of the tone. The crucial element in the experiment is the feeding of the animal when the animal's heart rate raises a given amount above the previous average, say, when the heart rate reaches 500 beats per minute, *in the presence of the tone*. The tone becomes the conditioned stimulus for food. After a number of pairings of the food and the tone, contingent on heart rate, the average heart rate per minute rises, for example, to an average of 500 beats per minute (b /min); but the heart rate remains at an average of 450 b /min *in the absence of the tone*. The animal has thus been taught to increase its heart rate from an average of 450 b /min in its quiet, non-tone state, to an average of 500 b /min in the presence of the tone (Black, Cott, & Pavloskin 1977). The tone has become a discriminative stimulus; the "payoff" for the animal is to get food under this contingent state. Thus, a normally physiological "given" condition of a fairly constant heart rate in an animal has been changed to one in which the rate has been systematically and reliably increased under a given set of experimental conditions.

Can this be done similarly with humans? The answer is yes. Black, Cott, and Pavloski (1977) explain:

> The response to be trained is occipital alpha electroencephalographic activity (EEG) recorded from scalp electrodes. The subjects are instructed to sit quietly in a room with their eyes closed. They are also instructed to rest during periods in which white noise is present and to produce occipital alpha activity during periods in which the white noise is absent. In addition, they are informed that when the white noise is absent, a tone will be presented when they successfully produce the required pattern of brain electrical activ-

ity, and that their task is to keep the tone on as long as possible. Before training begins, alpha activity is measured during a baseline period and found to be present 20% of the time. Then training is carried out for 80 minutes. At the end of training, alpha activity is present only 20% of the time during a 2-minute rest period in the presence of the white noise, and is present 80% of the time during a 2-minute period when the white noise is absent. (p. 90)[4]

The basic similarity in these two illustrations, with an animal and a human learning to respond under biofeedback control of some internal physiological state, is that the presence or absence of an external stimulus, the tone, accounts for the physiological changes in heart rate (animal) and in the alpha brain activity (human). This demonstration does not equate the animal and the human across-the-board, nor does it say that there are not other important differences in the control of internal process via biofeedback between animals and humans. What it does say is that "awareness," a kind of subjective state—"Yes, I'm ready," "Yes, I approve," "Yes, I want to do this"—is not necessary for the institution of control of physiological processes through biofeed-back. In fact, if the experimenters in the two instances (animal and human) did not differentiate between the tone-on and tone-off conditions with some reinforcement (or the white noise-on, white noise-off condition), presumably no change in the respective physiological processes would have been produced.

The internal state of volition or will, so often posited by psychologists and other clinicians, is not an easy answer to the changes brought about via biofeedback. While the types of studies discussed above may leave more intricate questions about the basics of biofeedback, they do suggest that it is not necessary to always posit mediational (often simply "mentalistic") processes of a volitional or willful nature to account for behavior change based on biofeedback or otherwise. Even when we "will" a change, there are some stimuli antecedent to this apparent voli-tional act: Somebody challenges you to do something and you respond pro or con, as you prefer; you observe that your piano-playing errors have to be corrected or you will not be invited to play at the recital, so you set about to improve; you are told you are a most welcome person at a dinner party, so you accept the offer and put on your best attire. The volitional change is, itself, a response to some stimulating condition; environmental changes

---

[4] Reprinted with permission from Black, A.H., Cott, A., & Pavloski, R. The operant learning theory approach to biofeedback. In G.E. Schwartz, & J. Beatty (eds.). *Biofeedback: Theory and research.* New York: Academic Press, 1977.

are always going on, and it is often hard to tell at first glance just what elicits our behavior. If there were indeed no eliciting conditions for some behaviors, it would be up to those who suggest this alternative explanation to show cases and causes for so believing.

There are also instances where we try to change our behavior, knowing how to do so, or knowing the outcome we desire, without being able to do so. The willful or volitional changes that try to mediate between a given condition and some future one may not come off well. For example, we may try to control our anger on verbal command (our own or another's) without success; we may try to sing or play a difficult passage on a musical instrument without being able; we may "say" we are going to study, promise to do so, then fail to follow through. If will or volition were a necessary condition for behavior change, of a biofeedback or other type, it certainly would not be a *sufficient* condition. It is not difficult to find stronger evidence that volitional control of our behavior is easily faulted (take, for example, the intended smoking-stopper, the intended gambler-quitter, the intended alcoholic-abstinencer, and so on).

The meaning, then, of biofeedback for the so-called internal problem and, in turn, for the social skills basis of psychopathology, is as follows:

1. What has been long regarded as outside "conscious control," namely the activities of the autonomic nervous system, are now being brought under deliberate control. While the control is not as pervasive or as certain as control over the striated or skeletal muscular system, the beginning of more consummate control and regulation are present, and the future of enhancing such control is very promising.

2. Biofeedback will tell us more about "emotional or visceral learning," a topic clouded over many years with speculation, myth, and difficult experimental problems.

3. Matters that are usually left to experiential and cognitive speculation are now capable of being brought not only under the control of the individual, as this control affects his or her emotional state, but also under experimental control in ways that can be studied for the best means of regulation of

internal states (e.g., maintaining a steady autonomic condition, lowering an internal condition so as to reduce stress, changing the locus of control from one part of the body to another, and so on).

4. Biofeedback is pivoted on instructions and information fed back to the person (and to an observer such as a therapist) through precise instrumentation, such as a dial registering the electrical potential on the skin surface, with this information being related to something the person can do to reduce stress while receiving proper guidance as to how much the stress is actually reduced. The calibration of the instrument (dial, tone, etc.) keeps the person posted at all times on the internal state and how well this state is being regulated. Similar attempts at self-control (or internal control), such as negative or positive imagery, are left completely up to one's intuitive observations and cannot be made public, nor can the experiential elements of imagery tell the person in objective terms how successful he or she is in the stress-reducing operation.

5. Biofeedback fits well with other knowledge of learning, physiological functioning, and the development and exercise of self-control skills. Persons learning biofeedback control (of tension or whatever) are employing measures, with the help of instrumentation, which are needed to measure the internal state, similar to those employed when they learn and polish any other skill of a motoric or physiological nature.

6. The results from biofeedback research and clinical applications are extremely versatile, covering a large variety of areas of self-control related to headaches, hypertension, ulcers, insomnia, colitis, free-floating or specific anxieties, depression, and so on. No other recent single group of therapeutic measures (biofeedback is a collection of skills and devices, not a single entity), other

than the operant applications to various problems such as autism, mental retardation, physical handicaps, the reduction of habit disorders, etc., has proved so heuristic in such a short period of time.

7. Biofeedback puts the person in control of his or her own resources and brings the presenting problem (headaches, etc.) under self-control. No other therapeutic modality has as great a likelihood of instilling self-control as does biofeedback, an objective shared in principle by therapists of all persuasions, but not as often realized by them.

8. As biofeedback proceeds in the effort to control a given problem, scientific data are accumulated along the way which can be used in comparison with the same person's behavior on other occasions or with other people. Similarly, various biofeedback measures and various ways of reporting data can be utilized and compared for purposes of economy, effectiveness, and reliability. The whole biofeedback operation is a kind of Siamese twin, cementing scientific accuracy and objectivity with clinical applications and humane benefits; it constitutes an ideal amalgamation of science and applied technology.

9. Once the person has gained some degree of self-control via biofeedback measures over such a problem as headaches, the boost in confidence allows him or her to relate more effectively in social skills situations by either reinforcing more precisely and consistently already existing skills that may have been inhibited by personal discomfort, or by affording the opportunity to acquire and develop social skills without the pervasive reservation that says, "I can't function well in social groups because I always get these splitting headaches—so why try." The reservations people hold that often inhibit their social development—"I can't do it," "It won't work," "I'll panic," "I'll collapse,"

and so on—can be set aside or materially reduced via biofeedback, thus freeing them to move on to more complex social functioning of which they are perfectly capable but have lacked the opportunity heretofore to develop. The ultimate payoff is the social skills objective, but a necessary precondition may be the reduction of consummate tension via a biofeedback route.

10. All of the "internal" subtleties of expectations, imagery, self-reference, etc., are focused on as the individual learns, through biofeedback, to observe him- or herself better and in ways more saliently related to actual functioning. The so-called internal processes (thoughts, images, emotions) and self-reflection, among disturbed persons, most often serve purposes related to escape and avoidance; hence, they are maintained owing to tension reduction associated with escape /avoidance. Biofeedback approaches are constructed in a way that changes the negative and escape connotations of tension into positive ones by providing for feedback (positive reinforcement) of selective efforts to reduce the tension.

A CLINICAL EXAMPLE OF BIOFEEDBACK[3]

Biofeedback, a technique for displaying usually unnoticed physiological variables, such as blood pressure, blood vessel pulse amplitude, and brain alpha activity, is now finding useful clinical applications. At one time it was believed that these variables—products of the autonomic nervous system—could not be directly controlled. In a series of brilliant experiments, DiCara and Miller (1968a, 1968b, 1968c) and Miller (1969) showed that if an organism could discriminate these physiological variables, they could be brought under control through operant methods. In one experiment, DiCara and Miller (1968c) succeeded in training a rat to blush one ear and blanch the other. This result showed

---

[3]This section was written in collaboration with George W. Cherry.

that, given appropriate feedback, the animal could self-regulate physiological variables formerly considered to be beyond "voluntary" control. The clinical applications follow fairly straightforwardly from knowledge of how the disturbance of a physiological variable mediates a psychosomatic symptom or complaint. An example at the human clinical level is seen in the following migraine case.

It has been widely believed for some time that the final common pathway for migraine headache is the profound dilation of the extracranial blood vessels. At the onset of a headache, pulsating cranial pain results from increased amplitude of hydraulic pulsations of the extracranial blood vessels that press on surrounding pain-sensitive fibers, especially around the eyes. A secondary swelling and sterile inflammation transforms the pain from the initial pulsations to a steady uninterrupted throb. The precipitating factors can be dietary (chocolate, cheese, and alcohol are especially implicated), situational (socially conflictful situations are often the precursors), or physical fatigue. However, the migraine headache is often multiply determined and the migraineur has to live a restricted life in order to avoid all precipitants. For example, one student's headaches seemed to be precipitated by not drinking a cup of coffee in the morning, getting less than 6 hours sleep, or not obtaining an "A" on every paper, test, or course.

Migraine is often treated with pharmacological agents (such as ergotamine tartrate mixed with caffeine), which are vasoconstrictors; however, these agents do not always work well with all migraineurs, and they may have untoward side effects. Other therapies are therefore needed. Since migraine is one of the most common psychosomatic disorders, afflicting about 5% of the population, an inexpensive, effective, and safe therapy is sorely needed. The bases for a better therapy began in a series of biofeedback experiments at the Menninger Clinic beginning in the early 1970s. Biofeedback, as a result, has been employed in various ways to reduce the extracranial vasodilation which appears directly to mediate the migraine headache. Theoretically, the most directly effective physiological variable to regulate is cranial blood vessel pulse amplitude. Friar and Beatty (1976) described an experiment that successfully reduced major headache attacks by training migraineurs to constrict extracranial blood vessels by means of feedback of arterial pulse waves recorded from the surface of the skin with a pressure plethysmograph (a device for determining and registering variations in the size of an organ and in the amount of blood present or passing through it). While this technique is effective and is based directly on regulating the physiological variable deemed responsible for the migraine, plethysmographic feedback is expensive and complex. Therefore the clinical researchers have investigated substituting an easier variable to monitor the arterial blood volume—skin temperature, where feedback thermometers are more practical and less expensive than plethysmographs. Measurement of skin temperature is principally influenced by two factors: the air temperature around the patient and the degree of vasodilation of peripheral blood vessels. In a comprehensive report on self-regulation of human tissue temperature, Taub (1977) has documented very high effectiveness of biofeedback training of subjects to control hand temperature of forehead temperature. Hand *vasoconstriction* covaries with extracranial *vasodilation;* therefore, biofeedback clinicians have sought to reduce migraine by any of the following: increased hand temperature; reduced forehead temperature; increased difference between hand temperature and head temperature. In the following clinical example, the patient was trained to increase the temperature of the index finger of his right (dominant) hand.

The patient was a graduate student with a 15-year history of migraine. There was apparently a hereditary predisposition because the patient's mother was also a migraineur. The patient's personality was almost classically characteristic of migraine sufferers, i.e., he was obsessional with high ambition, efficiency, and rigidity. Although intellectually combative and hostile toward professors and students who disagreed with his rigid intellectual viewpoints, he seldom expressed hostility openly. At times of conflict, he became progressively more anxious, frustrated, and resentful. A year of client-centered therapy, the use of tranquilizers and antidepressants, along with assertive training, failed to reduce the frequency, duration, or intensity of his migraine attacks. He had also learned Transcendental Meditation (TM), trying relaxation to reduce his headaches, but it proved of little value. In our treatment of him, we were intent on establishing that biofeedback was the causative factor in any improvement noted. This was posited on demonstrating that biofeedback was the essential factor in vascular (hand and forehead) control; in turn, this control would provide for mitigating or aborting the headache. To establish that the biofeedback was responsible for the temperature control, the patient was hooked up to the device but prevented from receiving its output (the therapist-experimenter noted and recorded the temperature). Procedurally, the therapist took a baseline (no instructions to patient); he then instructed the patient to meditate (TM); then the therapist instructed the patient to relax while listening to soothing music; finally, he allowed the patient to monitor the feedback and asked the patient to try to increase the temperature of his hand. The initial trials of all methods to increase hand temperature were strikingly in favor of the TM procedure, whereby the patient was able to increase hand temperature by more than 17 ° F (from under 75 ° F to over 92 ° F). It was then decided to exploit this already learned response; we demonstrated to him on the biofeedback instrument that he could control his hand temperature by meditation, and assured him that if he exercised this control early in a migraine cycle (during the first prodromal signs), he could reduce or abort his headache. During the ensuing month, the patient followed the hand-warming discipline and experienced an 80% reduction in the number of migraine attacks. However, TM was not feasible in social situations; he could not always close his eyes and relax in situations that cued the possibility of a migraine. We then taught him a modified TM technique through biofeedback where he kept his eyes open, and later, where he not only did this but carried on a conversation with the therapist. During the second month of therapy, the patient used this technique and experienced no migraine attacks, although he did encounter many occasions that formerly would have resulted in migraine headaches.

CRISIS INTERVENTION

Crises in people's lives have occurred for as long as anyone can remember and far longer than anyone can document. In recent years, however, crisis intervention, as a special mental health service, has surfaced and become an important adjunct (in some cases) to already existing clinics (such as out-patient clinics in hospitals), or a separate service in the community, existing independent of (but interrelated with) other mental health facilities. In either instance (as a separate service or as an adjunct to other mental health services) crisis intervention has evolved as a viable intervention setting and, in so doing, it has embraced a number of mental health and behavioral change postures that are of interest in understanding social skills in relation to psychopathology.

A *crisis* means that a number of stressful factors have come to confluence in a person's life, factors that may or may not have been present before, or whose importance may have been overlooked until then. Crises challenge a person's confidence and self-esteem, adaptability, resourcefulness, and the ability to maintain at least a modicum of balance in everyday life. Crises are calls for help, because if the crisis is not met with some degree of relevance and helpfulness, the person's plight may worsen or may even result in suicide.

Crises may also present opportunities for a new start, for settling issues that have been neglected too long. In the solution to problems under crisis motivation, an individual may advance his or her self-understanding and relevance in living. Crises are not always "bad," but may constitute more of a challenge and a washing out of old tendencies that have needed the scrub brush for some time.

Crisis intervention centers have been located in colleges and universities, sometimes as part of counseling centers of mental health centers (Berman, Davis, & Phillips, 1973) and sometimes as separate services (Brook, 1973). Community-run crisis centers (sometimes called "Hot Lines") may make no effort to offer therapy but are essentially referral services (Delworth, Rudow, & Taub, 1972). Since the time of professionals is at a premium for diagnosis and therapy in most mental health settings, paraprofessionals appear to run most crisis centers (Dorr, Cowen, & Kraus, 1973). The training of volunteers and paraprofessionals then becomes a major issue and one that is addressed often in the crisis intervention literature (Getz, Fujita, & Allen, 1975). As a result of calling on volunteers, special crisis-oriented training programs have arisen in a number of settings to prepare paraprofessionals for their roles (Kelly, Snowden, & Munoz, 1977).

Crisis intervention may be viewed as a way of guiding persons into more regular and less emergent treatment of a longer term nature (Hardman, 1975). Not only do volunteers often "man" the crisis intervention centers, many other professionals, such as nurses (Nelson & Mowry, 1976; Cunningham, 1975) and undergraduate and graduate students in psychology and social work, do limited therapy and/or referral (Messersmith & Huessy, 1975) and are on a standby relationship to the relatively less trained volunteers, as are the police in some instances. The contact with a crisis center may lead to a single session psychotherapy (Specter & Claiborn, 1973; Spoerl, 1975).

A variety of therapeutic persuasions are utilized in crisis centers. Workers in such centers are trained in rational-emotive psychotherapy (Tosi & Moleski, 1975), in transactional analysis (Klingbeil & Alvandi, 1975), in more general behavioral approaches to anxiety management (Berman, Davis, & Phillips, 1973; Phillips, 1977b), and in Rogerian-based orientations (Gray, Nida, & Coonfield, 1976). Once volunteers and subprofessionally trained workers are encouraged to function in crisis centers, care must be taken to train these practitioners in ways that do not strain their capacities. Resourcefulness in training measures includes extensive use of video taping and telephone calls to clients (Termansen & Bywater, 1975), postdischarge contacts in person

(Cast & Zitrin, 1975), professional monitoring of calls received by less experienced clinicians (Berman, Davis, & Phillips, 1973), and continuous feedback to the worker regarding how the communication between worker and client might be improved (Brook, 1973).

In some respects, crisis centers operate much like mental health clinics and university counseling centers in that they have attrition rates, show recidivism, observe people failing to show up for appointments or for call-backs, and so on. Barber (1975) found that the recidivism rate for the first year of study in a crisis youth center with mostly psychotic offenders was a little better than the average figures for such mental health treatment facilities on a state-wide comparison. Ewing (1976) compared 30 crisis intervention child guidance cases with the same number treated by conventional clinical procedures and found that the two sets of procedures did not yield different outcome results, but that the time and costs associated with crisis intervention were less. Dropout rates were found to be less in crisis intervention cases than with long-term out-patient psychotherapy cases (Lorber & Satow, 1975).

As has been implied above, crisis work may accept, refer, and sometimes treat target populations such as older people (Strickler, 1975), children in relation to parental disability (Romano, 1976), family members in relation to a dying member (Grady, 1975), rape victims (Burgess & Homstrom 1975; McCombie, 1975), persons from the counterculture (Brooke & Heligman, 1975), emergencies related to sudden death in a family (Polak, Egan, Vandenberg, & Williams, 1975), and the development of resources related to common disasters such as floods and tornados (Zarle, Hartsough, & Ottinger, 1974).

Implied in the above review of studies relating to a variety of topics in crisis intervention is the importance of social skills. The importance of social skills is demonstrated in several ways: in the successful training of lay or non-professional workers; in comparative data showing that crisis intervention may compare favorably in limited ways with more intensive or longer term treatment; and in the attempt to meet a crisis by resolving a problem, thereby helping the person to remain under his or her own control and avoiding hospitalization or other dependency status.

The goals of crisis intervention are to restore the person to his or her precrisis status; to prevent the development of more serious emotional disturbances; to enact as many problem-solving procedures as possible; to put an emphasis on outcome instead of on the more complicated processes of one's whole life; to work in the context of a time-limited treatment; to refer the person to community resources as readily as possible (e.g., employment agencies, legal aid); to offer the services in settings not associated with long-term, dependent care such as hospitals and institutions; and to provide appropriate referral services that will likely monitor the person in ways commensurate with the intervention procedure itself (Berman, Davis, & Phillips, 1973; Hoffman & Remmel, 1975; Kapp & Weiss, 1975; Langsley & Yarvis, 1975). Each of these emphases is a skill in its own right, a skill that begins with the training of the professional worker or his or her surrogate and proceeds through the contacts with the patient in short-term, functional ways, to the construction of therapy programs that emphasize the problem-solving potential of the person, and provide follow-up to see that some measure of practicality has been achieved. An emphasis on diagnosis is almost entirely absent in crisis intervention work; seldom is a patient referred or treated for other than immediate problem-solving objectives; much skill on the part of crisis intervention workers is in evidence when and as these objectives are attained. Crisis intervention as a mental health service has arisen precisely to meet these functional needs and is not dependent on traditional concepts of personality, psychotherapy, diagnosis, psychopathology, or the like. The movement of crisis intervention strategies away from traditional thinking about clinical problems has been its strength; using fully qualified professional workers only as back-up persons appears not to be a handicap, and in some instances it may be an asset.

Why is it possible for crisis intervention procedures to work? If a depth view of human personality and behavioral functioning were true—if all the psychopathological underpinnings alleged to be the case with psychological disturbances were the case—crisis intervention would not only not work, it would be unrealistic and even harmful. Instead of being discouraged by a depth view of human functioning, crisis intervention work has proceeded very successfully on the basis of an alternate set of hypotheses, namely hypotheses related to timeliness of intervention as being constructive, teaching problem-solving skills, and so forth.

There are a number of signs of the maturity of the crisis intervention movement (Berman, Davis, & Phillips, 1973; Brockopp & Lester, 1973; Delworth, Rudow, & Taub, 1972; Kelley, Snowden, & Munoz, 1977; McGee, 1974; Spector & Claiborn, 1973). These reports study the problems of establishing, running, and evaluating the work of crisis centers. A number of problems are in evidence when a crisis center is inaugurated: selecting paraprofessionals; training paraprofessionals in telephone answering, in referral services, and in short-term therapy; developing counseling or interpersonal techniques where the person is not seen face-to-face in most instances; developing a referral policy and follow-up; and dealing with problems related to other mental health services, such as community clinics or counseling centers and private practice mental health workers. Crisis center services can force a kind of rearrangement of the delivery of mental health services in a community by showing that their viability is well established, that they are not simply "Band-aides" among the mental health services, and that their services are more than a kind of "traffic cop on the street corner of mental health activities."

Not only are crisis centers showing these signs of maturity, they are also growing in new directions, taking on innovative dimensions, and discovering new things about the delivery of mental health services. Attempts are being made to remove destructive elements in the client's or patient's social milieu (Kiev, 1974; King, Morgan, & Smith, 1974; Wold & Litman, 1973). Planned intervention in the client's social environment is occasionally being practiced (Brook, 1973). "Hot Line" services for dormitory students who have encountered intractible roommates and unwholesome living conditions have been developed (Berman, Davis, & Phillips, 1973). Telephone counseling has been carried on in some crisis centers where lonely people are invited to call in periodically for "just talking it out" or for referral to social activities, potential companions, or other community services (Paull, 1972).

What would the social skills needs be if one were to actively pursue the establishment and operation of a crisis intervention center? These might be extensive, depending on the range of services, the contractual nature of services, and the community-related characteristics of the services. Some brief excursions into social skills training would reveal among others the relevant considerations presented in Table 7-1.

In general, the number of social skill lacks on the part of patients would have to be identified, responded to, and moved toward tentative solutions on the part of a crisis center worker. The skills required by the worker match those needed by lay counselors and therapists, volunteer workers, and others in the training modality discussed in Table 7-1. The whole armamentarium of worker /crisis center skills revolves around such mental health considerations as helping in the establishment of target behaviors; attitudes toward the patient such as acceptance, warmth; ability to detect significant statements from the caller; and a host of more objectively defined skills relating to knowledge

Table 7–1
Social Skills Deficits Seen at a Crisis
Intervention Center and the Social
Skills Needs of Center Workers

CRISIS CENTER ACTIVITIES	SOCIAL SKILLS DEFICITS/PATIENTS	SOCIAL SKILLS/ WORKERS
Telephone interviewing	Loneliness, anxiety, hesitancy, self-doubt, resentment	Acceptance; knowledge of referral sources; ways to help patient develop contact
Prolonged phone calls	(Same as above) Active rejection by/of others	skills; counseling skills; moving patient to action, as well as showing acceptance
Repeated intermittent calls	(Same as above) Dependency on (and confidence in) brief therapy relationship; lacking other therapy sources	Approximates regular therapy; many skills to convert patient's inaction into action, and reinforcing same; community referral knowledge
Getting patient into new environment	Assertiveness; lack of information on legal, housing, etc., matters	Teaching assertiveness; knowledge of community resources; teaching approach skills and follow-up skills
Getting patient into therapy	Decision/assertiveness/ planning, taking responsibility for self-improvement	Interview skills; therapy planning; referral knowledge; skills involving patience and perseverance

of community resources and how to conduct both formal and informal follow-up. The crisis center worker must constantly detect signs of weakness and /or strength, or potential action, on the part of the caller /patient, implement and reinforce positive signs, try to reduce emphasis on the negative signs in the caller, and show the tenacity to continue on with refractory cases until some additional measure of contact and planfulness is forthcoming. Since the crisis worker cannot easily refer the patient /caller for a diagnostic work-up or for other considerations, the crisis worker has to be ready on-the-spot with considerable interpersonal skills of a timely nature, modulated with a realistic and somewhat positive view of what can be done for the caller/patient.

In summary, the crisis center is a relatively new mental health and community resource that plays a highly preventive role against more serious consequences in the lives of troubled people, while at the same time reflecting a positive thrust toward practical problem solving. The crisis center operates on the assumption that functional social and interpersonal skills in the hands of properly coached lay workers can help mobilize the needy person in ways that capitalize on the present or potential resources of that person and thereby avert more dire and serious consequences. But equally important is the fact that the crisis center is nonpathology oriented. It is social skills oriented in that it teaches these skills to the lay workers who, in turn, teach them to the clients who call in by emphasizing here-and-now efforts and solutions to problems, and by stressing the relationship between the client and his environment as a present and future challenge.

8

Taking social skills as an alternative way of viewing psychopathology has considerable implications for the practice of psychotherapy. The focus of this chapter is on some ways in which these implications might be realized.

People present themselves for therapy on being persuaded (by themselves or by others) that there is more wrong in their lives than need be the case, that the personal losses they experience are greater than their personal gains, and often in hopes that reexamining some or many facets of their lives (aside from other depressing issues) will lead to more gainful living. People do not have to be "down and out" or suicidal or on the verge of drastic action to be propelled into therapy; in fact, the *serious* crisis situations may sometimes militate against seeking therapy, as an overall rejection of help often accompanies feelings of desperation and doom. Most people enter therapy hoping to develop some skills in dealing with their interactions with others, because these interactions have led to depression, anger outbursts, anxiety attacks, capriciousness or risk-taking, and so forth.

The old way of looking at therapy is to see the verbal exchange between patient and therapist as a way of finding out what memories or repressed materials in the patient's life *make* the person react in given unwanted and unacceptable ways (Wachtel, 1977), with the emphasis on uncovering these "unconscious" factors. The therapist is passive, occasionally inquiring, and occasionally interpreting. The manner of conducting psychotherapy from a social skills vantage point is quite different: It is based on the premise that unwanted or psychopathological behavior is learned, as is any other behavior, and can therefore be "unlearned" or relearned. It assumes that problems are extant, ob-

200

Social Skills
and Psychotherapy

servable, manipulable, and open to specific change because they are contingent upon a number of ascertainable factors in the person's life. In the behavioral /social skills framework, nobody is persuaded (although there may often be subtle factors that account for one's behavior in critical situations) into thinking that the causes are mentalistic or repressed; they are, indeed, available more or less immediately to scrutiny by the patient and by the therapist (in the context of the therapy and /or inferentially from many known and knowable factors in the patient's life). The "trick" in the behavioral and social skills framework is to know what and how to observe, to look for reinforcing conditions and for the contingencies controlling behavior. These reinforcement contingencies are currently operative and available, not matters of repressed memory or the like. Therapists taking a behavioral and social skills vantage point interact more vigorously with the patient, thereby increasing the likelihood that the patient's problems will show up in the therapy context. The interaction leads to more problem-solving efforts, so that the chances of finding acceptable and useful solutions pivot on a forward thrust in the patient's life, an experimenting with new behaviors, and not a retrospective musing or searching about the past.

People, as patients, speak about their problems of not being able to *do* things, to *feel* certain ways, to *experience* the kind of pleasure they wish, to *achieve,* to *rise to the occasions* and *opportunities* they feel they have before them; and they also complain about not getting *others to do* (or be or act) as they, the patients, wish. Control, management, skill, setting achievable goals for self and others—all these weigh heavily in the verbal reports of patients as they enter into and move along with therapy.

It is hypothesized here that all of the patients' problems are in the category of social skills. If they knew how and could do so and so, they would; if they could persuade or influence others, they would; patients lack the skills to bring about the ends they desire. Also, they lack the skills useful in deciding on and trying out the ends they wish to pursue, in knowing whether the ends are achievable or simply fantasies or exaggerations of what might reasonably be expected to occur. Patients do not know or observe themselves accurately or realistically, hence they have to be taught to observe and to use these observations for problem-solving purposes.

Part of the skill deficit in patients, then, is setting up expectations or goals or extrapolating from known situations to unknown ones serving modest and achievable goals. The use of the word *extrapolation* here is important as it takes the place of many mentalistic and fuzzy notions about why people behave as they do. All science extrapolates from the known to the unknown (also known by other names, such as prediction, trend setting, projecting results, stating probabilities for this or that set of events, and so on). The patient operates like a scientist does—extrapolating—except in the former case the data-base, the means to the ends, and the calculability of the results are much less well attended. The whole set of operations that go into extrapolation are made up of skills; they have to be learned, tried out, and modified along the way, always being kept open for new considerations. Patients lack the flexibility that science teaches in these respects, but patients can learn these skills through therapy.

Psychotherapy that takes a social skills standpoint would consider the patient as a set of behavioral probabilities with emotional overtones (not really separating the two, but giving a nod to traditional ways of describing the plight of the patient) that are "up for change." What the patient is doing, how the problems are stated (verbally and otherwise), are open to observation, or to some form of direct data collection by the therapist and by the patient. Ideally, a therapist working in a school for handicapped children and making home observations comes on the data directly and clearly; although, of course, one has to decide what data to collect, how to collect it, and how to arrange it in meaningful ways. When the therapist is beholden only to the patient's report and to other indirect measures, such as tests and inventories, the data-base is less secure. We do the best with what we have, including learning to better observe the patient *in situ* in order to extend the data-base and to use the data available for purposes of promoting change. Patients "tell" the therapists what the problems are; but one has to observe, listen, compare, and check the reliability of such "telling." Ordinarily, there is no mystery about people's problems and to think that there is a mystery is, itself, an unnecessary obfuscation.[1]

The assertion that there is no mystery about human problems and problem solving—of a psychological nature—arises in part from the outlook of those who contend that the morals, the ethics, the religions, and the literature of the past (the wisdom of the ages) are well able, in principle, to set the person on reasonable paths toward reasonable goals. But sometimes the wisdom of the past may set both the paths and goals too rigidly; consequently, changing times throw these prescriptions about living into conflict or disrepute. Issues in living inevitably arise along the way, many of which are related to conflicting messages and interpretations from the wise minds of the past. The therapist, and /or other institutions provided by society, can help the patient clear up conflicting goals and means to them, and thereby help him or her utilize the wisdom of the ages more effectively. Likely the therapist cannot set the specific goals for the patient (nor can others speak entirely for the person) and probably should not attempt to do so. One's goals can be seen as complex derivatives from one's socialization experiences; they reflect many biases and preferences that may have to be called into question if one is to develop and function more nearly optimally in life. (We will have more to say about this point in chapter 10 on the "Social Curriculum.")

Another interpretation of the assertion that human problems are less mysterious than they are often regarded as arises from a problem-solving interpretation and from the social skills vantage point of this book. The "problem situation" is based on a set of skills, however misfiring or deficit; and the solution to problems lies in the arena of teaching more adequate social skills to replace the poorly functioning ones. Therapy becomes, in large part, the skill of teaching social skills, the latter being based on an analysis

---

[1]Psychologists trained to view abnormal or psychopathological behavior as learned behavior (comparable to any other learned behavior) look more readily for natural circumstances that might be related to the unwanted problems. Supporting this viewpoint is the training of many psychologists who are also proficient in experimental work, research design, educational and clinical work with children, all of which give them a more natural science as well as a more humanistic outlook. Transferring, then, to problems of adolescents and adults is not a giant leap from simpler organisms, but rather, equips the psychological clinician with practical concepts, theories, and intervention methods that are more productive of change in clients or patients.

of the person's problems status and the environmental pos- sibilities for change. The therapist's skills are those of looking at the patient in terms of modifying behavior and in developing the repertoire to promote change in the patient.

SOME METHODOLOGICAL CONSIDERATIONS

The vantage point of this book, that social skills underlie psychopathology, can be further supported in the psychotherapy situation. Given the presenting complaints of persons applying for therapy (see chapters 2, 3, 4, and 5), one can preoccupy oneself with traditional diagnostic efforts and depth therapy, or one can go directly to a social skills determination of the problem condi- tion. If by proceeding via social skills one can then remediate or substantially relieve the patient's presenting complaints, and make gains in a short time, confidence is established in this ap- proach.

One might also apply a more strict behavior modification methodology, following an ABAB design. "A" refers to the pre- senting complaint, the baseline in more formal terms; "B" refers to a "reversal" of the reinforcement contingencies considered to be responsible for the occurrence and maintenance of "A" (the baseline or initial behavior); and "A" is a return to baseline in order to further test the notion that the suspected reinforcement conditions are, indeed, operative; the final "B" in this paradigm represents a second effort at changing the reinforcement con- tingencies to those that are problem solving oriented. These me- thodological procedures have been used in the study of normal and handicapped children and adolescents (Baer, Wolf, & Risley, 1968; Ramp & Semb, 1975) to considerable advantage, but they await more convincing applications to more complex behavior change, as is found in the out-patient, psychotherapy clinic. The reason more rigorous methodological procedures have not been utilized with the more complex adult clinical cases, in talking types of psychotherapy, is that we use speech and verbal com- munication to take the place of experimentation.

Verbal communication may be easier and more facile in many ways than trying to treat the psychotherapy case as a laboratory one (or even one similar to that used in field studies of preschool children or in studies of severely handicapped chil- dren), but it does not yield the data that are needed to cinch the case for more precise methodology and more convincing evidence of behavior change. However, we must use the verbal therapeutic exchange as appropriately as we can to move from and with it toward social skills changes for the patient. The case presented below emphasizes this tact in verbal psychotherapy (it can apply as well to writing therapy, see Phillips, 1977a). Verbal, face-to-face therapy is the most common form of therapy and will be with us for a long time; switching its emphasis away from exploring the past, unconscious motivation, repressed anxiety, and the like, to the development of social skills for problem solving is a relatively new and much needed effort. Following the first case, two others will be presented which give some methodological advantage over simple verbal exchanges (even though they emphasize social skills development), in that these cases take account of "natural reversals" in the contingencies supportive of behavior change.

> M. H. was a 27-year-old male, graduate student who worked part-time in the emergency ward of a local hospital. He was estranged from his wife after 3 years of marriage, was unsure of his progress in graduate work, was lonely, depressed, and angry at the world. Upon presenting himself for therapy, he wrote a four-page, longhand version of his problem status in which he mentioned the following concerns: "anxiety, depression, anger at my wife, doubt that I should continue on with school this fall, looking for another job with less blood and guts and better hours, concern that I do not seem to have many friends, and often I am unable to concentrate, study or set any stable goals for myself."
>
> Ten therapy sessions, each for one-half hour, were conducted over about 6 months. The young man kept a log that he valued highly not only for the therapy hour itself but as a guide to how to handle his emotional upsets during the interim. When he finished therapy, he wrote the following resume:
>
> Therapy was for me my first honest relationship, and may remain for a while my only totally honest relationship with another person because of the unique nature of the experience. Neither I nor the therapist had anything to gain from anything less than honesty. The only other place where one can be totally revealing is in one's journal. That is the blessing of the journal; all sides can be considered, even the dark and negative ones that I would rather not show to others. With that totality considered, I know what I think about a particular subject (person, goal, myself, etc.). I can be ahead of the game, instead of being *reactive*. I can *anticipate* problems and work out solutions on paper; writing gives me a feeling of clarity that is (or was) a new experience for me. I have, in fact, decided to continue the journal,

expand it, and I'm seriously feeling that writing might become my principle mode of (emotional) expression—even though I hope to continue my work in other fields as well. When I began therapy, I think I was in the throes of a nervous breakdown. I was highly emotional and felt that the world was swallowing me up. Without bragging, I feel that I've gone through the nervous breakdown, gone past that and grown up, now no longer a boy, but a man! The role of therapy, in this instance, functioned the way the role of the elder of a tribe does—I was ushered into manhood through ordeals, and helped through the ordeals by an elder with a good outlook on life. This is not to say that I think I have arrived anywhere, but that I have begun . . .

How were social skills part of the regular face-to-face psychotherapy sessions? Some of the many answers to this question follow:

1. In the first meeting, *several problem areas were delineated*, to wit: relationship with estranged wife, what to do about the job, what to do about his future in graduate school, and how he could achieve better relationships with others as well as overcome his depression and anxiety.

2. A *log* was suggested and its use explained to him (he called it his journal); he agreed to keep it and to set down thoughts and observations about the areas of concern delineated. He was advised that self-observation, via the log, was a skill in learning to know himself better and to see how his "ups" and "downs" were related to events in the environment, especially to others of importance to him.

3. He agreed to *assert himself* by arranging to see his estranged wife, talk with her about their relationship (he'd been reluctant to do this for several weeks, all the while anxious and depressed about this vacillation or conflict), and tell her how angry he'd been toward her, owing to their sexual problems, his lack of assertiveness toward her (his own admission), and his efforts to try to make her finally decide their marital fate. The meetings that took place between them over sev-

eral weeks gave him greater confidence in his ability to pose problems to and with her and to state how he felt about her, both pro and con. As a result of this skill in interacting with her candidly, he felt "loosened from her control" and able to say that he did not feel they should reconstitute their marriage.

4. While he was grappling with the issues with his wife, he *increased his social life,* met some new people, became friendly with them by trying to see them as persons (and not just using them as crutches), by inviting them to his apartment, by making overtures toward them, whereas before he had always waited for others to demonstrate interest first. He began an active social life after about 2 months of therapy, and found himself responsive to and interested in several eligible women. He also made a closer friendship with a former male acquaintance through playing various musical instruments together, sharing culinary experiments, and socializing with women.

5. He said he had *gained enough confidence in his personal life* to now attempt, after 3 months of therapy, to have a "down-home talk" with his boss as to his future on the job, whether he could transfer to a more agreeable position, and whether he could stay on his income level until he finished his M.A. program. He had been afraid of his boss prior to this interview with him; the interview was rehearsed in therapy and vicariously in his journal. He made three anxiety-burdened attempts to speak with his boss before he was finally successful.

6. He was able to *structure his time* between work, class, study, and socializing in more balanced ways—"not staying home and moaning over my plight all weekend, neither studying nor going out—a horrible waste." During this time, he was able to

make up an "incomplete" grade from the previous spring semester after he achieved a schedule of work and play that suited his objectives. This one goal was about the hardest for him, as it was not a matter of prodigious effort at one time—"like psyching myself up to talk to Leslie" (his wife), or the boss, hard as these were on occasion—but a matter of sustained effort over time. He remarked toward the end of therapy that he had "conquered himself" in that he could put himself to whatever objective he desired with reasonable reliability and perseverence.

7. When asked once in therapy (about the seventh or eighth of ten sessions) how he could now approach others (wife, boss, acquaintances, friends) whereas before he had been unable to do so, he remarked: "Well, I did know before what to do, but I lacked the *actual skill* in carrying out the things I wanted—it was like hearing a piece of music and recognizing it, but not being able—without practice, without skill—to actually play the music on the piano or on the guitar." He added later, in further explanation, "I now know I can carry out something, that I have the skill and confidence, but before I had only vague dreams or hopes, mixed with anger and resentment and depression over not being able to control myself."

8. As part of the discussion in therapy about how he would tackle a given problem, there was much discussion of the pros and cons of the efforts—*the conflict paradigm rehearsed*—so that he could admit to the therapist and to himself such sentences as, "I know I am scared (or anxious, or reluctant) to do this, but I have to accept that I feel that way and not allow the anxiety to scare me off *completely*—I have to still go through with it." This admission, this facing up to

the conflict allowed for both facets, the pros and the cons, to come under his control, plus the fact that he gradually learned that he could carry out his intentions and did not have to be driven off by anxiety. Knowing that he could bring an objective to some kind of conclusion was a source of confidence, and he saw he could set goals and attain them without much emotional flack.

9. None of the discourse in therapy was directed backward in time, as if the past could explain his problems; *all efforts* (log, in-therapy rehearsals, agendas for therapy meetings and for interim periods) *were forward-looking, problem-solving, skill-developing*. The therapist acted as a strong reinforcer not only for the effort itself, but for the preparation for the effort and for its evaluation and realignment as each problem fell under his control and paved the way for additional success.

10. Among the *social skills* he developed, or increased in proficiency, were: observing himself better; discerning the conflictful nature of his relationships with those close to or important to him (wife, boss, new girl friends); seeing that he had to approach others and attempt to sustain the relationships long enough to determine their value to him (whereas before he had avoided opportunities, summarily dismissed them after short encounters, feeling they were not worth the effort); attempting to do things for others rather than waiting for signals first from others; seeing that his depression was due to his inability to set, achieve, and properly evaluate his goals; learning to study and work wholeheartedly at each without preoccupations that he should be doing better, or doing something else; developing some long-range goals of a vocational nature with present studies and work becoming better articulated subgoals; and becoming more re-

laxed in the setting of goals and in their pursuit (prior goals had been set in panic, reacted to in haste, followed by depressive aftermaths, with anxiety predominant when he felt he should take up the effort again).

Had the therapy with this patient concentrated on the past, on simply how he felt about his experiences and conflicts, without putting all these in a context of how he actually behaved, in therapy and out of it, it is extremely doubtful that as much progress in as short a time could have been made.

A still stronger case for the emphasis on social skills is afforded when the natural contingencies are manipulated due to unforeseen events in a person's life. Two other cases where social skills were the hallmark of the therapy also allowed for changes in the natural contingencies governing unacceptable behavior; these are now reported.

"Michael" was a six-year-old boy of average intelligence, the eldest in a family of three boys who was said by his parents to have been a bedwetter all of his life—"He never did get trained," his father said. The parents tended to blame each other for their respective methods in dealing with Michael. Upon application for therapy, the boy had been wetting the bed each night, sometimes twice each evening, once before midnight and again in the early morning. He had been denied camping out privileges and sleeping-over privileges with friends owing to the "terrible stink he makes" according to the mother's report from other children and their parents. As expected, Michael was confused about himself, resentful of his loss of social opportunities, and somewhat withdrawn in the family and in his bearing when he first came for therapy. The therapy consisted of two sets of efforts to help Michael and his family: First, to call off all punishment by the parents, helping them to ignore Michael's transgressions except in terms of the second part of the therapy. Secondly, Michael was to have a regular bedtime, getting up time, daily responsibilities, and to have a prospective set of rewards in the form of attending "picture shows" (as he put it), going to museums, and working on model cars and airplanes, contingent upon his daily performance. A chart was set up for his duties, a star awarded at the end of each day for his good performance and a special treat at the end of the week when at least four stars had been achieved (Monday through Friday). His schoolwork was also attended to in the same structured way. It was explained to the parents that Michael's bedwetting was not due to some unconscious effort on his part to punish the parents, he was not sexually confused; he was simply unsocialized in important ways and, to be sure, their parental handling had not helped the situation, but the remedy lay in teaching him some self-management skills, including his night-time management of voiding, and evidence that the management (on their part as well as on Michael's part) was going well through the rewards made available.

Figure 8-1 shows Michael's bedwetting throughout his treatment period. This figure shows the baseline, the beginning of the treatment regimen, the "natural reversal" that resulted in Michael's lapse when he was uprooted from his bed and his own room during the grandmother's 2-week visit at Christmas time, then the return to the treatment regimen. A follow-up a year later showed that Michael seldom wet the bed and usually only when he was ill, extremely tired, or in relation to the family's traveling. This case shows that an ABAB design (Baseline, Treatment, Reversal or Return to Baseline, and then Resumption of Treatment) can sometimes occur "in nature," and that an alert therapist can relate the reversal to changes in the social reinforcement contingencies, which, of course, govern the social skills involved. One does not only have to create a reversal effect to know that substantial changes may occur through practical treatment of unwanted behaviors.

In Michael's case, what were the social skills taught? First, the parents were instructed in the proposition that the bedwetting was due to a lack of social maturity (skill in handling one's bodily needs appropriately) and not due to some very pathological (sexual) state. Secondly, skills were then taught Michael via the parents' structuring of duties and rewards on a contingency basis. Third, distracting stimuli before going to bed were avoided (such as pillow fights, viewing of exciting TV shows, excessive eating and drinking, etc.), so that bedtime was approached slowly, not directly upon a period of utter exhaustion from which it was difficult to awaken. Fourth, the child was rewarded (reinforced) with cherished pleasures and objects when and as his record gradually improved, which he was told about in advance; the chart for this record was made by Michael. Fifth, no censorship or punishment by the parents was allowed. Sixth, the record spoke for itself, and both parents and Michael were pleased with results. Michael said on one therapy visit that he was going to get to go on an "overnight" for his birthday in March "because my record is so much better."

Another case of a "natural reversal" in the treatment of alcoholism, partly through some social skills improvement, was seen with "Sam" a 45-year-old father of two children, ages 10 and 12.

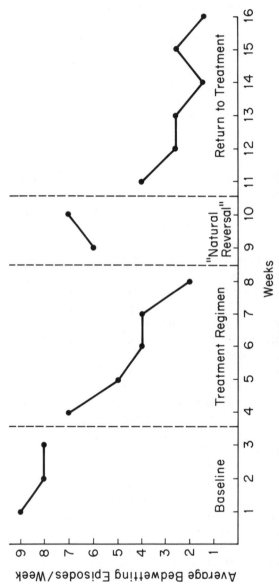

Figure 8-1. Baseline, Treatment Period, Natural Reversal, Return to Treatment, for Michael's bedwetting over a 16-week period.

Sam had been an excessive drinker for years, and his marriage had been threatened by his wife (Sarah) leaving on several occasions, only to return "because I felt sorry for him and thought he'd really go to pot if I stayed away with the kids." In the first interview, it was evident that Sam was disinterested in any social life in his home, that he declined to go out with the family, and that he was shy to a painful degree among peers. While the therapy did not attempt to remedy all of Sam's problems, one fact of importance aimed to reduce the drinking and to increase Sam's social behavior. The contingency here was based on Sarah's stating in the initial therapy hour that if Sam would make a serious effort to improve in these two major directions, she would stay with him as long as he improved or maintained a reasonable level of self-control and social obligation. Were he to not try and to fall back on his old practices, Sarah said she would leave within a short time and be unwilling after that to try any other corrective or therapeutic measures.

The baseline for Sam's drinking, at the beginning of therapy and for several years prior, had been "several beers a day," to which his wife commented, "at least a six-pack and often more." We used the baseline of six beers a day as the best approximation. Beginning with active therapy, the couple (Sam and Sarah) were to have a cocktail hour in which no more than 2.5 ounces of alcohol, per person, in whatever form, would be drunk. They would talk over events of the day, family problems, things to do with the children, entertainment plans, and the like during this hour period, "a daily redress of all grievances," as Sam at first uncooperatively and grudgingly put it. A record of all alcohol consumption was made the basis of data-taking; a second part of the new regimen was that Sam and Sarah would plan to have guests in for dinner one Saturday night each month, would go out to others' homes if invited once or twice a month, and would take in a movie or the theater once a month. In addition, they agreed as a family to make two trips each month of interest to the children—to museums, skating rinks, ball games, or the like. Sam's social obligations in his home were difficult for him to perform as he had always turned everything over to Sarah, letting her cook the dinner, make the drinks, introduce people, and so on, while he sat mostly passively in occasional conversation with others but hardly ever active or socially assertive. After whatever parties they did hold in their home, Sam's practice had been to go to bed and leave all the chores and clean-up jobs to Sarah; often he was too inebriated at the end of a party to engage in any activity other than sleep, Sarah complained and Sam admitted.

Figure 8-2 shows two activities: alcohol consumption in ounces and specific instances of Sam engaging in social or helpful

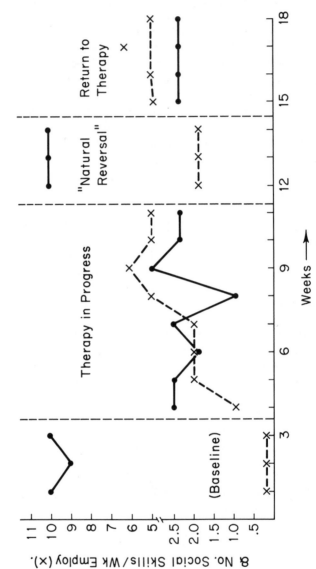

Figure 8-2. Eighteen weeks of a double regimen to decrease Sam's alcohol consumption and to increase his social skills (social obligations in the home). The daily alcohol consumption is averaged for weekly reports; social skills data were accumulated mostly on weekends but show a weekly average.

activities, such as introducing at least one person at a social gathering, getting drinks ready for the guests, helping his wife Sarah into her chair at dinner or into and out of the car when they went out, helping to clean up the table after a party, and similar items.

While anyone might admit that these objectives were of some value in helping Sam to grow in personal and family responsibilities, did these measures "really go to the heart of Sam's inferiority feelings and related problems of dependency and the like"? It is not easy to answer such a question, as posed. Rather, it is easier to reply in terms of specific objectives (such as change in alcohol consumption and an increase in social responsibilities) and see whether these improvements also bode well for Sam and Sarah's relationship and for Sam's psychology in general. The results cited above seem to support the contention that a social skills emphasis did have an ameliorative and gainful effect on Sam's behavior. The natural reversal in Sam's progress came, as indicated in Figure 8-2, when his mother came for a visit. However, Sam was later able to recover his initiative and to continue on with his newly acquired skills and self-control. Although data on Sam's behavior were collected daily as to alcohol consumption (summarized as weekly averages in Figure 8-2), most of his practical efforts at improving his social obligations were confined to weekends when special events occurred. Sam's social efforts at skill development were much more complex than his controlled drinking, since the social skills were quite varied (introducing others at parties, attending to guests' needs, helping with dinner, helping with chores related to entertaining such as clean-up, and so on), but the variety was also an encouragement to Sam as he could "try on different skills, and not have to do the very same things each week." He began to report in his weekly therapy session with his wife that he felt more "whole, and less sneaky about my drinking and turning everything over to Sarah like I did for so long."

The natural reversal, as cited above, resulted in more loss of self-control over drinking than in a decrement in practicing his social obligations. The reversal showed that contingent effort and wife's approval of his behavior were influences which helped him improve his behavior and attitude; but the mother's presence threw a negative cast over his efforts, "made me feel like a kid at home again." For a brief time, he felt all was lost and he might as well salvage his drinking pleasures and let all else go by the board. When Sam's mother's visit was over, Sarah and Sam drew up another contract similar to the one before and got started again on a more constructive relationship, reinstating the contingent control over drinking and social obligation.

Although the questions of why Sam drank, why he was so dependent, and the "whys" of many other of his behaviors might be considered, there is no way to answer these except in relation to actual behavior change. Even if we knew the whole story of Sam's dependency needs and the like, this would not be tantamount to changing his habits—he would still have to show that the "understanding of why he behaved thus and so" had a practical effect on his daily behavior. The answer, then, to the "why" questions resides in finding ways to change his behavior. The development of social skills applicable to common situations and the control of his drinking enabled Sam to begin to solve the perpetual problems of the past and, in the solution, to feel better and to grow to be more assertive and less dependent.

Three vantage points contrast the practice of psychotherapy from a social skills vantage point compared to more "uncovering" types of therapy. First, the therapy moves from the generalities inherent in the presenting complaints to specific social skills lacks which are approached in the manner illustrated above, or in similar ways delineated in earlier chapters in this book. As these specific target behaviors in the form of developing skills are better managed, there is a lessening of symptoms (pathology is reduced) and the individual begins to again generalize his or her improvement. We move then from the general to the specific and back to the general again. It is this latter generalization that really counts for the most in the lives of people and in assessment of behavior change; it is, however, pivoted on specific problem areas or target behaviors because a wholly general approach will not attack the problems present in ways that will promote behavior change or in ways salient in the individual's life.

A second contrasting procedure separating social skills / psychotherapy from more conventional modalities is that the reluctances the person has ("resistance" in psychoanalytic parlance), characteristic as they are of conflict, are approached in gradual skill-developing terms. As discussed in the chapter on psychopathology (see chapter 5), the gradual increase of approach tendencies via successive approximations through social skills development encompasses at once the "resistance" and the motivation to act, to assert, etc., in one package. One does not have to first overcome pathology before gaining social competence; the two are complementary and the task of a therapy based on social skills is, indeed, to recognize this reciprocity and to increase approach tendencies while reducing avoidance ones.

The plethora of internal distress and subjective anxiety (as well as overtly expressed anxiety) gives way to social reinforcement as the individual gains in his or her social competence. The internal events, the subjective elements that so many psychotherapies hold so near and dear, are but the off-shoots of poor social skills. As the social skills are increased and as reinforcement based on assertiveness increases, the "need" for rumination, self-abnegation, worry, compulsion (all inadequate attempts to solve problems because they are not based on or located in the social matrix) decreases. Gradually, more adequate problem solving takes over, and the individual functions in a more integrated way in his natural social orbit, gaining reinforcement for self-satisfying and socially appropriate behaviors.

DEVELOPMENTAL COUNSELING AS SOCIAL SKILLS TRAINING

In addition to applying social skills to standard face-to-face psychotherapy situations, as illustrated above, it is important to recognize a large scale movement that has arisen in regard to counseling students with common complaints, where these students are treated in small structured groups of a time-limited nature with very specific therapeutic objectives (Drum & Figler, 1975; Ewing, 1978). Some refer to these activities as "developmental counseling," recognizing that many of the problems faced during the college years do not require individual therapy, even of a nonintensive nature, but that requirements for greater student maturity may be served by and through small structured groups. Topics for these small structured groups include assertiveness training, anxiety management, dating skills, life planning, career planning, getting to know themselves vis-à-vis the college or university, developing social relationships in new settings (living in dorms instead of homes), and many more. These highly structured groups put an emphasis on defining common problems (determining student needs), setting up ways and means for overcoming the problems or meeting the needs, and organizing the whole counseling enterprise on a practical, time-limited, focused basis. Structured or focused groups of these sorts tend to cut down on the need for individual therapy, reach a larger number of potential clients than do standard clinical procedures of a psychotherapeutic nature, and closely parallel efforts in peer counseling, lay therapy training, and the like. The conceptual organization of the structured or focused group approach is one of teaching social

skills and reinforcing them through the actions and approval of
the group itself (approaching a behavior modification group
therapy model) and through catching students at developmental
junctures where the focused groups can be particularly germane.
Some of the outcomes from these types of groups are that students
are sometimes prepared for more involved therapy (if that is
needed); they may learn to know themselves better, relate and
share their common problems with one another, and seek common solutions; they can learn that life is filled with opportunities,
problems, crises, important junctures, and stressful periods and
that most of these challenging events can be dealt with through
persistent, modest efforts of a practical social nature—in short,
through improving of social skills.

9

It is often profitable to examine another field of specialization or inquiry in order to place one's own area up against the structure of the allied area of knowledge. Although at first blush, one might wonder why psychotherapy could be compared with the law, further scrutiny shows that each area of knowledge and application seeks to control and to change behavior. If each area—law and psychotherapy—is obligated to the same objectives, it should be interesting and instructive to compare and contrast them.

LAW

The law seeks to regulate the relationships between persons or entities (corporations, for example). This regulation takes several forms: A body of rules or principles is laid down (laws); the principles are defined as to the conditions under which they apply (the limits of the law, which law or principle applies in a given practical circumstance, and so on); a set of precedents are extant on which the current judgment is based (previous cases of a similar nature; and the law seeks to resolve conflict between persons or between persons and entities (the entities may be corporations, the state or some other legally constituted group). The law "functions" by applying all of these conditions to a particular case.

In addition, the law operates through the medium of courts. These courts may vary in composition and complexity all the way from traffic court to the United States Supreme Court; the cases

Law and Psychotherapy
in the Light
of Social Skills

they review may range from very transitory ones, such as minor traffic offenses, to broad social policy and ramifying political and jurisdictional decisions. Courts may consist of a judge and jury, a judge only, or a panel of judges. These courts are arranged in a hierarchy, and the citizen may have access to "higher" courts if he or she can point to improper handling of a given case in a "lower" court. Courts also have special areas of competence (domestic cases are heard in courts with the same name, not in criminal courts, and so forth).

Of even greater importance than this sketchy outline of how the law and courts are structured vis-à-vis society and the individual, is the way evidence and information are admitted, processed, and evaluated. This is the most complex part of our legal apparatus. Not all evidence is admissible; and even evidence that is, in principle, admissible, must be obtained under controlled and regulated conditions (the police, upon arresting a suspect in a crime; cannot force a confession from the suspect—that judgment is reserved for the courts under "due process"). Courts, then, require a set of criteria for entry into the court system, they employ a set of criteria for processing a case, and they have rules for arriving at decisions, judgments, sentencing, and the like. The only condition in the court system in which some of these rules are suspended is in the case of juvenile courts and /or domestic relations courts adjudicating conflicts between juveniles and their families or between juveniles and society. Although rules, in the strict legal sense, are somewhat suspended in the case of juvenile and domestic relations cases, there are other rules, so to speak, which address the welfare of the juvenile and in which society, in the instrumentation of the court, seeks the welfare of the juvenile, judging that this welfare is also the welfare of society at large. Punishment, redress of grievances, or the like are often suspended in the case of juvenile cases.

Courts also have to judge whether individuals in some instances are capable of standing trial. When the suspect is psychotic, not "responsible" for his or her behavior, then that person may not be tried in the usual legal manner, but is remanded to a hospital for observation over an extended time, or permanantly, or put into some kind of psychological or medical treatment regimen so as to help improve the personal integrity of the offender (or alleged offender), whereupon that person may later be brought to trial, or with sufficient progress and rehabilitation, the case (the person and his or her offenses) may be dismissed.

The law has grown up over centuries, has been modified continuously, and can truthfully be said to represent not only political theories (e.g., how the law and courts operate in a democratic society compared to their operation in an authoritarian society) but also represents a philosophy of mankind or a theory of human behavior. If the law says thus-and-so and a person violates this law, then, perforce, that person is in conflict with the law (hence with society) and is to be punished (if found guilty) in order to "correct" his or her behavior. Thus, the law and the instrumentation of the courts are entities established by society to regulate and control human behavior, ranging all the way from trivial acts ("do not walk on the grass," "do not enter this door," etc.) to offenses against the government, treason, blatant crime, and the like.

It is interesting to speculate at this point on why we need any regulations concerning human behavior other than the law. Why isn't the law sufficient in all cases of regulating or controlling human behavior and adjusting offenses or conflicts between parties? What does the law hold to be important that is not important (or may not be important), and what does the law hold to be unimportant that is important, in the light of a science of human behavior? Does the law know all it is supposed to know in order to carry out its mission? If not, where are its weaknesses and gaps? More will be said on this topic below.

PSYCHOTHERAPY

Psychotherapy or behavior change in one form or another (we are not concerned in this immediate discussion with "schools" of psychotherapy but simply with any formal attempt to change behavior, improve the person's "psyche," or redirect the person's relationships with others) also seeks to resolve conflict between persons (or "within" a person, although this is an essentially doctrinaire version of human difficulties) and to adjust this conflict so that it is reduced in form or intensity or frequency, or fully extinguished.

Psychotherapy has its rules as well. Some of these rules and procedures are based on social precedence, even constrained by the law on occasion, and to some extent are based on empirical study (laws, generalizations, rules, principles, etc.) of human behavior in a general sense. Psychotherapy seeks to redress grievances or complaints between persons, but in many instances, the parties to the complaints may not both (or severally) be present in psychotherapy—maybe only one party to the complaint may be in therapy. There is no rule that says only one party to a dispute, conflict, or complaint may, or should, enter psychotherapy; in fact, the drift of theory and practice is to include as many parties to a complaint as possible (e.g., include the whole family, not just the "disturbed" or "disturbing" child).

In redressing complaints or dissatisfactions, psychotherapy seeks to change the behavior of the person in therapy—the patient or client—the one presently identified as the instigator of complaints and the one who desires change. In psychotherapy, one can only hope to change the behavior of the patient (or client) and leave change on the part of others (unless they, too, are in therapy) to chance or to some relatively feeble design derived in the therapy enterprise. Psychotherapists are prone to saying, "In therapy, we have only you and your behavior to work with—what changes that might come from the others may or may not accrue to you, and they are most likely to be related to your changing first." Psychotherapy, unlike the law, has no external power to provoke or require change (as the law can force an employer to pay a minimum wage to a complaining employee).

Psychotherapy asserts that if a person "understands" his behavior, that understanding will bring the behavior under control. Just how understanding is achieved is, of course, subject to many interpretations and schools of thought, but in a broad sense, when a person observes, regulates, and controls his or her own behavior, that state of affairs theoretically puts the person in control of him- or herself and thereby reduces the likelihood of conflict with others, the intensity of conflict that may arise, or the frequency of any possible conflict. Although it is not possible to guarantee social adjustment and emotional equanimity for anyone, the better one regulates his own behavior, the less likely there is to be social conflict, except for exigencies that may develop in anyone's life.

In the conduct of psychotherapy, the therapist and the patient act as a kind of "prosecuting attorney," as judge and jury,
somewhat as a court would act in admonishing one to behave a
certain way and cease behaving a different way. The frame of
reference, the rules, the principles, the objectives, the desired
change are "there on the table top" in psychotherapy, with society
as a more distant frame of reference. In prosecuting the law, the
frame of reference is society at large, as the court represents society; while individual rights of the offender or complainant are
respected, the unyielding frame of reference (despite individual
differences in the complainant or defendent) is society and its
welfare.

Psychotherapy says that people behave "wrongly" because
they do not understand themselves; the law says that the law tells
one what to do and thus "wrongdoing" is punishable because the
rules and regulations are extant. This is an area of considerable
conflict between law and psychotherapy. It is an area of conflict
that is potentially reducible through a more systematic teaching
and reinforcing of social skills that not only serve the individual's
purposes but do not conflict with others, or society. Broad positive social purposes are also served thereby. More will be said on
this thesis later.

Some of what has been said, and some other considerations
as well, are summarized in Table 9-1. This juxtaposition of the law
and psychotherapy will help further in this discussion of how
each attempts to manage (control) and change human behavior.

Table 9-1 presents some ways in which law and psychotherapy, as ways of controlling or changing behavior, are alike and
different. Both law and psychotherapy enter the process of
socialization, for purposes of correcting maladaptation at different
junctures in the lives of people and for somewhat different
reasons, although their objectives may be quite similar. Both law
and psychotherapy seek to correct that which has gone astray, so
to speak, without clearly extant norms, without a social developmental process that can be pointed to with clarity, and without
convincing evidence as to how change can be economically
brought about and maintained. There is no absence of theory
about change within the domain of psychotherapy, but the law is
rather deficient on this score.

Even prior to the formulation of legal codes, as such, and
before psychotherapy developed as we know it today, religion
performed the function of setting up social norms and objectives.
Law and religion have intermingled almost inextricably over the
centuries to set standards, distribute punishment, and direct

Table 9–1
**How Law and Psychotherapy Are Similar
and Different in Important Ways**

LAW	PSYCHOTHERAPY
Provides rules regarding conduct under a variety of circumstances	Provides behavioral principles; social norms; subjective standards of the individual
States how rules or laws apply (e.g., domestic relations/juvenile courts versus criminal courts)	Applies itself via interviews, in office; frequency conditions, etc.
Utilizes precedents (relies heavily on cases of the same or similar nature)	Some reliance on precedent; uses current diagnosis, other criteria linking present case to extant knowledge; relies on past less than the law, except in traditional therapy
Seeks to resolve conflict between persons, between persons and entities (corporations, the state, etc.), and between entities	Seeks to resolve conflict between persons (the patient and others), sometimes between patient and society (juvenile/adult offenders), or "within" the person (which, of course reflects extant social norms)
"Functional" role of the law is to put these characteristics into action in regard to a case (or cases)	"Functional" role of therapy is to use past and present (sometimes future information) to resolve conflict
Clients, before the law, state their cases or positions	Patients (clients) state their cases (for self, for self vis-à-vis others), sometimes for others (as with children) before the therapist
The law applies principles to resolve conflicts and acts on these principles	Psychotherapy applies principles, makes (shrewd?) guesses as to origin of conflict, with less emphasis (except in behavior therapy) on how to resolve same

225

Table 9-1 *(continued)*

LAW	PSYCHOTHERAPY
Law accepts only narrowly defined data or information in order to reach conclusions, make judgments	Theoretically, psychotherapy is open to all kinds of data (perhaps too broadly so?) as basis for decision (diagnostic, therapeutic, administrative)
Says you shall/will do/not do certain things to resolve conflict or to prevent conflict reoccurrence	May recommend but generally tends to avoid will/shall and do/not do recommendations unless patient (client) addresses these issues forcefully by choice
Choice of client in resolving conflicts is seldom (or only peripherally) considered	Client's choice, preference as to goals and procedures is of utmost importance
Law declares "You are guilty and responsible..." and then acts on this judgment (a complex premise)	Patient may report *feeling* guilty, but therapy does not emphasize guilt; recognizes guilt as conflict between social norms and actual behavior
Law emphasizes guilt	Psychotherapy plays down guilt as much as possible but recognizes its role in conflict production and resolution
If found guilty, punishment in one form or another ensues (fine, sentence, combinations, etc.)	Again, in psychotherapy, guilt is played down, regarded as an exacerbater of conflict, inimical to selfhood and independence
Guilt status is intended as being informational, to lead to change	Guilt is to be resolved, not emphasized; leads to "hardening" of conflictful plight

Table 9-1 *(continued)*

LAW	PSYCHOTHERAPY
After adjudication, law says, "Go...and sin no more."	Psychotherapy says change your behavior by self-understanding (in more traditional "depth" sense) or by altering the environment (hence own behavior) in behavioral therapy
Law increases pressure on offender—increases fines, sentences, abrogates rights (e.g., takes away driver's license) upon repetition of offense—"You know better via this punishment."	Repetition of conflict (problem) may be seen as a by-product of unconscious motivation (in "depth" psychology), or at least not understanding self; behaviorally speaking, the repetitiveness needs to be more carefully analyzed, subtle contingencies noted, etc.
Offenses generally viewed as deliberate	Offenses (or other unwanted behavior) may be due to unrecognized or changing conditions, as well as due to behavior not yet under control (e.g., temper outbursts that create difficulty with others)
Tends to see change as an all-or-none-matter (for most part), with fines, sentences, etc., the instrument of change; or with prospects of same preventing misbehavior	Psychotherapy is both behavioral and concerned with subjective (private) experiences; allows private events to loom large to explain observable events; often fails to conceptually clarify private versus public events, even in the interest of changing a person; psychotherapy is seldom-if-ever-all-or-none in promoting change.
Asserts causality is a matter of "will power" plus knowing what to do (even diminishes in importance the person "not knowing the law..."); is scientifically and psychologically very naive	Asserts causality is a matter of past events, native endowment, and present understanding; varies from a depth/historical view to environmental consequences (reinforcement contingencies)

Table 9-1 *(continued)*

LAW	PSYCHOTHERAPY
Admits some scientific data as evidence (fingerprints, "lie detectors", x-rays, and medical findings), but is very choosy in this regard	Theoretically admits any scientific data, but may not always be sophisticated in how regarded or used (e.g., psychometric data may not be properly scrutinized)
Law creates and implements an adversary position between conflicting parties, although it attempts to ameliorate and judge same	Seeks to ameliorate, to compromise, to understand differences, to "explain" differences on individual differences basis, hoping the latter will resolve the conflicts; or pave way for behavior change via an environmentally controlled program (not eschewing the former, however)
Law is intolerant of repeated transgressions—steps up aversive consequences via increased fines, sentences, etc.	Psychotherapy is confused on extent to which responsibility is placed on the individual, the role of the environment, the person, social factors, etc.; confusion is shown among various "schools" of psychotherapy but also across procedures used for changing a person regardless of the theories followed
Places responsibility directly on the individual; intolerant of "social explanations" for the most part	Psychotherapy tolerates (perhaps too much at times) "backsliding" and seeks to understand it better; or to revise environmental/contingency management; is generally accepting of irregular growth toward self-control

Table 9-1 (continued)

LAW	PSYCHOTHERAPY
The law applies control through the promise of adverse consequences — punishment (some cases of reducing sentences with "good conduct")	Uses adverseness very little; uses punishment very little; uses negative reinforcement a lot; puts control in hands of positive incentives and rewards
Permits redress to a "higher" court under some limiting conditions	Open to change of therapist, therapeutic modality, type of therapy, etc.
Falls back on old laws, principles, in spite of failure to change behavior of offender; older laws more hoary	Continually explores new avenues of therapy; precedent is important mainly to the orthodox; may spawn too many theories and procedures
Maintains a somewhat rigid position regarding the social relevance of the law (e.g., in regard to marijuana legislation), saying, "The law is the law..." and resisting change	Keeps an open, scientifically, empirical attitude; keeps studying its results; views knowledge as incomplete and provisional
Seems never to throw up hands in perplexity, defeat; seems to grind away and repeat past behavior	Admits defeat; may become resigned to producing little positive change, but just maintaining a modicum of control and absence of a worsening condition

Table 9-1 *(continued)*

LAW	PSYCHOTHERAPY
Bears a very strong, direct relationship to society, despite seeming insularity at times	Admits responsibility to patient, to society, to the profession, but these responsibilities have few direct lines of positive affirmation, they are mainly the avoidance of untoward ethical or moral consequences
Seldom regards (and almost never emphasizes) motivation to do well, perceptions, intention, etc., in explaining "error" in action	Considers motivation, perception of conditions, intention as valid premises for understanding behavior and that these act both as cause and effect in changing behavior
Law stresses legal versus illegal acts (if a behavior is not illegal it is of no concern to the court, save in domestic and juvenile cases), narrowing its quest as much as possible as to what constitutes a problem	Psychotherapy is virtually the opposite to law in this respect, addressing itself almost entirely to nonlegal considerations, but addressing legal issues with patients under the rules of the court only

mankind's individual and social behavior. But here, too, there has been an absence of instruction as to how the individual was to be socialized, what social skills were to be developed and how, and who was to hold the responsibility for developing whatever social skills might grow out of informal contact in the family, the school, and more broadly in society. Social instruction has been a no-man's land, yet it is the basis for the law, for religion, and for psychotherapy as they are all thought of as systems for promoting behavior change and stability. We might ask: Change for what? Stability for what?

Social philosophies then have been more adept at setting social goals than they have been adept in proffering means to achieve such goals. Socialization and the development of social skills might be regarded as the embodiment of the means toward social ends, but they have not been fully recognized as performing, or being able to perform, this role. The social ends we desire just come about, or fail to come about, and we lack a strong leg up on the problem of why we fail or succeed. The means–ends relationships are not clearly known or understood. This very role— the development of a social curriculum—is the missing link between social intention and purpose on the one hand, and social consequences on the other hand. It is this missing link that gives rise to psychopathology *and* to the technologies (psychotherapy) and social regulations (the law) which purport to correct social lacks and supply social skills. Psychotherapy and the law have erected enormous scaffoldings to deal with the problems of psychopathology (whether viewed from an individual or a social standpoint), but the supporting structure is weaker than it need be because of the absence of a social curriculum. Working toward the development of social curriculum will not only aid in the reduction of psychopathology but will shore up the systemic nature of corrective efforts, such as those represented in the law and in psychotherapy. More will be said on this issue in the following chapter.

10

At present, there is no body of knowledge suitable to the construction of a social curriculum, where social curriculum refers not only to developmental characteristics from infancy to adulthood, but also to a kind of cultural ecology or social economy that would guide all facets of social development throughout all ages and conditions. A social curriculum implies a broad social philosophy of how people might optimally behave if constructive social living is to be realized; wherein knowledge of human behavior from the laboratory, the field, and the clinic are put to the service of the social philosophy, developing in the process an ecology or economy that would interrelate parts and the whole. Guiding this overall social economy and the social curriculum would be a number of aspects of cybernetic thinking. A general systemic approach to social living would be taken, and the content and details of social living would be provided empirically over time by social and developmental psychology, by biology, sociology, and anthropology. The end result—rather, the ever-expanding objective—would be to provide social "ultrastability" (Ashby, 1956; Boulding, 1953; Barker, 1963; Bronfenbrenner, 1977; Cadwallader, 1964; Carothers, 1953; Gouldner, 1960; Klapp, 1973; Rogers, 1972).

SOCIAL ORGANIZATIONS AS CYBERNETIC SYSTEMS

In order to understand the notion of a social curriculum and place it in the proper context, it is important to first note the nature of social systems from a cybernetic standpoint. If the systemic nature

Toward a Social Curriculum: A Proposed Flight into the Future

of social organizations is better understood, then the rationale for a social curriculum becomes clearer.

Cybernetics has been applied to a variety of scientific fields: communications, automation, neurology, psychology, electronics, and others. It is evident from these areas of application that cybernetics can be used in a theoretical way to understand social processes, as they are systemic in nature and thus lend themselves to a holistic analysis (Cadwallader, 1964). Several principles of cybernetics appear applicable to the study of social systems and to the development of social curriculum as a constructive approach to the problem of human psychopathology viewed from a social skills standpoint.

Cybernetics is concerned with regulation and control in open systems. The establishment of equilibrium and stability are the products of a well-functioning system—social, individual, or otherwise. Stability does not preclude change, but proposes openness to change in calculable and controllable ways ("ultra-stability" is a term used by Ashby [1956] to refer to the maintenance of stability through change, applying to biological and social systems alike). In everyday parlance, the reference is to *controlled change*, where it is recognized that individuals change, the social system changes, and the nonsocial environment changes. All of these changes can be understood and ordered through some kind of over-arching stability or control. Put another way, change in the parts of a system need not destroy the larger system—just as the body as a total organization can accommodate rapid growth in extremities, or illness or infirmity in various parts, without destroying the integrity of the whole, so changes in social organiza- 233 tions and in society generally can be accommodated without destroying the integrity of the whole.

Another idea from cybernetics is that systems must change—either they change or they perish (entropy). The only way for individual organisms to survive is to change; likewise, species must change, and social organizations and structures must change. Not to change is to die. Therefore, the inevitability of change requires that we "roll with the punches" and capitalize on and understand change; we can learn to harness the energy of change to achieve an overall stability (ultrastability). This notion can apply equally well to individuals, to social institutions such as schools, families and organizations, to still larger segments of society, and to society as a whole. Since we cannot stop change, and would not want to do so, we learn to live with change and to see its fruitfulness.

A third cybernetic point is that change forces adaptation. As the child grows and matures and changes, adaptations take place, relationships with others change, and the child grows from a totally dependent person to one fairly independent and interrelated to others in more adaptive and innovative ways. Satisfying the needs of an infant are far less complex than satisfying the needs of an adult; changes throughout the life span require adaptation. Sometimes, too, adaptation requires innovation, the invention of relatively novel ways to adapt, not simply reactions to pressure from the environment, but new structures or new constellations of relationships with the environment. Sometimes people refer to this innovative adaptation process as creativity. Throughout phylogenetic history, species that have not adapted or been innovative have perished; again, reemphasizing that not to change (adaptively or creatively) is to die. Another point, possibly a corollary to the above, is that once one can understand change and the nature of adaptation and creative or innovative activities, one then can anticipate the need for change and make adaptations before one is forced to do so by pressing circumstances. Thus, in nature, animals store up food for the winter, make dams to preserve habitats, migrate to warmer climates—all on small signals of change in the weather or other ecological indices, allowing for adaptation before circumstances become critical. If man can see the need for social changes in institutions before the institutions become moribund and disintegrate, then man can preserve some of the benefits of the institutions (e.g., the family) and adapt and reintegrate before dire outcomes prevail. Not to organize for change is to be vulnerable to history (rather than learning from it), and to risk impoverishment or worse. This point can be further illustrated by saying that we must learn how to change, and that this learning is one of the most important of adaptive and creative processes. In learning how to change, we gain an over-arching view of the change process, see its elements and demands, then change by creating new solutions. This is more than a passive adaptation to change or adjustment, like sitting differently in a chair to relieve numbness or boredom or pressure, it is designing a new and more comfortable chair, only to try it out, use it, and adapt it further as newer insights are gained.

Where the physical environment is concerned, man has actually learned to some extent how to change: we dig wells and construct reservoires in order to have water for drinking, cooking, and cleaning; we no longer just find a stream and use it without harnessing its potential. We contrive new ways to heat our abodes, not relying alone on the noonday sun, then suffering the cold of night unprotected. We have adapted creatively and innovatively in meeting these needs and most other "basic" or primary needs (physical survival, food, warmth, extracting nutriment from the soil and from plants, and so forth). But we have not created social systems or adaptations of the creative type now apparently needed if we are to gain the potential from social living which we find available to us.

This discussion implies that innovation and change can be proffered by groups as well as by individuals. Before recorded history, group adaptations were probably more important than individual change and innovation. We do not know who or what group first discovered the wheel or harnessed the power of fire; later in history, as communication and written records became more precise, we became able to account for individual innovations and to attribute monumental discoveries or inventions to given individuals, even though the group contributions to these leaps forward must have been significant.

In order for these principles of change and innovation to be recognized and capitalized on, we need what cybernetic theorists call a "network of information" (Cadwallader, Homans, 1961; Pask, 1961). We must have some ways of receiving, recording, and measuring change, as the thermometer is an obviously practical device for receiving, recording, and measuring change in the temperature of the air. Much of applied science consists in the inventions of such devices, some of which are highly technical and intricate, as the physical environment is exceedingly complex.

After the information is acquired, i.e., is measured and recorded, there has to be some way in which it is stored, assigned to categories, or collated in ways that are useful. It is a matter of sorting information so that it is retrievable on demand for some useful purpose. We do not just throw all our clothes, groceries, tools, and garbage into a closet in the house, we have certain places for each of these items so that their presence can be easily identified and the articles retrieved (finding the gloves you need for the cold weather, the hoe to turn up the soil, the garbage bag of use in disposing of waste, etc.). Information is collected and stored in books, files, ledgers, tables, and the like; larger storage is found in vaults, libraries, on sound records, and on microtapes of various kinds. Information is so voluminous that large collating and retrieval systems have been invented to handle the information (cybernetic's contributions to information systems has been profound in this respect, exemplified in the form of vast and intricate computers that have data-bases in terms of millions of bits of information).

Information that is stored, however tidily, is of less value to mankind than information retrieved and put to some function, purpose, or problem-solving end. So what if weather charts are collected for all regions of the country for years or decades if these charts do not tell us something relevant about energy uses, conservation, the need for new power supplies, and about the distribution of energy sources to homes, factories, schools, and other human settings? Some kind of priority system has to be invented—itself an informational matter, since we make decisions, set priorities and take practical steps on the basis of knowledge we have or might somehow obtain—so that we do not use our efforts unparsimoniously. We may have, for example, vast quantities of information about student achievement in basic subject matter fields (English, science, languages, geography) throughout the United States; this information is of little value if it does not help us to set new curriculum and teaching objectives, to evaluate the effectiveness of schooling, and to predict the usefulness of certain fields of information for later vocational, cultural, and personal uses.

The informational network is expanded to get still more information fed back to us when we have retrieved previous information from the data-base, used it to make predictions (were the predictions accurate to an acceptable degree?), and set courses of action. The data on weather from season to season and year to year may allow us to conserve and store fuel and to selectively use other energy sources, so that over a decade or more we may find ways to economize on our natural resources (use of fossil fuels, for example), or be forced to invent new sources of energy (utilize the sun's heat more fully). Collated and stored information is used in certain practical ways, the data from which then constitutes still another part of the vast informational network. This network of information is limitless, since we are adding new information all of the time, correcting old information on the basis of its usefulness, and seeing the need for still more innovative items of information for upcoming problems we confront. The quest is endless; change is ever-present; survival is forever based on adaptive and innovative responses to change. There is great challenge in meeting these continuing problems. The social sphere is no different from the physical world in this respect and requires even more adaptiveness and inventiveness if we are to optimize individual development and live more harmoniously.

The above remarks apply to what we might call the social macrocosm, wherein change and its regulation are most important. In the microcosm of the individual and his or her relationship to society, we confront similar problems. Change—orderly change—and the reduction of entropy are equally important at this level, in the individual's relationship to society. The reason many if not most problems of individual psychopathology occur (these, too, are entropic processes) is because the systemic nature of the individual's behavior is not seen in context with the larger system. We treat individual behavior, and consequently the study of psychopathology, too much in isolation, burrowing into the "mind" of the individual, and thereby fail to see both the interrelationship between the individual and society, and the change requirements placed on the individual if he or she is to function optimally in society. If we are to view psychopathology as a function of individual–social relationships in a systemic way, and if we are to place importance on orderly change (trying for ultrastability) for the individual in relation to society, then some movement toward a social curriculum as a way of relating the individual to society more integrally must be attempted. This individual–social relationship recognizes and emphasizes the social nature of what we usually call individual psychopathology. It is the thesis of this book that the problems of the individual in regard to psychopathology are more open to social solutions (social skills training) and to social preventive work (hence the need for a social curriculum) than they are open to solutions at the level of the individual, per se, where psychotherapy is conducted primarily as an uncovering of internal processes.

What information do we need in psychology and the social sciences if we are to advance the importance of a social curriculum? What kinds of information are to be gleaned, stored, tested, revised, and extended, and how will we know if our efforts are fruitful? There are no easy answers to these problems, and details await extensive empirical studies, but some stabs at them will be taken in the remainder of this chapter, since our social skills framework will suggest ways in which a social curriculum can be proposed that may have an ameliorative and (hopefully) a preventive effect on what we call psychopathology.

SOCIAL CURRICULUM PROPOSALS

As students of developmental psychology have noted (Hartup, 1976), the fuller nature of social development in children and the contributions of the social matrix to child development characteristics have not been very well attended by scholars and researchers (Sroufe, 1966). Essentially, we have seen child development as a series of stages, punctuated by learning certain things, all broadly but vaguely influenced by the sociocultural settings. The child's development has been construed often as a set of "givens" with the social framework having one or another effect, based largely on viewing the child as *reacting to* the environment, in a manner similar to one reacting to the cold by buttoning up an overcoat or wrapping a scarf more completely around the neck and face (Barker & Wright, 1954; Brim, 1975; Bronfenbrenner, 1977; Jones, 1972; Piaget, 1932; Sroufe, 1966). Lacking in the studies of children as social organisms are studies and theories about what is integral in the social environment and in acculturation processes that influence, perhaps even determine and direct, children as social beings in their movement from infancy and childhood, through adolescence to adulthood, in systemic ways.

Further, we have not noted as fully as we might how we can build social environments to suit our purposes (Skinner, 1948). Although utopian speculation has been around for a long time, most utopian thinking has been excessively idealistic (as the term "utopian" indicates) and not sufficiently concerned with efforts to find practical ways to better man's social and physical environments. (Bennis, Benne, & Chin, 1961; Coleman, 1973; Klapp, 1973; Rogers, 1973; Zaltman, 1973; Zaltman, Kotler, & Kaul, 1972). Most environmental and planned changes (as with "model cities" like Reston, Va. and Columbia, Md.) have surrendered to economic needs and planning, with social needs getting only an occasional nod. Utopian theories have often assumed that man could more or less jump to some idealized state if he could be persuaded that the change was good; but these theories failed to recognize the vast intricacies of the socialization process, how the individual influences the social environment, and vice versa, and the gradualness of change. The cybernetic and over-arching notions of change available to us today were, of course, not available to Plato or Thoreau, or any of the great utopian planners throughout history. This is not to say that we have in hand all we need to know to blueprint a utopian order (or that we even desire a utopian society), but we have better principles of change available that allow us to bypass utopian orders as they have been traditionally conceived and to see change more clearly in terms of the informational networks suggested by cybernetic theory. Also, we know today that we could not just drop people into some idealized social order and have them automatically acculturated and socialized, largely because we would not know how to create the idealized order and implement the organism–social environmental changes well enough to meet the many exigencies that would surely occur. We are, then, dealing with a very provisional set of propositions when we talk about creating social influences that help prevent later psychopathology—or provide means for correcting the psychopathology. We are working very modestly to try to recognize not only the necessity and vast potential for change but also the substantial problems associated with change.

Some of the general propositions likely of value in teaching social skills through a social curriculum would include the following. These are very mundane behavioral goals but they are the same behaviors out of which psychotherapy and social skills training are wrought; if they are of corrective or remedial value, then they would surely be of value in a basic social curriculum.

1. Teach That Conflict Is Pervasive and Ever-Present

We have seen how *conflict* is the conceptual basis for psychopathology. Full cognizance of how basic conflict is to human distress (as well as to gainful problem solving) requires lifting this notion to full awareness and making it central in self-knowledge, in individual problem solving, and in understanding social problems and their resolution. In this way, the fundamental role of conflict in human affairs would service the most constructive of purposes—prevention, amelioration, and sensitizing society to interesting problems that are up for study and solution before they get out of hand. This view of conflict helps unite its conceptualization as the cause of psychopathology with its stimulus value for innovative and creative problem solving into one whole. The importance of conflict and its resolution would be characterized at all levels of social growth and social organization. At every problem level—individual and social, dyadic or group—we would pose the questions: What are the conflicts and what are their dimensions? What data do we need to better understand and solve the conflicts? How will we know if the conflict resolution is reliable, gainful, constructive and generalizable to other situations? The whole informational network can be put to the service of conflict resolution. The results of conflict resolution, as new information, can then be fed back into the informational network, enhancing knowledge, improving practical affairs, and enlarging social and individual life. We would know the value of the conceptualization of conflict by its fruits, and would live enhanced by them.

2. Build Tolerance for Adverseness and Annoyances

Since the avoidance of noxious aspects of conflict are those giving rise to social and personal annoyances—from excess street garbage to rampant crime as social pathology, and from facial tics to disturbances of psychotic proportions as examples of individual pathology—it is important to recognize early in a social curriculum that these features of life do, indeed, exist and must be coped with. The first coping might well be *tolerant understanding*. The discerned adverseness of life, (in personal affairs and in social organizations) is the first sign of conflictful distress of a possibly psychopathological degree; and the annoyance of not being able to solve problems of an intellectual or abstract nature is the first stimulus that acquaints us with the challenges of nonpsychopathological problem solving and the reach for higher levels of understanding. In either case, psychopathological possibilities or intriguing intellectual stimulation toward problem solving, the tolerance for adverseness and annoyance is the hallmark of readiness for problem solving. This tolerance tends to soften the problem in the case of personal and social distress and to enlarge the starting ground for intellectual challenge. Exercising tolerance provides the best attitude for acting on the wisdom one might have at the outset of a problem of whatever nature, and the best stance for gaining new information and improving on the informational network in order to move forward on the problems. Tolerance is the best assuager of early anxiety while still preserving some discomfort of a motivating or enabling nature. Tolerance, conceptualized, taught, and exemplified, keeps the fires of problem solving burning while not enflaming the person or the social group to disabling panic, hatred, impatience, or constriction (Skinner, 1948).

3. Instruct Clearly in the Differences between Problem Tolerance and Problem Solving

Unless the individual and /or society become so tolerant that they react passively and unrealistically to problems signifying conflict, the differences between watchful waiting and preparation for problem resolution have to be distinguished from boredom, numbness, passive acquiescence, or unrealistic (possibly psychotic-like) resignation and avoidance. Problem tolerance is a period of gathering information, a period for musing about problems or investigating them vicariously (reading, talking with others, exploring similar problems in other aspects of science or life or personal affairs), not a time for undue postponement or avoidance. Problem tolerance is also a hedge against impulsivity in trying to solve problems before one is ready, before one has the requisite information of a reliable nature, and is a time for trying vicarious solutions. Tolerance allows one to be relatively unemotional in facing problems and in giving one's energies, and those of society, over to the substantive aspects of a problem, the proper framing of the problem-question, and the determination of what would constitute a solution if one moved in any of several directions. Characteristic of the young and the immature is impulsive problem solving; we would want early in life, and early in the trajectory of social institutions, to teach this problem tolerance before going off like the proverbial headless rider into further conflicting and ill advised courses of action. Tolerance, then, is a readying or preparatory period; problem solving is an action-taking stance; both are needed, but they should not be confused.

4. Build Cautiously and Slowly toward Expectations That Are Real and Testable

As indicated previously, the expectations (extrapolations) so characteristic of human life can often get out of line, become unrealistic and untestable; and in this excess, increase conflict (both artificial and real), leaving in their wake a vast range of psychopathology. It is asserted here that the conflicts underlying psychopathology are derived from a variety of circumstances, one of the most important of which are those expectations we learn of a grandiose nature (nurtured by society and our common socialization) which are reinforced on one level but easily disconfirmed at a different level. It is true that folklore ("Hitch your wagon to a star," "There is always room at the top," "Be number one," "Only the first is good enough," "My country, right or wrong," and so on), the theater, novels, American history (perhaps the history of other countries as well), and other important avenues of socialization beget and strongly emphasize the setting of personal and social goals well beyond the reach of nearly all, if not all, people. People break down, emotionally speaking, when their expectations soar beyond all reason, when they become paralyzed by the discrepancy between expectations and realizations, and when the depressive aftermaths and disclaimers disengage them from social life and the normal gratifications of daily living.

It would be necessary, then, in building a social curriculum, to recognize the relevance of the old statement, "A man's reach is greater than his grasp," or equivalent statements, to savor what is constructive and useful in this statement, and to separate as well as possible the differences between self-defeating and grandiose expectations and those that may be improvable or difficult to attain but which are, in principle, reachable and constructive. If we never stretch ourselves and try for higher goals, we will less likely learn of our potentialities, which are always up for testing under the conditions of constant change, emphasized herein as basic to reality. We do not, then, want to dampen human aspirations, creative flights, and the like in order to caution against grandiosity, vanity, unilateralness of purpose, and intractability in setting goals. The line between these two extremes may be very subtle and hard to define in many instances; we know the differences often only when the consequences are observed, failing in advance to predict the outcome of the flights into creativity of a Thomas Edison versus a visionary inventor who fails to produce working plans or models for his or her fantasies. One clue to many of the problems in the area of too high expectations is that people harboring such beliefs, and acting on them in ways that seem impervious to correction, are probably reinforced on a basis other than that related to their performance and action. Thus, "beautiful people" are reinforced for their "looks" without regard to what they do or how they relate to others; they get empty benefits (said another way, their social reinforcement is random, noncontingent on observable or intentional behavior on their part) based on how they appear rather than on what they do. This social reinforcement may be very confusing because it is not under their control—they are simply "beautiful" and they need not do anything to relate to others, serve the needs of others—hence they often float in an impersonal vacuum, feel "empty," and life often appears meaningless. Possibly adulation for whatever reason can bring about this emptiness, perhaps arising through continuous over-satiation and effortless living. The expectation is that benefits to adulation will come to them unrelentingly; when these expectations are dashed, untoward consequences follow—the person is variously unhappy, depressed, dejected, suicidal.

Since our abilities to construct theories about ourselves are highly potent and active, especially when society and the socialization process so strongly support high aspirations, it would be a wise matter to train children to create and aspire and expect in terms of testable aspects of themselves and the world around them, and to *do* what they talk about doing and to talk about only what they in fact *do*. To unify talking-about and acting-on the intriguing aspects of nature, human actions and potentialities and the phenomenal world would be the model way to handle expectations.

The role of fantasy, myths, allegorical accounts of human motivation and activities should be looked at searchingly.[1] Is it wise to foster fantasy in children when, due to their reality-testing capabilities, the fantasy may already be rampant and ever-present? Coralling the fantasy for useful social and personal development purposes might be given the higher priority. Instead of teaching children all the paraphernalia of "Mother Goose," moralistic stories of high motivation and great deeds that are brought about by luck or noncontingent effort, the child's imagination should be aroused by what are highly imaginative "real" stories of animals, people, human events, and the like. There is much mystery in nature that is not harnessed for social curriculum or child-rearing instructional or educational purposes. Dealing with the "mysteries" of the real world will simultaneously intrigue the child and stimulate the child's imagination, yet at the same time hold to reality. The old adage, "Truth is stranger than fiction," applies here.

Many parents and teachers might be surprised to learn that there could well be a nontraditional–fantasy emphasis in education and in teaching the child the wonders of life. The perpetuation of fantasy is largely an adult activity—they are the ones who are socially reinforced by the child's responses, by vicarious

---

[1]Bettelheim (1976) has written persuasively regarding the uses of enchantment. However, enchantment may come as well from "real" life as from fairy tales, myths, and similar fiction; the child could well learn that there is more enchantment in the lives of animals, the customs of other people, the marvels of the world than in Rumpelstiltskin, gnomes, witches, and other fictional brews.

stimulation in the mythology taught children, and by the comfort of knowing the differences between reality and fantasy. Also, parents and teachers do not often have the purpose of accelerating the child's imagination about the real world, a matter they would have to think about and ferret out literature to support, whereas the standard fantasies are all too available in stores, shops, and libraries; so they take the easier course.

5. Direct the Solutions to Frustrations (Conflicts, in the Larger Sense) and Emotional Reactions toward Objectively Discernible Circumstances, Reducing Personal Reactions and Hostility toward Others

This is a problem-solving stricture. The first four points refer to preparation for problem solving; this point refers more to the actual efforts to solve or reduce problems. While most interpersonal conflict assumes enormous emotional and personalized implications, the solutions are usually found in more objective statements of the problem, in roles that people might play in remediating or correcting frustrations and conflicts, and in programming efforts to carry out solutions. A lot of interpersonal conflict and frustration revolve around intractible positions that people take; mediators and the establishment of policy (rules and regulations and laws) often reduce the intensity of the conflict and place solutions on more objective grounds. In school settings, conflicts between children are, of course, common; teachers learn rapidly that each child in the conflict is likely holding up only his or her own perspective and is not ready, willing, or able to assume an objective stance—the teacher has to do that. Solutions usually follow some revival of a rule, some social planning, some talking about the conflict so that the emotional and non-problem-solving aspects are reduced in intensity and real solutions become more likely. Under good guidance from an adult, children can learn interpersonal problem solving, can learn the importance of the role of the mediator (sometimes a therapist) in marshalling evidence, weighing it, and arriving at tentative solutions. In this way, children can learn that the emotional aftermath from conflict need not prevail; that problems can be solved, and that one of the most important transactions between people is simply that of working out solutions to problems (Almy, 1970).

While there is nothing very original about the preceding discussion of this topic, what is unusual is that we do not raise the problem solving to a higher conceptual and practical level; we tend more to stumble on to solutions, to let fortuitous circumstances contribute to or smother problems, and to harbor great prejudices and biases as a result of failure to solve or settle problems. The grudges, the complaints, the paranoid reactions of adults to life's vicissitudes probably arise out of the mess accompanying non-problem-solving. In turn, the emotionalized reactions harden into attitudes that are often intractable and self-righteous. As a possible correction to this state of affairs, one approach is to have the school curriculum of children include as much emphasis on interpersonal problem solving, on handling frustrations and conflict, and on recourse that helps to develop clear structures where emotionalized reactions are noted, as is spent on any other study of life. When people engage in psychotherapy, it is precisely this clarification of structure that arises, and some objectivity hopefully takes the place of previous subjectivity. Therapy is a social skill, but the skills of therapy can be packaged and taught in any curriculum and related to the problem solving that goes on in other departments of life such as in science, politics, community affairs, and in administrative matters (Haley, 1976; Mink, 1970; Phillips, 1977a; Thoresen & Mahoney, 1974).

6. Work toward Solutions to Problems That Have Heuristic, Stable, and Long-Range Effects; Avoid Temporizing; Build Equity for the Future

One reason society gets into innumerable crises (and this applies to individuals as well) is that problem solving is more temporizing than long range. Crisis intervention is useful and important (see chapters 6, 7, and 8) and must of necessity be the first approach to many problems; but if crisis resolution does not contribute to longer term solutions and to less vulnerability to frustration and conflict, the intervention may have to be repeated, perhaps accumulating a record of waste and worsening conditions.

There are several contributions to all-too-temporary solutions to problems: First is the failure to define the problem satisfactorily. If the dimensions of a problem are not well understood, then solutions are bound to go awry in one or several ways (Adler, 1961; Bartlett, 1958; Bruner, Goodenough, & Austin, 1956). Failure to define a problem correctly means that the data-base is in error, conclusions that follow are not applicable to the problem solution, and observations that follow from the logical sequence supporting problem solving are not on the mark. Children can be

46

Basis of
Psychopathology

taught the problem-solving seqence, perhaps using Dewey's steps in solving a problem as a model (Almy, 1970), and can learn to check out each step. Applying such a sequence to human interactions and interpersonal problem solving are altogether understandable by elementary age children and could be fit easily into many curricular offerings during this developmental period.

There are many problems extant today in society (energy, pollution, fossil fuel supplies, the delivery of health services and health care, social security, the treatment of the aged and infirm, the plight of the handicapped, and so on) that children as well as adults could tackle from the standpoint of analyzing the problems, marshalling evidence, and drawing a number of testable conclusions. This kind of exercise is not only instructive about the nature of the real social world, but it is a cogent exercise in applying problem solving for longer range purposes than just making next month's car payment, deciding what record to buy for a friend's birthday present, or what to do about pornographic movies in the downtown city area, interesting and commonplace as these problems are.

There is, however, no easy formula instructing us on how to shoot for long-range benefits, but there is merit in setting forth this objective as a criterion for a social curriculum. How can long-range benefits be included in problem solving, especially of a societal nature? How can individual problem solving meet needs that stretch well into the future? How are individuals and groups able to assess questions that require long-range solutions and keep these considerations foremost in mind? These are some of the questions a social curriculum can address (Cadwallader, 1964).

We can take some stock in the value of long-range health and educational planning, especially the former. Epidemiological data, health records, disease courses over decades in relation to social and industrial conditions, and the like, offer models of how long-range data gathering preliminary to decision making might take place. Perhaps as computers are used to accumulate more than economic data and can move into health, social, and political areas, we will gain data-bases for making better decisions and for instructing people on the importance of a social curriculum that is founded on cumulative records of wide social import. The recent crises in the supply of energy show how poorly society and governments have faced up to energy needs, trends, and projections. We do not have a "curriculum" for information gathering and processing about these vital issues at this time; it may be a while before we gain the momentum to include in a social curriculum all the basic data areas of social importance, but the problems of supplying these areas of information have to be clearly realized, and the earlier the better (Cadwallader, 1964).

7. Make Ethical Training Integral to All Social and Interpersonal Instruction and Problem Solving

Children are very open to instruction in terms of fairness, personal ethics, and consideration of principles of social justice if given a reasonable opportunity to learn and implement these notions. Teaching children ethical principles might gain a foothold in their awareness via helping animals, as well as through stories and actual contacts with other children. Nursery schools normally instruct children in taking turns, in sharing, and the like. While children under the impact of frustration usually behave emotionally, the overall instruction about fair play does make an impression on them, and they can often be observed invoking principles to govern the behavior of other children if not their own behavior (adults are generally good at this discrimination as well!) (Brophy, 1977; Danziger, 1973; Mussen & Eisenberg-Berg, 1977).

Stories with a moral are of interest to children, and questions and discussions about various principles (suited to their level of understanding) are sometimes intriguingly responded to by children. If the instruction is concrete and based on actual interactions between people that tap into the repertoire of children, they can learn the principles involved. If instruction is too abstract (emphasizing the nature of justice, or heavily based on retaliative moral principles), the child will be confused and discouraged. Also, principles of fair play that can be implemented by adults as models are of considerable value: We are not then saying to the child, "Do as I say but not as I do." Many of the complaints of adolescents about adult ethical, moral, or social behavior stems from the fact that adults verbalize one set of ethical guidelines but often act inappropriately to these strictures. Cleaning-up-the-adult-act will go a long way toward setting examples for children and implementing the ethical standards we wish to teach.

As with many points cited above, novelty for this point is not claimed; what is claimed is that we can articulate moral and ethical principles better for children than we now do, and we can put this set of objectives high on the social curriculum "must" list. If a curriculum of the usual educational type in the preschool setting and during the elementary years were to place a high priority on ethical instruction of a very concrete nature (Damon, 1977), we would not only have a way of teaching children better self-control, it is hypothesized that we would also enhance social skills to a noticeable degree (Damon, 1977; Goldstein, Sprafkin, & Gershaw, 1976; Goslin, 1969). Presumably, if ethical behaviors were regarded as social skills and taught for this reason, stressing continuity during the developmental years, we would have a larger number of adults reaching Kohlberg's sixth stage of moral development—"The universal ethical principle orientation"— and possibly greater reliability in maintaining highly acceptable moral and ethical behavior in a variety of situations; or, alternatively, some level comparable to Kohlberg's schema if culturally salient (Damon, 1977; Kohlberg, 1971).

The rest of the list of possible contributions to a social curriculum hinges on more specific educational items and more specific attitudes toward social problem solving. These follow from the already presented list of general strictures but take into account the fact that not all of the strictures will work out favorably and that many stop-gap measures must be provided to offset "slippage" in the system that regulates society and that purports to prepare persons through a social curriculum to live gainfully.

1. Social interaction is reciprocal—neither the child nor the adult simply reacts; the person both shapes the environment and is shaped by it. Recent work on the selective behaviors of infants is an item supporting this point (Damon, 1977; Haith Bergman, & Moore, 1977). Our efforts to instruct are not one-way streets aimed *at* the person, but complex cybernetic loops that expand and contract in relation to the reciprocity involved.

2. Organism and organism–environmental interactions will not inevitably produce good results just because we aim for them— mishaps will occur. There is need, then, for backup systems, prosthetic systems, and "rest area" circumstances to fit in when and where the on-going major systems of socialization default. For example, in the area of educating and treating handicapped children (orthopedic and /or sensory defective cases) there is need for prosthetic environments of a complex and perhaps permanent nature. Similarly, among all members of a society, efforts to increase the relevance and validity of

the social curriculum will be followed; but entropy, conflict, and other exigencies will occur beyond the control of the system at given times. Treating these spun-off, subsystems as integrally to the larger system as possible is desirable. At least moderately fail-safe systems are needed at all levels of social curriculum instruction and functioning.

3. Since the larger physical environment is also not under complete control (catastrophies do occur), there will need to be social curriculum adjustments to phenomenal changes in the physical environment and preparatory readiness at the social level to meet these exigencies (severe climactic or weather-induced changes, for example), otherwise sheer survival may be at stake. A wise social curriculum would take out social and psychological "insurance" against such catastrophic happenings.

Withal, movement toward a general social curriculum would be a staggering undertaking and a continuing obligation. But such a prospect must be faced. Our world is growing more complex and populous daily, problems of a stark survival nature stall us at every turn and with many decisions made at individual and social levels throughout the world. There is no escape from the reality of the need for general social planning and for continuing instruction and experimentation on how such planning can be actualized (Wiener, 1950). Beginning now to think in terms of a social curriculum will foster clarity about mankind's interrelationships and the preservation and extention of life on as fulfilling a basis as possible. Awareness of the need for a social curriculum applies equally to the development of social skills among people (and the concomitant ability to control psychopathology) and to the implementation of a whole social structure that is entirely geared to mankind's shared needs.

References

Adler, I. *Thinking machines.* New York: John Day, 1961.

Almy, M. *Logical thinking in second grade.* New York: Columbia University Teachers College Press, 1970.

Ansbacher, H., Ansbacher, R. *The individual psychology of Alfred Adler.* New York: Basic Books, 1956.

Arbes, B. H., Hubbell, R. N. Packaged impact: A structured communication skills workshop. *Journal of Counselling Psychology,* 1973, **20,** 332–337.

Argyle, M. *Social interaction.* New York: Atherton Press, 1969.

Argyle, M. *Bodily communication.* London: Methuen, 1975.

Arkowitz, H., Lichtenstein, E., McGovern. K., et al. The behavioral assessment of social competence in males. *Behavior Therapy,* 1975, **6,** 3–13.

Ashby, W. R. *An introduction to cybernetics.* New York: Wiley, 1956.

Ayllon, T., & Azrin, N. H. *The token economy: A motivational system for therapy and rehabilitation.* New York: Appleton-Century-Crofts, 1968.

Baer, D. M., Wolf, M. M., & Risley, T. R. Some current dimensions of applied behavior analysis. *Journal of Applied Behavior Analysis,* 1968, **1,** 91–97.

Bales, R. F. *Interaction process analysis: A method for the study of small groups.* Reading, Mass: Addison-Wesley, 1950.

Balzer, F. J., Jr. The development of psychiatric inpatient peer-helpers through a systematic human relations training program. *Dissertation Abstracts International,* 1975, (University Microfilms No. 75–8086)

Bander, K. W., Steinke, G., Allen, G. J., et al. Evaluation of three dating-specific treatment approaches for heterosexual dating anxiety. *Journal of Counselling and Clinical Psychology,* 1975, **43,** 259–265.

Bandura, A. *Principles of behavior modification.* New York: Holt, Rinehart & Winston, 1969.

Bandura, A. *Aggression: A social learning analysis.* Englewood Cliffs, N.J.: Prentice-Hall, 1973.

Bandura, A. Self-efficacy: Toward a unifying theory of behavior change. *Psychological Review*, 1977, **84**, 191–215.

Barber, M. A system for psychotic offenders. *California Youth Authority Quarterly*, 1975, **28**, 45–48.

Barker, R. *The stream of behavior*. New York: Appleton-Century-Crofts, 1963.

Barker, R. G., & Wright, H. F. *Midwest and its children*. Evanston: Row Peterson, 1954.

Barmash, I. *For the good of the company: Work and interplay in a major American corporation*. New York: Grossett & Dunlap, 1976.

Bartlett, S. F. *Thinking*. New York: Basic Books, 1958.

Baruch, D. W. *New ways in discipline*. New York: McGraw-Hill, 1949.

Beck, A. *Depression: Causes & Treatment*. Philadelphia: University of Pennsylvania Press, 1967. (a)

Beck, A. T. *Depression: Clinical, experimental and theoretical aspects*. New York: Harper, 1967. (b)

Beck, A. T., Ward, C. H., Mendelson, M., Mock, J. E., & Erbaugh, J. K. Reliability of psychiatric diagnosis. 2. a study of consistency of clinical adjustments & ratings. *American Journal of Psychiatry*, 1962, **119**, 351–357.

Becker, R. D. C. Review of Hobbs' The Futures of Children. *Contemporary Psychology*, 1977, **22**, 179.

Bellack, A. S. Internal vs external locus of control and the use of self-reinforcement. *Psychological Reports*, 1972, **31**, 723–733.

Bellack, A. S. Self-evaluation, self-reinforcement, and locus of control. *Journal of Research in Personality*, 1975, **9**, 158–167.

Bennis, W. G., Benne, K. D., & Chin, R. (Eds.). *The planning of change*. New York: Holt, Rinehart & Winston, 1961.

Bergman, J. S., & Doland, D. J. The effectiveness of college students as therapeutic agents with chronic hospitalized patients. *American Journal of Orthopsychiatry*, 1974, **44**, 92–96.

Berkowitz, L. (Ed.). *Advances in experimental social psychology (Vol. 7)*. New York: Academic Press, 1972.

Berman, P., Davis, A., & Phillips, E. L. George Washington University volunteer hotline, a descriptive study. *Psychological Reports*, 1973, **33**, 364–366.

Bettelheim, B. *The uses of enchantment: The meaning and importance of fairy tales.* New York: Vintage Books, 1976.

Bhanthumnavin, D. L. Sex and cultural differences in perceived locus of control among students in five countries. *Journal of Consulting and Clinical Psychology*, 1974, **42**, 451–455.

Black, A. H., Cott, A., & Pavloski, R. The operant learning theory approach to biofeedback. In G. E. Schwartz, & J. Beatty (Eds.), *Biofeedback: Theory and research.* New York: Academic Press, 1977.

Blatz, W. E., & Bott, E. A. Studies in mental hygiene of children: I Behavior of public school children—a description of method. *Journal of Genetic Psychology*, 1927, **34**, 552–582.

Bolen, L. M. G. An experimental study of the influence of locus of control, dyadic interaction, and sex on creative thinking. *Dissertation Abstracts International*, 1976, (University Microfilms No. 76-6374)

Boles, B. K. The effect of personality factors and training on the development of interpersonal skills by freshman medical students. *Dissertation Abstracts International*, 1976, (University Microfilms No. 76-3386)

Bonnard, A. The mother as therapist, in a case of obsessional neurosis. In *The psychoanalytic study of the child.* New York: International Universities Press, 1950.

Boulding, K. E. *The organizational revolution.* New York: Harper & Bros, 1953.

Boykin, M. F. L. Systematic desensitization and assertive training as methods of increasing emotional control among extraverts, ambiverts, and introverts. *Dissertation Abstracts International*, 1975, (University Microfilms No. 75–22159)

Brendell, M. Changes in positive personality traits as a function of teaching encouraging transactions. *Dissertation Abstracts International*, 1974, (University Microfilms No. 74-11851)

Brenner, J. Sensory and perceptual determinants of voluntary visceral control. In G. E. Schwartz & J. Beatty (Eds.). *Biofeedback: Theory and research.* New York: Academic Press, 1977.

Brim, O. G. Macro-structural influences on child development and the need for childhood social indicators. *American Journal of Orthopsychiatry*, 1975, **45**, 516–524.

Brockopp, G. W., & Lester, D. (Eds.). *Crisis intervention and counseling by telephone.* Springfield, Ill.: Charles C. Thomas, 1973.

Bronfenbrenner, U. Toward an experimental ecology of human development. *American Psychology*, 1977, **32**, 513–531.

Brook, B. D. Crisis hostel: An alternative to psychiatric hospitalization for emergency patients. *Hospital and Community Psychiatry*, 1973, **24**, 621–624.

Brooke, B. A., Heiligman, A. C. Can professionals work in the counter culture? *Social Work*, 1975, **20**, 400–401.

Brophy, J. E. *Child development and socialization.* Chicago: Science Research Associates, 1977.

Bruner, J. S., Goodenough, J. J., & Austin, G. A. *A study of thinking.* New York: Wiley, 1956.

Burgess, A. W., & Homstrom, L. L. Counseling the rape victim. *Scientific Proceedings in Summary Form.* Washington, D.C.: American Psychiatric Association, 1975.

Buros, O. K. (Ed.). *The seventh mental measurements yearbook* (Vol. I & II). Highland Park, N. J.: Gryphon Press, 1972.

Cadwallader, M. L.: The cybernetic analysis of change. In A. Etzioni (Ed.). *Social change: Sources, patterns and consequences.* New York: Basic Books, 1964, 159–164.

Calhoun, J. E. (Ed.) *Abnormal psychology: Current perspectives* (2nd ed). New York: CRM /Random House, 1977.

Calhoun, L. G., Cheney, T., & Dawes, A. S. Locus of control, self-reported depression and perceived causes of depression. *Journal of Consulting and Clinical Psychology*, 1974, **42**, 736.

Cameron, N. The functional psychosis. In J. McV. Hunt (Ed.). *Personality and the behavior disorders.* New York: Ronald, 1944.

Cameron, N. *The psychology of the behavior disorders.* Boston: Houghton Mifflin, 1947.

Campbell, A. A. A study of the personality adjustments of only and intermediate children. *Journal of Genetic Psychology*, 1933, **43**, 197–206.

Carkhuff, R. R. *Helping and human relations: A primer for lay and professional helpers* (Vol. I & II). New York: Holt, Rinehart & Winston, 1969.

Carkhuff, R. R. Training as a preferred mode of treatment. *Journal of Counseling and Psychology*, 1971, **18**, 123–131.

Carkhuff, R. R., & Berenson, B. G. *Beyond counseling and therapy.* New York: Holt, Rinehart & Winston, 1967.

Carkhuff, R. R., & Bierman, R. Training as a preferred mode of treatment of parents of emotionally disturbed children. *Journal of Counseling and Psychology*, 1970, **17**, 157–161.

Carkhuff, R. R., & Truax, C. B. Lay mental health counseling: The effectiveness of lay group counseling. *Journal of Consulting Psychology*, 1965, **29**, 426–431. (a)

Carkhuff, R. R., & Truax, C. B. Training in counseling and psychotherapy: An evaluation of an integrated didactic and experimental approach. *Journal of Consulting Psychology*, 1965, **29**, 333–336. (b)

Carothers, J. C. The African mind in health and disease. Monograph No. 17. Geneva: World Health Organization, 1953.

Carson, R. *Interaction concepts of personality.* Chicago: Aldine, 1969.

Cash, T. F., & Stack, J. J. Locus of control among schizophrenics and other hospitalized psychiatric patients. *Genetic Psychology Monographs,* 1973, **87,** 15–122.

Cast, S. P., & Zitrin, A. A public health approach to suicide prevention. *American Journal of Public Health,* 1975, **65,** 144–147.

Cherry, F., & Byrne, D. Authoritarianism. In T. Blass (Ed.), *Personality variables in social behavior.* New York: Lawrence Erlbaum Associates, 1977.

Childers, J. H. Jr. Comparison of competency in counseling skills developed through two types of training of internal-external oriented counselor-trainees. *Dissertation Abstracts International,* 1975, (University Microfilms No. 75-1575)

Clark, G. W. The effects of internal–external locus of control on intrinsic–extrinsic motivation with contingent–noncontingent reinforcements. *Dissertation Abstracts International,* 1975, (University Microfilms No. 75-11555)

Clark, R. D. The effects of reinforcement, punishment and dependency on helping behavior. *Bulletin on Personality and Social Psychology,* 1975, **1,** 596–599.

Clark, R. W. *The life of Bertrand Russell.* New York: Knopf, 1975.

Clark, J. V., & Arkowitz H. Social anxiety and self-evaluation of interpersonal performance. *Psychological Reports,* 1975, **36,** 211–221.

Clarke, A. M., & Clarke, A.D.B. *Early experience: Myth and evidence.* Riverside, N.J.: Free Press, 1977.

Clore, G. L. *Interpersonal attraction: An overview.* Morristown, N. J.: General Learning Press, 1975.

Coleman, J. S. Conflicting theories of social change. In G. Zaltman (Ed.), *Processes and phenomena of social change.* New York: Wiley, 1973.

Coleman, J. C. *Abnormal psychology and modern life (5th ed.).* Glenville, Ill.: Scott, Foresman & Co., 1976.

Collins, H. A., Taylor, G. A., & Burger, G. K. Locus of control as predictive of goal-directed behavior. *Journal of Clinical Psychology,* 1976, **32,** 29–293.

Collingwood, G. S. Retention and retraining of interpersonal communication skills. *Journal of Clinical Psychology,* 1971, **27,** 294–296.

Cone, J. D. Social desirability scale values and ease of responding to personality statements. *Proceedings of the Annual Convention of the American Psychological Association,* 1971, **6,** 119–120.

Connolly, S. G. The effects of human relations training using Gestalt therapy techniques upon selected personality variables in rehabilitation clients. *Dissertation Abstracts International,* 1975, (University Microfilms No 75-11913)

Coopersmith, S. *The antecedents of self-esteem.* New York: Freeman & Freeman, 1967.

Craighead, W. E., Kazdin, A. E., & Mahoney, M. J. *Behavior modification: Principles, issues and applications.* Boston: Houghton-Mifflin, 1976.

Cunningham, R. What do nurses do to help patients who attempt suicide? *Canadian Nurse*, 1975, **71**, 27–29.

Curran, J. P. Social skills training and systematic desensitization in reducing dating anxiety. *Behavior Research and Therapy*, 1975, **13**, 65–68.

Curran, J. P., & Gilbert, F. S. A test of the relative effectiveness of a systematic desensitization program and an interpersonal skills training program with date anxious subjects. *Behavior Therapy*, 1975, **6**, 510–521.

Dahlstrom, W. G., Welsh, G. S., & Dahlstrom, L. E. *An MMPI handbook* (Vol. 1). *Clinical Inter* (Rev. ed.). Minneapolis: University of Minnesota Press, 1972.

Damon, W. *The social world of the child*. San Francisco: Jossey-Bass, 1977.

Danziger, K. *Socialization*. Middlesex, England: Penguin, 1973.

Davison, G. C., & Neale, J. M. *Abnormal psychology: An experimental clinical approach*. New York: Wiley, 1974.

De Latil, P. *Thinking by machine*. Boston: Houghton-Mifflin, 1956.

Delworth, U., Rudow, E. G., & Taub, J. *Crisis center hotline: A guidebook to beginning and operating*. Springfield, Ill., Charles C Thomas, 1972.

Diagnostic and Statistical Manual-II. Washington, D.C.: American Psychiatric Association, 1968.

DiCara, L., & Miller, N. Instrumental learning of peripheral vasomotor responses in the curarized rat. *Communications in Behavior and Biology*, 1968, **1**, 209. (a)

DiCara, L., & Miller, N. Instrumental learning of urine formation by rats: Changes in ural blood flow. *American Journal of Physiology*, 1968, **215**, 677–686. (b)

DiCara, L., & Miller, N. Instrumental learning of vasomotor responses by rats: Learning to respond differentially in the two ears. *Science*, 1968, **159**, 1485–1486. (c)

Dorr, D., Cowen, E. L., & Kraus, R. Mental health professionals view of nonprofessional mental health workers. *American Journal of Community Psychology*, 1973, **1**, 258–265.

Drake, L. D., & Oetting, E. R. *An MMPI codebook for counselors*. Minneapolis: University of Minnesota Press, 1959.

Drum, D. J., & Figler, H. E. *Outreach in counseling*. Cranston, R. I.: Carroll Press, 1976.

Duck, S. *Theory and practice in interpersonal attraction*. New York: Academic Press, 1977.

Duncan, S. D., Jr. Nonverbal communication. *Psychological Bulletin*, 1969, **72**, 118–137.

Duncan, S. D., Jr. Some signals and rules for taking speaking turns in conversations. *Journal of Personality and Social Psychology*, 1972, **23**, 283–292.

Duncan, S., Jr., & Fiske, D. W. *Face-to-face interactions: Research, method and theory.* New York: Wiley, 1977.

Duncan, S. D., Jr., & Niederehe, G. On signalling that it's your turn to speak. *Journal of Experimental Social Psychology.* 1974, **10,** 234–247.

Dye, C. A. Self-concept, anxiety and group participation as affected by human relations training. *Nursing Research,* 1974, **23,** 301–306.

Ekman, P., & Friesen, W. W. A tool for the analysis of motion picture film or video tape. *American Psychology,* 1969, **24,** 240–243.

Ekman, P., & Friesen, W. W. Non-verbal behavior in psychopathology. In R. J. Friedman, & M. M. Katz (Eds.), *The psychology of depression.* New York: Wiley, 1974.

Ellis, A. *Reason and emotion in psychotherapy.* N. Y.: Lyle Stuart, 1962.

English, H. B., & English, A. C. *A comprehensive dictionary of psychological and psychoanalytical terms.* New York: Longmans, Green, 1958.

Ewing, C. P. Family crisis intervention and traditional child guidance: A comparison of outcomes and factors related to success in treatment. *Dissertation Abstracts International,* 1976, (University Microfilms No. 76-5933)

Ewing, C. P. *Crisis intervention as psychotherapy.* New York: Oxford University Press, 1978.

Farina, A., Arenberg, D., & Guskin, S. A scale for measuring minimal social behavior. *Journal of Consulting Psychology,* 1957, **21,** 265–268.

Ferster, C. B. Classification of behavior pathology. In L. Krasner, & L. P. Ullman (Eds.), *Research in behavior modification.* New York: Holt, Rinehart & Winston, 1965.

Ferster, C. B. A functional analysis of depression. *American Psychology,* 1973, **28,** 857–870.

Foulds, G. A. *Personality and personal illness.* London: Tavistok, 1965.

Freud, A. *The ego and the mechanisms of defense.* New York: International Universities Press, 1936.

Freud, S. Analysis of a phobia in a five-year-old boy. In *Collected papers.* New York: Basic Books, 1959.

Friar, L. R., & Beatty, J. Migraine: Management by trained control of vasoconstriction. *Journal of Consulting and Clinical Psychology,* 1976, **44,** 46–53.

Fuchs, N. R. Play therapy at home. *Merrill-Palmer Quarterly,* 1957, **3,** 89–95.

Furman, E. Treatment of under-fives by way of their parents. In *The psychoanalytic study of the child.* New York: International Universities Press, 1950.

Garmezy, N. The study of competence in children at risk for severe psychopathology. In E. J. Anthony, & C. Koupernick (Eds.). *The child in his family: Children at psychiatric risk* (Vol. 3). New York: Wiley, 1974.

Getz, W. L., Fujita, B. N., & Allen, D. The use of paraprofessionals in crisis intervention: Evaluation of an innovative program. *American Journal of Community Psychology*, 1975, **3**, 135–144.

Goldberg, E. M. I–E expectancy and perception of interpersonal control. *Dissertation Abstracts*, (University Microfilms No. 72-7787)

Goldsmith, J. B., & McFall, R. M. Development and evaluation of an interpersonal skill-training program for psychiatric inpatients. *Journal of Abnormal Psychology*, 1975, **84**, 51–58.

Goldstein, A. R., Sprafkin, R. P., & Gershaw, N. J. *Skill training for community living: Applying structure learning theory.* New York: Pergamon Press, 1976.

Goslin, D. (Ed.). *Handbook of socialization theory and research.* Chicago: Rand McNally, 1969.

Gouldner, A. W. The norm of reciprocity: A preliminary statement. *American Sociological Review*, 1960, **25**, 161–178.

Grady, M. An assessment of the behavioral scientist's role with the dying patient and the family. *Military Medicine*, 1975, **11**, 789–792.

Gray, B., Nida, R. A., & Coonfield, T. J. Emphatic listening test: An instrument for the selection and training of telephone crisis workers. *Journal of Community Psychology*, 1976, **4**, 199–205.

Haith, M. M., Bergman, T., & Moore, M. J. Eye contact and face scanning early infancy. *Science*, 1977, **198**, 853–855.

Haley, J. *Problem-solving therapy: New strategies for effective family therapy.* San Francisco: Jossey-Bass, 1976.

Hamilton, G. *Psychotherapy in child guidance.* New York: Columbia University Press, 1947.

Hardman, G. L. Utilizing crises for treatment. *International Journal of Offender Therapy and Comprehensive Criminology*, 1975, **19**, 42–52.

Harper, R. A. *The new psychotherapies.* Englewood Cliffs, N.J.: Prentice-Hall, 1975.

Hartup, W. W. Toward a social psychology of childhood. Presidential address. Division Seven. Amer. Psychological Assn. meeting. Washington, D.C., Sept. 1976.

Hayden, D. M. The internal–external control construct: Implications for psychotherapy. *Dissertation Abstracts International*, (University Microfilms No. 75-17807).

Henle, J., Jaynes, J., & Sullivan, J. J. *Historical conceptions of psychology.* New York: Springer, 1973.

Himle, D. P., & Barch, W. Behavioral indices of anxiety and locus of control. *Psychological Reports*, 1975, **37**, 1008.

Hinchliff, M. M., Lancashire, M., & Roberts, F. J. Depression: Defense mechanisms in speech. *British Journal of Psychiatry*, 1971, **118**, 501–511.

Hobbs, N. *The future of children.* San Francisco: Jossey-Bass, 1975.

Hoffman, D. L., & Remmel, M. L. Uncovering the precipitant in crisis intervention. *Social Casework*, 1975, **56**, 259–267.

Homans, G. C. *Social behavior: Its elementary forms.* New York: Harcourt, Brace & World, 1961.

Homans, G. C. *Social behavior: Its elementary forms* (Rev. ed.). New York: Harcourt, Brace, Jovanovich, 1974.

Hooker, J. F. The study of the only child at school. *Journal of Genetic Psychology,* 1931, **39,** 122–126.

Jack, L. M. An experimental study of ascendent behavior in pre-school children. Univ. of Iowa *Studies in Child Welfare,* 1934, **9**(3).

Jacobs, K. W. 16 PF correlates of locus of control. *Psychological Reports,* 1976, **38,** 1170.

Jones, N. B. *Ethological studies of child behavior.* Cambridge, England: University of Cambridge Press, 1972.

Jourard, S. M., & Lasakow, P. Some factors in self-disclosure. *Journal of Abnormal and Social Psychology,* 1958, **56,** 91–98.

Jung, C. G. *Psychological types.* New York: Harcourt Brace, 1923.

Kapp, R. A., & Weiss, S. D. An interdisciplinary, crisis-oriented graduate training program within a student health service mental health clinic. *Journal of American College Health Associations,* 1975, **23,** 340–344.

Kazdin, A. E. *The token economy.* New York: Plenum, 1977.

Kelly, J. G., Snowden, L. R., & Munoz, R. F. Social and community interventions. In *Annual review of psychology.* Palo Alto: Annual Reviews, 1977.

Kelvin, P. *The bases of social behavior: An approach in terms of order and value.* London: Holt, Rinehart & Winston, 1970.

Kiev, A. Prognostic factors in attempted suicide. *American Journal of Psychiatry,* 1974, **131,** 989–990.

King, G. D., Morgan, J. P., & Smith, B. The telephone counseling center as a community mental health assessment tool. *American Journal of Community Psychology,* 1974, **2,** 53–60.

King, G. F., Armitage, S. G., Tilton, J. R. A therapeutic approach to schizophrenics of extreme pathology: An operant-interpersonal method. *Journal of Abnormal and Social Psychology,* 1960, **61,** 276–286.

Klapp, O. E. *Models of social order.* Palo Alto: National Press Books, 1973.

Kleinmuntz, B. *Essentials of abnormal psychology.* New York: Harper & Row, 1974.

Klingbeil, G. A., & Alvandi, O. M. Concepts of transactional analysis and anxiety with persons in crisis. *Journal of Psychiatric Nursing and Mental Health Services,* 1975, **13,** 5–10.

Kohlberg, L. From is to ought. In T. Mischel (Ed.), *Cognitive development and epistemology.* New York: Academic Press, 1971.

Korchin, S. J. *Modern clinical psychology: Principles of intervention in the clinic and community.* New York: Basic Books, 1976.

Langsley, D. C., & Yarvis, R. M. Evaluation of crisis intervention. *Current Psychiatric Therapy,* 1975, **15,** 247–252.

Lazarus, A. A. *Behavior therapy and beyond.* New York: McGraw-Hill, 1971.

Lazarus, A. A. (Ed.). *Clinical behavior therapy.* New York: Brunner/Mazel, 1972.

Lazarus, A. A. Multimodal behavioral treatment of depression. *Behavior Therapy,* 1974, **5,** 549–554.

Lazarus, A. A. *Multi-modal behavior therapy.* New York: Springer, 1976.

Lazarus, A. A., & Rosen, R. C. Behavior therapy techniques in the treatment of sexual disabilities. In J. K. Meyer (Ed.), *Clinical management of sexual disorders.* Baltimore: Williams & Wilkins, 1976.

Lefcourt, H. M. Internal versus external control of reinforcement: A review. *Psychological Bulletin,* 1966, **65,** 206–220.

Lefcourt, H. M. *Locus of control: Current trends in theory and research.* Hillsdale, N. J.: Lawrence Erlbaum, 1976.

Lerner, M. J. Social psychology of justice and interpersonal attractions. In T. L. Huston (Ed.), *Foundations of interpersonal attraction.* New York: Academic Press, 1974.

Lester, D. Suicide and internal–external orientation. *Psychology,* 1973, **10,** 35–39.

Levine, J., & Zigler, E. The essential–reactive distinction in alcoholism: A developmental approach. *Journal of Abnormal Psychology,* 1973, **81,** 242–249.

Levitt, E. E., & Lubin, B. *Depression: Concepts, controversies and some new facts.* New York: Springer, 1975.

Libet, J. M., & Lewinsohn, P. M. Concept of social skill with specific reference to the behavior of depressed persons. *Journal of Consulting and Clinical Psychology,* 1973, **40,** 304–312.

Lock, J. *Some thoughts concerning education.* London: Ward, Lock, 1963.

Long, J., & Madsen, C. H., Jr. Five-year-olds as behavioral engineers for students in a day-care center. In E. Ramp, & G. Semb (Eds.), *Behavior analysis: Areas of research and application.* Englewood Cliffs, N. J.: Prentice-Hall, 1975.

Lorber, J., & Satow, R. Dropout rates in mental health centers. *Social Work,* 1975, **20,** 308–312.

Maccoby, M. *The gamesman: The new corporate leaders.* New York: Simon & Schuster, 1976.

Maher, B. A. *Principles of psychopathology.* New York: McGraw-Hill, 1966.

Mahoney, M. J. *Cognition and behavior modification.* Cambridge: Ballinger, 1974.

Mahoney, M. J. Reflections on the cognitive–learning trend in psychotherapy. *American Psychology,* 1977, **32,** 5–13.

Maier, N. R. F. *Studies of abnormal behavior in the rat.* New York: Harpers, 1939.

Maier, N. R. F. *Frustration: A study of behavior without a goal.* New York: McGraw-Hill, 1949.

Manuck, S. B., Hinrichsen, J. J., & Ross, E. O. Life-stress, locus of control, and treatment-seeking. *Psychological Reports,* 1975, **37,** 589–590.

Martin, B. *Abnormal psychology: Clinical and scientific perspectives.* New York: Holt, Rinehart & Winston, 1977.

Masserman, J. H. *Behavior and neurosis.* Chicago: University of Chicago Press, 1943.

May, R. *The meaning of anxiety* (Rev.). New York: W. W. Norton, 1977.

McCombie, S. L. Characteristics of rape victims seen in crisis intervention. *Smith College Studies in Social Work,* 1975, **46,** 30–31.

McFall, R. M., & Lillesand, D. D. Behavioral rehearsal and modeling and coaching in assertion training. *Journal of Abnormal Psychology,* 1971, **77,** 313–323.

McGee, R. K. *Crisis intervention in the community.* Baltimore: University Park, 1974.

McGovern, K. B. The development and evaluation of a social skills training program for college male non-daters. *Dissertation Abstracts International,* 1973 (University Microfilms No. 73-7929).

McLaughlin, T. F., & Malaby, J. E. Elementary school children as behavioral engineers. In E. Ramp, & G. Semb (Eds.), *Behavior analysis: Areas of research and application.* Englewood Cliffs, N.J.: Prentice-Hall, 1975.

Meehl, P. *Clinical vs statistical prediction.* Minneapolis: University of Minnesota Press, 1954.

Meehl, P. Some ruminations on the validation of clinical procedures. *Canadian Journal of Psychology,* 1959, **13,** 103–128.

Meehl, P. The cognitive activity of the clinician. *American Psychology,* 1960, **15,** 19–27.

Messersmith, C., & Huessy, H. R. Methods of treating mental illness. In E. Lieberman (Ed.), *Mental health: The public health challenge.* Washington, D.C.: American Public Health Association, 1975.

Michenbaum, D. *Cognitive-behavior modification: An integrative approach.* New York: Plenum, 1977.

Miller, N. E. Experimental studies in conflict. In J. McV. Hunt (Ed.), *Personality and the behavior disorders* (Vol. 1). New York: Ronald, 1944.

Miller, N. E. Comments on theoretical models illustrated by the development of a theory of conflict. *Journal of Personality,* 1951, **20,** 82–100.

Miller, N. Learning of visceral and glandular responses. *Science,* 1969, **163,** 434–445.

Mink, O. G. *The behavior change process.* New York: Harper & Row, 1970.

Minuchin, S., Chamberlain, P., & Graubard, P. A project to teach learning skills to disturbed delinquent children. *American Journal of Ortho-psychiatry*, **37**, 558–567.

Morley, E. L., & Watkins, J. T. Locus of control and effectiveness of two rational-emotive therapy styles. *Rational Living*, 1974, **9**, 22–24.

Murphy, G., Murphy, L. B., Newcomb, T. M. *Experimental social psychology*. New York: Harper & Brothers, 1937.

Murstein, B. I. *Love, sex and marriage through the ages*. New York: Springer, 1974.

Murstein, B. I. *Who will marry whom? Theories and research in marital choice*. New York: Springer, 1976.

Mussen, P., & Eisenberg-Berg, N. *Roots of caring, sharing and helping*. San Francisco: Freeman, 1977.

Nathan, P. E., & Harris, S. L. *Psychopathology and society*. New York, McGraw-Hill, 1975.

National Institute of Mental Health Survey and Reports Section. Statistical Notes 26–50. September 1971.

Nay, W. R. *Behavioral intervention: Contemporary strategies*. New York: Gardener, 1976.

Nelson, Z. P., & Mowry, D. D. Contracting in crisis intervention. *Community Mental Health Journal*, 1976, **12**, 37–44.

Orford, J. *The social psychology of mental disorder*. Marmondsworth, England: Penguin, 1976.

Orlansky, H. Infant care and personality. *Psychological Bulletin*, 1949, **46**, 1–48.

Page, J. D. Psychopathology: *The science of understanding deviance* (Ed. 2). Chicago: Aldine, 1975.

Parloff, M. B. The psychotherapy marketplace. In A. Rosenfeld (Ed.), *Mind and supermind*. New York: Holt, Rinehart & Winston, 1977.

Pask, G. *An approach to cybernetics*. New York: Harper & Bros, 1961.

Patterson, C. H. *Theories of counseling and psychotherapy* (Ed. 2). New York: Harper & Row, 1973.

Paull, H. RX for loneliness: A plan for establishing a social network of individualized caring through care-ring. *Crisis Intervention*, 1972, **4**, 63–68.

Pavlov, I. *Lectures on conditioned reflexes: Conditioned reflexes and psychiatry*. W. H. Gantt (trans.). New York: International Publishers, 1941.

Pendleton, L. R., Shelton, J. L., & Wilson, S. E. Social interaction training using systematic homework. *Personality and Guidance Journal*, 1976, **54**, 484–487.

Peterson, D. R. *The clinical study of social behavior*. New York: Appleton-Century-Crofts, 1968.

Phares, E. J. Expectancy changes in skill and change situations. *Journal of Abnormal and Social Psychology*, 1957, **54**, 339–342.

Phares, E. J. *Locus of control in personality*. Morristown, N. J.: General Learning Press, 1976.

Phares, E. J., & Lamiell, J. T. Relationship of internal–external control to defensive preferences. *Journal of Consulting and Clinical Psychology*, 1974, **42**, 23–38.

Phares, E. J., & Lamiell, J. T. Personality. In *Annual Reviews in Psychology*. Palo Alto: Annual Reviews, 1977.

Phillips, E. L. Parent-child similarities in personality disturbances. *Journal of Clinical Psychology*, 1951, **7**, 188–190.

Phillips, E. L. *Psychotherapy: A modern theory and practice*. Englewood Cliffs, N.J.: Prentice-Hall, 1956.

Phillips, E. L. The use of the teacher as adjunct therapist in child guidance. *Psychiatry*, 1957, **20**, 407–410.

Phillips, E. L. *Counseling and psychotherapy: A behavioral approach*. New York: Wiley Interscience, 1977. (a)

Phillips, E. L. *Day to day anxiety management*. New York: Krieger, 1977. (b)

Phillips, E. L., & Ferster, C. B. The role of feelings in a world of behavioral fact. Discussion Hour, Association for Advancement of Behavior Therapy, New York, 1976.

Phillips, E. L., Gershenson, J., & Lyons, G. On time-limited writing therapy. *Psychological Reports*, 1977, **41**, 707–712.

Phillips, E. L., & Haring, N. G. Results from special techniques for teaching emotionally disturbed children. *Exceptional Children*, 1959, **26**, 64–67.

Phillips, E. L., & Johnston, M. H. S. Theory and development of short-term, parent–child psychotherapy. *Psychiatry*, 1954, **17**, 267–275.

Phillips, E. L., Wiener, D. N., & Haring, N. G. *Discipline, achievement and mental health*. Englewood Cliffs, N.J.: Prentice-Hall, 1962.

Phillips, E. L., & Wiener, D. N. *Short-term psychotherapy and structured behavior change*. New York: McGraw-Hill, 1966.

Phillips, E. L., & Wiener, D. N. *Discipline, achievement and mental health* (Ed. 2). Englewood Cliffs, N.J.: Prentice-Hall, 1972.

Phillips, L., & Zigler, E. Social competence: The action-thought parameter and vicariousness in normal and pathological behaviors. *Journal of Abnormal and Social Psychology*, 1961, **63**, 137–146.

Piaget, J. *The moral judgement of the child*. New York: Harcourt, Brace & World, 1932.

Polak, P. R., Egan, D., Vandenberg, R., & Williams. Prevention in mental health: A controlled study. *American Journal of Psychiatry*, 1975, **132**, 146–149.

Premack, D. Toward empirical behavior laws: Positive reinforcement. *Psychological Review*, 1959, **66**, 219–233.

Premack, D. Reinforcement theory. In D. Levin (Ed.), *Nebraska symposium on motivation*. Lincoln: University of Nebraska Press, 1965.

Premack, D. Catching up with common sense or two sides of a generalization: Reinforcement and punishment. In R. Glaser (Ed.), *The nature
of reinforcement.* New York: Academic Press, 1971.

Prociuk, T. J., & Breen, L. J. Locus of control, study habits and attitudes,
and college academic performance. *Journal of Personality,* 1974, **88,**
91–95.

Prociuk, T. J., Breen, L. J., & Lussier, R. J. Hopelessness, internal–external
locus of control, and depression. *Journal of Clinical Psychology,*
1976, **32,** 299–300.

Ramp, E., & Semb, G. (Eds.). *Behavior analysis: Areas of research and
application.* Englewood Cliffs, N.J.: Prentice-Hall, 1975.

Rioch, M. J. Changing concepts in the training of therapists. *Journal of
Consulting Psychology,* 1966, **30,** 292–294.

Rioch, M. J. Pilot projects in training mental health counselors. In E. L.
Cowen, E. A. Gardner, & M. Zax (Eds.), *Emergent approaches to
mental health.* New York: Appleton-Century-Crofts, 1967.

Rioch, M. J., Elkes, C., Flint, A. A., et al. National Institute of Mental
Health pilot study in training of mental health counselors. *American
Journal of Orthopsychiatry,* 1963, **33,** 678–689.

Rogers, E. M. The change agency and change target. In G. Zaltman, P.
Kotler, & I. Kaufman (Eds.), *Creating social change.* New York: Holt,
Rinehart & Winston, 1972.

Rogers, E. M. Social structure and social change. In G. Zaltman (Ed.),
Processes and phenomena of social change. New York: Wiley, 1973.

Romano, M. D. Preparing children for parental disability. *Social Work in
Health Care,* 1976, **1,** 309–315.

Rosen, R. C. Operant control of sexual responses in man. In G. E.
Schwartz & J. Beatty (Eds.), *Biofeedback: theory and research.* New
York: Academic Press, 1977.

Rotter, J. B. *Social learning and clinical psychology.* Englewood Cliffs,
N.J.: Prentice-Hall, 1954.

Rotter, J. B. Generalized expectancies for internal versus external control
of reinforcement. *Psychological Monographs,* 1966, **80** (1, whole No.
609).

Rotter, J. B. Some problems and misconceptions related to the construct
of internal versus external control of reinforcement. *Journal of Consulting and Clinical Psychology,* 1975, **43,** 56–67.

Rycroft, C. *Anxiety and neurosis.* Middlesex, England: Penguin, 1971.

Sameroff, A. J. Concepts of humanity in primary prevention. In G. W.
Albee, & J. M. Jaffee (Eds.), *Primary prevention of psychopathology.*
Hanover, N. H.: University Press of New England, 1977.

Schmidt, H. O., & Fonda, C. P. The reliability of psychiatric diagnosis: A
new look. *Journal of Abnormal and Social Psychology,* 1956, **52,**
262–267.

Schuette, C. G. Life change, locus of control, needs, and academic performance of college freshmen. *Dissertation Abstracts International,* 1976, (University Microfilms No. 76–4656).

Schwartz, G. E. Biofeedback as therapy: Some theoretical and practical issues. *American Psychology,* 1973, **28,** 666–673.

Schwartz, G. E., & Beatty, J. (Eds.). *Biofeedback: theory and research.* New York: Academic Press, 1977.

Seitz, F. C. Five psychological measures of neurotic depression: A correlational study, *Journal of Clinical Psychology,* 1970, **26,** 504–505.

Seligman, M. E. P. Depression and learned helplessness. In R. J. Friedman & M. M. Katz (Eds.), *The psychology of depression: Contemporary theory and research.* Washington, D.C.: Winston, 1973.

Seligman, M. E. P. *Helplessness.* San Francisco: Freeman, 1975.

Seligman, M. E. P., & Maier, S. F. Failure to escape traumatic shock. *Journal of Experimental Psychology,* 1976, **74,** 1–9.

Shaw, B. F. A systematic investigation of two psychological treatments of depression. *Dissertation Abstracts International,* 1975, Ottawa, National Library of Canada.

Sheldon, W. N. *Atlas of men.* New York: Harper & Row, 1954.

Shinedling, M. M., Terry, D. W., & Ravsten, L. A. Short-range hedonism: Therapy for patients who cannot delay gratification. *Hospital and Community Psychiatry,* 1975, **26,** 133–136.

Siegel, L. J., & Steinman, W. M. The modification of a peer-observer's classroom behavior as a function of his serving as a reinforcing agent. In E. Ramp & G. Semb (Eds.), *Behavior analysis: Areas of research and application.* Englewood-Cliffs, N.J.: Prentice-Hall, 1975.

Skinner, B. F. *Walden two.* New York: Macmillan, 1948.

Skinner, B. F. *About behaviorism.* New York: Knopf, 1974.

Sloane, R. B., Staples, F. R., Cristal, A. H., et al. *Psychotherapy vs behavior therapy.* Cambridge: Harvard University Press, 1975.

Solomon, R. I. Punishment. *American Psychology,* 1964, **19,** 239–253.

Sommer, R., & Osmond, H. The schizophrenic no society. *Psychiatry,* 1962, **25,** 244–255.

Sowards, S., & Phillips, E. L. Social skills deficit as a critical element in depression: A preliminary investigation. Paper presented George Washington University Counseling Center (unpublished), 1973.

Spector, G. A., & Claiborn, W. L. (Eds.), *Crisis intervention.* New York: Behavioral Press, 1973.

Spoerl, O. H. Single session psychotherapy. *Diseases of the Nervous System,* 1975, **36,** 283–385.

Sroufe, L. A. A methodological and philosophical critique of intervention-oriented research. *Monograph of the Society for Research in Child Development,* 1966, **31,** 3 (Series No. 112).

Stampfl, T. G., & Lewis, D. J. Essentials of implosive therapy: A learning-theory-based psychodynamic behavioral therapy. *Journal of Abnormal Psychology*, 1967, **72**, 496–503.

Stanton, A. H., & Schwartz, M. S. *The mental hospital: A study of institutional participation in psychiatric illness and treatment*. London: Tavistock, 1954.

Steiner, I. D. Perceived freedom. In L. Berkowitz (Ed.), *Advances in Experimental Social Psychology* (Vol. 5). New York: Academic Press, 1970.

Strahan, R., & Huth, H. Relations between embedded figures test performance and dimensions of the I–E scale. *Journal of Personality Ass.*, 1975. **39**, 523–524.

Strickland, B. R. Internal–external control of reinforcement. In T. Blass (Ed.), *Personality variables in social behavior*. Hillsdale, N.J.: Lawrence Erlbaum Associates, 1977.

Strickler, M. Crisis intervention and the climacteric man. *Social Casework*, 1975, **56**, 85–89.

Sullivan, H. S. *Conceptions of modern psychiatry*. New York: Norton, 1954.

Szasz, T. S. *The myth of mental illness*. New York: Hoeber-Harper, 1961.

Taub, E. Self-regulation of human tissue temperature. In G. E. Schwartz & J. Beatty (Eds.), *Biofeedback: Theory and research*. New York: Academic Press, 1977.

Termansen, P. E., & Bywater, C. SAFER: A follow-up service for attempted suicide in Vancouver. *Canadian Psychiatric Association Journal*, 1975, **20**, 29–34.

Thoresen, C. E., & Mahoney, M. J. *Behavioral self-control*. New York: Holt, Rinehart & Winston, 1974.

Tooth, G. C. *Studies in mental illness in the Gold Coast*. London: Her Majesty's Stationary Office, 1950.

Tosi, D. J., & Moleski, R. L. Public forum: Rational-emotive crisis-intervention therapy. *Rational Living*, 1975, **10**, 32–37.

Ullman, L. P., & Krasner, L. *A psychological approach to abnormal behavior*. Englewood Cliffs, N.J.: Prentice-Hall, 1969.

Ullman, L. P., & Krasner, L. *A psychological approach to abnormal behavior* (Ed. 2): Englewood Cliffs, N.J.: Prentice-Hall, 1975.

Ulmer, R. A., & Lieberman, M. The children's Minimal Social Behavior Scale: A short objective measure of personality functioning. *International Journal of Psychology*, 1970, **5**, 269–274.

Updegraff, R., & Keister, M. E. A study of children's reactions to failure and an experimental attempt to modify them. *Iowa City, University Iowa Studies in Child Welfare*, 1937, **13**(4).

Vitalo, R. The effects of training in interpersonal functioning upon psychiatric patients. In R. R. Carkhuff (Ed.), *Helping and human relations*. New York: Holt, Rinehart & Winston, 1969.

Vuchinich, R. E., & Bass, B. A. Social desirability in Rotter's locus of control scale. *Psychological Reports*, 1974, **34**, 1124–1126.

Wachtel, P. L. *Psychoanalysis and behavior therapy: Toward an integrated approach.* New York: Basic Books, 1977.

Walder, L., Cohen, S., Breiter, D., et al. Teaching behavioral principles to parents of disturbed children. In A. M. Graziano (Ed.), *Behavior therapy with children.* Chicago: Aldine-Atherton, 1971.

Wallace, F. C. Anthropology and psychopathology. In J. Page (Ed.), *Approaches to psychopathology.* New York: Columbia University Press, 1966.

Ward, J. H., Jr. Hierarchical grouping to optimize an objective function. *Journal of the American Statistical Association*, 1968, **58**, 236–244.

Watson, D., & Friend, R. Measurement of social-evaluative anxiety. *Journal of Consulting and Clinical Psychology*, 1969, **33**, 448–457.

Waxer, P. Non-verbal cues for depression. *Journal of Abnormal Psychology*, 1974, **33**, 319–322.

Weisman, M. M., Paykel, E. G. *The depressed woman: A study of social relationships.* Chicago: University of Chicago Press, 1974.

Wickramasekera, I. *Biofeedback behavior therapy and hypnosis: Potentiating the verbal control of behavior for clinicians.* Chicago: Nelson-Hall, 1976.

Wiener, N. *The human use of human beings.* Boston: Houghton-Mifflin, 1950.

Wilkins, W. E. Trends in powerlessness: A ten year follow-up. *Journal of Psychology*, 1975, **91**, 15–18.

Williams, J. L. Implications of the rise of cognitive behaviorism. *American Psychology*, 1977, **32**, 895–896.

Wilson, G. Introversion /extraversion. In T. Blass (Ed.), *Personality variables in social behavior.* New York: Lawrence Erlbaum Associates, 1977.

Wold, C. I., & Litman, R. E. Suicide after contact with a suicide prevention center. *Archives of General Psychiatry*, 1973, **28**, 735–739.

Wolpe, J. *Psychotherapy by reciprocal inhibition.* Stanford University Press, 1958.

Wolpe, J. *The practice of behavior therapy.* N.Y.: Pergamon, 1969.

Wolpe, J., & Lazarus, A. A. *Behavior therapy techniques.* New York: Pergamon, 1966.

Zaltman, G. *Process and phenomena of social change.* New York: Wiley, 1973.

Zaltman, G., Kotler, P., & Kaufman, I. (Eds.). *Creating social change.* New York: Holt, Rinhart & Winston, 1972.

Zarle, T. H., Hartsough, D. M., & Ottinger, D. R. Tornado recovery: The development of a professional–paraprofessional response to a disaster. *Journal of Community Psychology*, 1974, **2**, 311–320.

Zax, M., & Cowen, E. L. *Abnormal psychology: Changing concepts* (Ed. 2). New York: Holt, Rinehart & Winston, 1972.

Zigler, E., & Phillips, L. Psychiatric diagnosis and symptomatology. *Journal of Abnormal and Social Psychology*, 1961, **63**, 69–75.

Index

268